NEW KOREAN CINEMA

NEW KOREAN CINEMA

Edited by
Chi-Yun Shin and Julian Stringer

NEW YORK UNIVERSITY PRESS
Washington Square, New York

Images from *Chunhyang* are courtesy of Taehung Pictures. The cover image from *Take Care of My Cat* is reproduced courtesy of Cinema Service Co. Ltd. All other images are reproduced courtesy of the Korean Film Archive. For their help in obtaining images, we should like to thank SooJeong Ahn, Jenny Chung and Choi Jae Won (Cinema Service), David E. James, Yi Tae-won (Taehung) and especially Kwon Young-taek of the Korean Film Archive.

First published in the U.S.A. in 2005 by
NEW YORK UNIVERSITY PRESS
Washington Square
New York, NY 10003
www.nyupress.org

First published in Great Britain in 2005 by
Edinburgh University Press Ltd
22 George Square
Edinburgh

Library of Congress Cataloging-in-Publication Data
New Korean cinema / edited by Chi-Yun Shin and Julian Stringer.
p. cm.
Includes bibliographical references and index.
ISBN-10: 0-8147-4029-4 (cloth : alk. paper)
ISBN-13: 978-0-8147-4029-3 (cloth : alk. paper)
ISBN-10: 0-8147-4030-8 (pbk. : alk. paper)
ISBN-13: 978-0-8147-4030-9 (pbk. : alk. paper)
1. Motion pictures–Korea (South)–History. I. Shin, Chi-Yun. II. Stringer, Julian, 1966-
PN1993.5.K6N48 2005
791.43′095195–dc22   2005006942

Typeset in Sabon and Gill Sans by
Servis Filmsetting Ltd, Manchester, and
printed and bound in Great Britain by
Antony Rowe Ltd, Chippenham, Wilts

p   10 9 8 7 6 5 4 3 2

CONTENTS

NOTES ON THE CONTRIBUTORS

Nancy Abelmann is an Associate Professor of Anthropology, East Asian Languages and Cultures, and Asian American Studies at the University of Illinois at Urbana–Champaign. She is the author of *The Melodrama of Mobility: Women, Talk and Class in Contemporary South Korea* (University of Hawai'i Press, 2003) and *Echoes of the Past, Epics of Dissent: A South Korean Social Movement* (University of California Press, 1996), and co-author (with John Lie) of *Blue Dreams: Korean Americans and the Los Angeles Riots* (Harvard University Press, 1995). She is co-editor (with Kathleen McHugh) of *Gender, Genre, and Nation: South Korean Golden Age Melodrama* (Wayne State University Press, forthcoming).

SooJeong Ahn has a BA degree from Sogang University and an MA degree from Goldsmiths College, and worked for the Pusan International Film Festival between 1998 and 2002. She is currently researching a Ph.D. on film festivals at the University of Nottingham.

Chris Berry is Professor of Film and Television Studies at Goldsmiths College, University of London. His work on Korean culture includes the website *The House of Kim Kiyoung* (http://www.knua.ac.kr/cinema/index.htm), which he compiled with Kim Soyoung, '"What's Big about the Big Film?": "De-Westernizing" the Blockbuster in Korea and China', in Julian Stringer (ed.), *Movie Blockbusters* (Routledge, 2003), and 'Syncretism and Synchronicity: Queer 'n' Asian Cyberspace in 1990s Taiwan and Korea', co-authored with Fran Martin in (ed., with Fran Martin and Audrey Yue) *Mobile Cultures: New Media and Queer Asia* (Duke University Press, 2003). He has also written widely on Chinese cinema.

Jung-ah Choi is an Assistant Professor in the School of Education at Grand Valley State University in Michigan. She earned her Ph.D. at the University of Illinois at Urbana–Champaign with her dissertation entitled 'Classed Schooling, Classless Identity: Schooling Stories of Returning Dropouts in South Korea' (2002). Her research interests include issues of social class, schooling and youth culture.

Hye Seung Chung is a post-doctoral fellow in Korean Studies at the University of Michigan. She has contributed to *Asian Cinema*, *Film Quarterly*, and *Film* *and Philosophy*. Her essays will appear in the forthcoming anthologies *Seoul Searching: Identity and Culture in Korean Cinema* (SUNY Press), *East Main Street: Asian American Popular Culture* (New York University Press), and *Gender, Genre, and Nation* (Wayne State University Press). Her Ph.D. dissertation investigates the politics of cross-ethnic performance and masquerade circulating around the Hollywood film and television images of Korean American actor Philip Ahn.

David Scott Diffrient is a Ph.D. candidate in the Department of Film, Television, and Digital Media at UCLA. His work has appeared in *Cineaction*, *Film Quarterly*, *Cineaste*, *Paradoxa*, and *Asian Cinema*. His essays will appear in the forthcoming anthologies *Seoul Searching: Identity and Culture in Korean Cinema* (SUNY Press), *Gender, Genre, and Nation* (Wayne State University Press), *Horror Film: Creating and Marketing Fear* (University of Mississippi Press), and *The Encyclopedia of Men and Masculinities* (ABC-Clio Press). His dissertation, entitled 'Episodes and Infinities', maps the international history of anthology, compilation, omnibus and portmanteau films.

Andrew Grossman is the editor of and a contributor to the anthology *Queer Asian Cinema: Shadows in the Shade* (Harrington Park Press, 2000). His writings on Asian cinema will appear in the forthcoming anthologies *24 Frames: Korea/Japan* (Wallflower Press) and *Chinese Connections: Critical Perspectives on Film, Identity, and Diaspora* (Temple University Press). He is also a regular contributor to *Bright Lights Film Journal*, *Scope: An Online Journal of Film Studies*, and *American Book Review*.

Kyu Hyun Kim is Assistant Professor of History and East Asian Languages and Cultures at the University of California at Davis. He has contributed to *Education About Asia*, *Journal of Asian Studies*, *New Directions in the Study of Meiji Japan* (Brill, 1997), and *Public Sphere Private Lives* (Harvard, 2003).

Kyung Hyun Kim is Associate Professor of Korean culture at the University of California at Irvine. He is the author of *The Remasculinization of Korean Cinema* (Duke University Press, 2004) and co-editor of *Im Kwon-Taek: The Making of a Korean National Cinema* (Wayne State University Press, 2002). He has published articles in *positions: east asian cultures critique*, *Cinema Journal*, and other journals.

Soyoung Kim is Professor of Cinema Studies at the Korean National University of Arts, chief editor of *Trans: Journal of Visual Culture Studies*, and editorial collective member for *Inter-Asia Cultural Studies* and *Traces: A Multilingual Journal of Cultural Theory and Translation*. Her books in Korean include *Specters of Modernity: Fantastic Korean Cinema* (2000), *Cinema: Blue Flower in the Land of Technology* (1997) and *Cine-Feminism: Reading Popular*

Cinema (ed., 1994). She is also director of *Koryu: Southern Women and South Korea*, among other short films, and has been a Visiting Professor at the University of California at Berkeley.

Hyangjin Lee is Lecturer in the School of East Asian Studies at the University of Sheffield. She is the author of *Contemporary Korean Cinema: Identity, Culture and Politics* (Manchester University Press, 2000).

Jooran Lee is a freelance writer who contributes to various journals, magazines and webzines in Korea, mainly on homosexual themes. She was Music Director and Advisory Committee member for Rainbow 2002, the Gay Pride Parade in Korea, as well as a founder member of the Korean Sexual Minority Culture and Rights Center. She contributed a chapter entitled 'Remembered Branches: Towards a Future of Korean Homosexual Film' to the anthology *Queer Asian Cinema* (Harrington Park Press, 2000).

Aaron Han Joon Magnan-Park is an Assistant Professor in the Department of Film, Television and Theatre at the University of Notre Dame. He previously taught at the University of Iowa, Illinois State University, the American University of Paris, and the Université de Paris IV-Sorbonne. His work focuses on transnationalism, diaspora, and pan-Asian cinema. He has published chapters in *The Politics of Community* (Davies, 2002) and *Chinese Connections* (Temple University Press, forthcoming).

Darcy Paquet is founder of the website Koreanfilm.org, and also writes for film trade magazine *Screen International*. He has served as programme consultant for the Far East Film Festival in Udine, Italy, since 2002. Forthcoming essays on *Christmas in August* and *Obaltan* will be included in *Seoul Searching: Identity and Culture in Korean Cinema* (SUNY Press) and *24 Frames: Korea/Japan* (Wallflower).

Michael Robinson has been teaching and writing about Korea since beginning his career at the University of Southern California in 1980. In 1995 Professor Robinson joined the East Asian Languages and Cultures Department at Indiana University where he currently teaches Modern Korean history as well as general and specialised courses on East Asian society and culture. He is the author or editor of three major works on Korea: *Cultural Nationalism in Colonial Korea* (University of Washington Press, 1988), *Korea Old and New: A History* (Harvard University Press, 1991), and (with Gi-Wook Shin) *Colonial Modernity in Korea* (Harvard University Press, 1999).

Chi-Yun Shin is a Lecturer in Film Studies and currently the BA Film Studies Course Leader at Sheffield Hallam University, UK. She is a contributor to the forthcoming anthology, *Seoul Searching: Identity and Culture in Korean*

Cinema (SUNY Press), and her articles have appeared in such journals as *Paragraph* and *Scope: An Online Journal of Film Studies*. She is currently working on a manuscript entitled *Diaspora and Cinematic Formation: Black British Cinema of the 1980s and 1990s*.

Jeeyoung Shin is a Ph.D. candidate in the Media Studies programme in the Department of Communication and Culture at Indiana University, Bloomington, working on the relationship between media globalisation and the phenomenon of South Korean media flows in East Asia. Her essay 'Contradiction in the Visible: Globalism and Nationalism in Two Contemporary South Korean Films' is included in the forthcoming anthology *Seoul Searching: Identity and Culture in Korean Cinema* (SUNY Press).

Julian Stringer is Lecturer in Film Studies at the University of Nottingham. He is editor of *Movie Blockbusters* (Routledge, 2003), co-editor (with Mark Jancovich, Antonio Lázaro Reboll, and Andy Willis) of *Defining Cult Movies: The Cultural Politics of Oppositional Taste* (Manchester University Press, 2003), and author of articles on Chinese, Japanese and Korean cinema. He is a General Editor of *Scope: An Online Journal of Film Studies* and a member of the Editorial Advisory Boards of *Screen, New Cinemas* and *Intensities: The Journal of Cult Media*.

ILLUSTRATIONS

INTRODUCTION

Julian Stringer

South Korean cinema is finding its place in the sun. At the dawn of the new millennium, the growing enthusiasm for Korean movies around the world is evidenced by intense activity on multiple fronts. Titles as varied as *Chihwaseon* (*Ch'wihwasŏn*, 2002), *Oasis* (*Oasisŭ*, 2002) and *Old Boy* (*Oldŭ poyi*, 2003) are winning prizes at major international film festivals. Others – including *Friend* (*Ch'in'gu*, 1999), *Spring, Summer, Fall, Winter . . . and Spring* (*Pom, yŏrŭm, kyŏul . . . kŭrigo pom*, 2003), and *The Way Home* (*Chip ŭro . . .*, 2001) – are opening hearts and purses in markets across Asia, Europe and North America. With hundreds more films circulating in subtitled versions on multi-region DVD and inexpensive VCD, Korean movie fandom is on the rise just about everywhere. Hollywood executives are also sitting up and taking notice. Stories concerning Korean cinema published in trade papers such as *Variety* reveal just why and how US studios are so eagerly gobbling up remake rights to domestic hits like *My Sassy Girl* (*Yŏpki chŏk-in kŭnyŏ*, 2001) and *A Tale of Two Sisters* (*Changhwa wa Horgryŏn*, 2003).

Film Studies, too, has responded to the interest and importance of contemporary Korean cinema. Until even a few years ago, there was a paucity of critical writing on the subject. Happily, this situation is now in the process of being reversed as pioneering books and articles have recently seen the light of day.[1] Following the publication of *Im Kwon-Taek: The Making of a Korean National Cinema* (James and Kim, 2002), *New Korean Cinema* is the second volume of academic essays dedicated solely to Korean film to appear in the English language outside Korea. Both books engage with key developments in the Korean movie industry over the past two decades. Each also foregrounds diverse critical voices by gathering contributions from established and emerging Korean cinema scholars on three continents. Fundamental differences nevertheless distinguish one from the other, however.

Figure 1 South Korean hits have been slated for US remakes: *My Sassy Girl* (2001).

Im Kwon-Taek: The Making of a Korean National Cinema focuses on the lifetime achievement of an extraordinary and symptomatic film-maker from the 'old' Korean cinema industry. It pays particular attention to Im's stature as a director of 1980s political art cinema, including modern classics such as *Mandala* (*Mandara*, 1981) and *Gilsottum* (*Kilsottŭm*, 1985), and to the cultural significance of his phenomenally successful period melodrama *Sopyonje* (*Sŏp'yŏnje*, 1993). Written in the mid- to late-1990s, at the very moment when Korean cinema was on the verge of 'breaking through' internationally, its overarching aim and accomplishment are to position Im's work within the context of four decades of post-1960s Korean society.

In contrast, *New Korean Cinema* restricts its focus to the momentous social changes which have swept across South Korea since the early 1990s – a period that may be thought of as the post-*Sopyonje* era. Hyangjin Lee's chapter in the present volume on Im's award-winning *Chunhyang* (*Ch'unhyangdyŏn*, 2000) testifies to the fact that Im Kwon-Taek continues to play a pivotal role in the Korean cinema of this time. The book's main argument, however, is that the cultural phenomenon which critics now routinely refer to as 'New Korean Cinema' is qualitatively different from the pre-1990s cultural cinema Im's name is habitually linked with. This volume's central ambition is therefore to understand the nature and source of the popular Korean cinema that began its rise to prominence at roughly the same time as the historic box-office success of *Sopyonje*.

The book therefore seeks answers to a two-sided question. What has happened to South Korean cinema since the early 1990s? And in what sense can it be said to be new? In response, its fourteen chapters collectively maintain that a distinct form of commercial film-making has indeed emerged since that time. Moreover, they explain where it came from and why it is taking the forms it is, and they assess what its defining characteristics are.

Before proceeding with the analysis, however, it is first necessary to make an important qualifying statement. In line with other work on the subject, *New Korean Cinema* is inevitably and unavoidably structured around a linguistic *faux pas*. The scholarly work represented here is almost exclusively concerned with the contemporary cinema industry of the Republic of Korea (South Korea) rather than with the cinematic output of the Democratic People's Republic of Korea (North Korea). Film historians and movie-goers alike remain fatally ignorant of the North Korean cinema for one perfectly good reason – it has yet to emerge on to the world stage.[2] Given this context of ignorance, as well as the continuing division of the Korean peninsula into two distinct nation-states, it should under no circumstances be assumed that the terms 'South Korean cinema' and 'Korean Cinema' are in any sense synonymous. Claims regarding Korean national cinema that fail to take into account the existence of a hitherto 'unknown' cinema in the North remain highly problematic. Suffice to say, then, that the New Korean Cinema now being so vociferously consumed at home and abroad is a product of recent developments in the culture of the South. In turn, the chapters of this book provide fresh and original perspectives on some of the titles produced in the Republic of Korea over the past decade or so. (Chris Berry's contribution also includes an in-depth, comparative analysis of the North Korean title *Soul's Protest* [*Sarainnŭm ryŏnghondŭl*, 2001].)

With this proviso in mind, the book advances discussion of two central themes. First, it argues that the dynamic and glamorous South Korean movie industry now being 'discovered' and celebrated all over the world has a past and a history. New Korean Cinema did not spring fully armoured from the ground. Instead, it is the product of a variety of structural changes which, over recent years, have transformed the Korean cinema industry and the wider culture of which it is a part. These changes may broadly be identified with the achievement of democratic civil governance from 1992 onwards after an extended period of military rule 1961–87.

Michael Robinson's introductory chapter to this volume traces the dominant narrative of South Korean society in the twentieth century. The defining characteristics of this narrative encompass the experience of successive national traumas. These include: colonial subjugation at the hands of Japan (1910–45), the division of the Korean peninsula, the Korean War (1950–3), and authoritarian rule by corrupt regimes visiting brutal repressions upon their own people – outrageous acts of state violence symbolised above all else by the bloody Kwangju Uprising of May 1980. Underpinning such extreme hardship has been an atmosphere of Cold War security paranoia. The North Korean Communist threat has provided the pretext for the imposition of oppressive laws by successive military governments in the South. The legitimacy and stability of these regimes have in turn been bolstered by the presence on Korean soil of neocolonialist US forces.

Human survival instincts, brave and committed acts of resistance, and intense democratisation struggles by the Korean people also constitute a vital part of this national narrative. After many long years of protest, endless pressure finally bore legal fruit at the tail-end of the twentieth century as South Korea moved towards becoming more and more open and pluralistic. In 1992, the election of the nation's first civilian president, Kim Young-sam (Kim Yŏng-sam), symbolically inaugurated the birth of a freer society.

These latter, epoch-making transformations also engendered the restructuring and formation of distinct social and cultural identities. With freedom in the air, new social actors representing dedicated political movements mounted the stage of history with increased assertiveness.[3] The heightened visibility in South Korea of protest groups – farmers, urban workers and trade unions alongside women, gays, lesbians and queers, and human rights activists – augmented the government's instigation of a new system of regional autonomy which threatened to undermine the long-standing financial and symbolic authority of the capital, Seoul. In unprecedented ways, Koreans of all shades and persuasions have been busily claiming a piece of the pie, and they now face a collective future free from many of the burdens of the bad old days. While the effects of such profound shifts in the organisation of society are only just beginning to be documented and assessed, cinema provides one powerful means of taking stock. Indeed, civil society in South Korea has undoubtedly found in the newly invigorated commercial film culture one of its most compelling and pleasurable forms of expression.

The second area of discussion that *New Korean Cinema* seeks to advance concerns the question of how, why and on what terms 'new cinemas' emerge and find their place within world film history.[4] This is a complex subject, and a difficult one to approach. Previous work on some of the other New national cinemas to have been spawned during the global age – for example, those from West Germany, the numerous Chinese societies, and Iran – has demonstrated a flurry of ambiguities and instabilities at the heart of the concept of *new-ness* itself. For example, in one of the most sustained and rigorous discussions of the subject to date, Yingjin Zhang dissects the multiple and contradictory ways in which various Chinese cinemas – Mainland, Hong Kong, Taiwan – have been described and classified over the past two decades. Zhang concludes that what he terms 'the problematic nature of naming' these distinct and separate New Chinese Cinemas can easily lead to rank confusion (Zhang 2002: 18).

Clearly, the very fact that 'Korea' encompasses a divided film industry – with both North and South claiming their own, very different production systems – testifies to the relevance of the 'problem of naming' in this particular national context as well. Yet beyond this primary linguistic issue, there is already enough evidence to suggest that written commentaries on New Korean Cinema are in danger of smearing themselves with a lack of clarity.

Consider in this regard the fact that, while the the phenomenon of New Korean Cinema may currently be an object of fascination all around the globe, not everyone appears to subscribe to a similar sense of what it actually refers to. A brief look at the subject of periodisation helps to illustrate this point. Upon invoking the name 'New Korean Cinema', *when* exactly do we mean? Attempting to answer this question proves to be a slippery business because some critics have been murmuring off-and-on about a 'new' cinema in Korea for quite some time now. However, there appears to be little consensus concerning when and how this cinema emerged, whether or not it is still in full bloom or in decline, or which films and activities comprise and define its core elements.

More specifically, some scholars correctly identify that the South Korean film industry spawned a 'New Wave' during the course of the early- to mid-1980s – this is characterised as a distinct movement by commentators such as Standish (1994). Yet at the same time, others perceive continuities across the 1980s (the years of intense democratisation campaigns and the brief years of the art-political cinema movement) and the 1990s (the years of civilian governance and a newly invigorated commercial cinema). For example, Park (2000) tracks what he variously terms the 'Korean New Wave Cinema' and the 'new cinema' across the years 1988–97. Kim (2004) employs the phrase 'New Korean Cinema' in a catch-as-catch-can way so as to describe developments from across the full period of the early 1980s to the present day. Similarly, Gateward (2003) claims that the 1980s saw the emergence of a 'New Wave' movement represented by titles such as

Figure 2 The 1980s Korean 'New Wave': *Chilsu and Mansu* (1988).

Mandala and *Chilsu and Mansu* (*Ch'il-su wa Man-su*, 1988). However, she also collapses this very specific linguistic usage in with developments in the later cinema, thus failing to differentiate in the process between the 1980s 'New Wave' movement and the 'New Korean Cinema' of 1990s titles such as *Hot Roof* (*Gyaegot Un Nalui Ohu*, 1996) and *Three Friends* (*Se Ch'ingu*, 1996).[5]

To be sure, there are, of course, continuities between distinct periods of contemporary South Korean cinema. For example, the career of director Jang Sun-woo (Chang Sŏn-u) extends from the 1980s New Wave to the 1990s New Korean Cinema, from *Seoul Jesus* (*Seoul Yesu*, 1986) to *Lies* (*Kŏjinmal*, 1999). Yet the point to underline here is that confusion over naming can easily and quickly breed ontological uncertainty over what critics and audiences in diverse locations actually mean when they talk about a new national cinema in the process of formation.

As a way of differentiating New Korean Cinema from the so-called New Wave of the 1980s, this book pays close and particular attention to a number of specific elements that define the commercial film industry as it now exists in the South. These elements include the impressive domestic box-office success of a range of recent home-grown films, together with changes in the availability of production capital and the emergence of concept movies such as the 'Korean blockbuster'.[6] They also include a generational shift in film-making which has created an industry dominated by young personnel in their twenties and thirties who became film-makers following their formal education in film, rather than through the industrial apprentice system that Im Kwon-Taek passed through. In addition, these elements encompass a generational shift in audiences (i.e. a domestic audience dominated by younger consumers), as well as the development of a committed film culture led by international festivals, movie magazines such as *Cine-21* and *Kino*, and the active production of short films. Last but by no means least, these elements also include both the short- and long-term effects of greater freedom of expression.

None of the above developments happened at the same time and in the same place, however. New Korean Cinema is not a distinct movement and it was not born at a precise moment. Moreover, in the age of global media flows, New Korean Cinema is revealing its dazzling colours to the world in multiple versions – at different paces, in varying ways, across diverse territories. The representative films released to date in Paris, for instance, are of a very different kind and quantity from the titles currently on offer to cinema patrons in other European cities such as Berlin and London (let alone Nottingham and Sheffield). In turn, culturally contingent and geographically specific distribution and programming practices decree that spectators in Hong Kong, Pusan and Tokyo are being exposed to different kinds of New Korean Cinemas from their counterparts in Los Angeles, Seattle and Toronto.

To summarise, this volume takes the transition away from military rule *circa* 1992 as the 'break' around which perceptions of contemporary Korean cinema's vitality and newness are structured. The post-authoritarian, post-political period of the post-1990s therefore constitutes the book's central site of engagement. Yet to repeat, the changes documented herein are complex and variously situated in terms of culture and history. *New Korean Cinema* resists the temptation arbitrarily to impose a neat sense of tidiness and closure upon developments in Korean society and international media culture that are both multi-faceted and ongoing. In other words, when discussing New Korean Cinema, no easy correspondence may be assumed between the political, the economic, and the cultural spheres.[7] Indeed, it is the very existence of such dauntingly complex webs of meaning that makes contemporary Korean cinema such an exciting yet simultaneously challenging object of study.

The key word in all of these regards is *change*. *New Korean Cinema* is organised in three parts, each of which explores different aspects of a film industry in a state of constant flux. The first section, 'Forging a New Cinema', provides discussions of Korean society and culture as well as the political economy of the South Korean film industry. Michael Robinson opens proceedings with a comprehensive overview of the defining characteristics of Korean cultural production throughout the twentieth century. Darcy Paquet then charts developments in the strucure and output of the South Korean film industry since the early 1990s. Jeeyoung Shin outlines the terms of the post-1992 government's globalisation (*Segyehwa*) drive which attempted to engineer a positive overseas reception for the products of Korea's culture industry. The final two chapters consider Korean cinema's fortunes at one of the key exhibition sites through which this much-anticipated global success has revealed itself – international film festivals. Hyangjin Lee considers different reactions in Seoul and Cannes to Im Kwon-Taek's historic *Chunhyang*; while Kim Soyoung offers a detailed discussion of the extent to which the rise of domestic film festivals since the 1990s provides fertile ground for the advancement of issues of identity politics.

In Part II, 'Generic Transformations', close attention to a diverse range of film genres provides evidence not just of structural changes in the cinema industry, but of innovative aesthetic mutations as well. In the first chapter of this section, Julian Stringer demonstrates how the classification of Korean genres enables the construction of variable social identities in specific reception environments. Kyu Hyun Kim considers the rise of the Korean horror film through in-depth analysis of two of its finest accomplishments, *Tell Me Something* (*T'elmissŏmding*, 1999) and *Sympathy for Mr. Vengeance* (*Poksu-nŭn na-ŭi kŏt*, 2002). Chi-Yun Shin then compares and contrasts the treatment of gender relations in two films concerning same-sex friendship. After that, Nancy Abelmann and Jung-ah Choi track the intermingling of generic components – comic, melodramatic and violent – in the anarchic youth film *Attack the Gas Station* (*Juyuso sǔpgyŏksagŏn*, 1999). Finally, Chris Berry discusses *Soul's Protest* in the context of the South Korean *Phantom, the Submarine* (*Yuryŏng*, 1999) – two films set on board boats in which the formal and narrative concerns have been shaped by the influence of Hollywood intertexts.

In the third and final section, 'Social Change and Civil Society', a number of powerful contemporary films are shown to provide evidence of the compelling new possibilities opened by the transition to civil governance. Aaron Han Joon Magnan-Park extends the book's engagement with themes of post-politics by showing how the reverse narrative structure of *Peppermint Candy* (*Bakhasat'ang*, 2000) engages issues of trauma and recovery. A concomitant emphasis on the sensory experiences of male subjectivity is also of interest to Kyung Hyun Kim in his meditation on the nature of the protagonist's vague wanderings in Hong Sang-su's masterpiece *Turning Gate* (*Saenghwalŭi palgyŏn*, 2002). Identifying an emerging gay, lesbian, and queer discourse in Korean cinema, Andrew Grossman and Jooran Lee then critically evaluate its nascent accomplishments by looking at two movies concerning spectral sexuality. Finally, Hye Seung Chung and David Scott Diffrient draw the book to a close with a wide-ranging and timely overview of transnational co-production trends in contemporary South Korean cinema, focusing in particular on the intriguing and highly original Korea–Japan collaborative venture *Asako in Ruby Shoes* (*Sunaebo*, 2000).

It is customary in an Introduction to proclaim one's desire that the appearance of a new volume of academic essays on a given topic will stimulate extensive and vigorous research in the field. New Korean Cinema is such a diverse phenomenon that the scope of critical analysis contained herein can only scratch the surface of its range of concerns. Certainly, this book is able to probe the depths of no more than a small fraction of the very many excellent films produced in South Korea in recent years. Titles not extended the courtesy of

Figure 3   A critical success: the deeply touching melodrama *Christmas in August* (1998).

detailed consideration, but which nevertheless repay close viewing and critical scrutiny, include *Ardor* (*Milae*, 2002), *Christmas in August* (*Palwŏl ŭi k'urisŭmasŭ*, 1998), *The Day a Pig Fell into the Well* (*Tweji ga umul e ppajin nal*, 1996), *The Foul King* (*Panch'ikwang*, 2000), *The Isle* (*Sŏm*, 2000), *Memories of Murder* (*Salin ŭi ch'uŏk*, 2003), *Nowhere to Hide* (*Injŏng sajŏng polgŏt ŏpta*, 1999), *A Petal* (*Kkotnip*, 1996), *Public Enemy* (*Kongkong ŭi chŏk*, 2002), *Push! Push!* (*Sanpuingwa*, 1997), *Shiri* (*Swiri*, 1999), *Untold Scandal* (*Sŭk'aendal*, 2003), and *Waikiki Brothers* (*Waik'ik'i Pŭradŏsŭ*, 2001) – to name no more than a baker's dozen of them.

Figure 4 The struggle for democracy in South Korea: *A Petal* (1996).

Behind the rush to look ahead, however, lurks a need to keep an eye on the past. *New Korean Cinema* emphasises that the democratisation struggles of the 1980s paved the way for the changes that marked the transitional society of the 1990s. As such, for all the connotations of newness that it unravels, the past – as memory, as lost fetish object – returns time and again. The processes through which some audiences outside Korea are at the present moment eagerly embracing the shimmering surfaces of this latest Asian pop culture 'fad' are fraught with dangers of objectification and exoticisation. Western teachers and scholars, in particular, should remain mindful of the ways and means by which the past is often just as important – if not more important – than the triumphs and youthful charms of the present.

This cautionary note is especially important given that social change in South Korea over the past few years has occurred at a blistering pace. In fact, change is occurring so rapidly that it is proving hard for even dedicated fans and specialist researchers to keep up. Yet it is concepts of equality, free speech, social justice and community that now dictate and structure the pace of political debate in South Korea. After years of hope and struggle, film-makers and audiences now face the challenges of inhabiting a pluralised society that is able and willing finally to look the rest of the world firmly in the eye. In liberal capitalist centres such as Hong Kong, New York, Paris and elsewhere, that gaze is being recognised and returned. The story that emerges across the course of this book, therefore, might be said to be the confirmation that Korean cinema is playing, and will continue to play, a vital role in constructing, mediating and reflecting the nature and allure of an enduringly powerful imaginative concept – Democracy. For the foreseeable future, the particular version of democracy put into practice in and around South Korea's commercial film industry will fascinate more and more foreign movie-goers and commentators, just as it will continue to drive the engine of social institutions and everyday life in Korea itself.

Yet there is another story, one linking democracy with reunification, that cannot yet be told – except as one among many possible scenarios in contemporary titles such as the famous blockbuster *Joint Security Area* (*Kongdong kyŏngbi kuyŏk JSA*, 2000). David E. James closes his preface to *Im Kwon-Taek: The Making of a Korean National Cinema* with the following words: 'For no less than in the political and social spheres, cultural work of any worth can be inspired and guided only by the hope of the eventual recovery of an integral freedom in Korea' (James 2002: 17). The contributors to *New Korean Cinema* echo and reiterate those sentiments. Like the New German Cinema of the 1960s and 1970s, New Korean Cinema is a product of its time and of a divided nation. In common with the achievements of stellar West German directors of the period, whose films anticipated and have outlived the collapse of the Berlin Wall, South Korean film-makers are at present making future history by remembering – not dwelling upon – the traumas of the past. In the early years of the twenty-first century, New Korean Cinema promises to be a chapter in an as yet unwritten history of rival celluloid siblings. At some unspecified point in the future, it may constitute a page in a larger history of a unified nation. By then, the sun could have set on an even more fundamentally reshaped Korean society.

A Note to the Reader All Korean names and titles in this book have been romanised according to the McCune–Reischauer system. In those cases where the preferred form of a name (e.g. Chun Doo Hwan, Park Kwang-su) or film title (e.g. *Attack the Gas Station*) already have currency in English, however, these particular usages have been retained. Korean names are presented in Korean style, i.e. surname first, given name last, except in cases where individual authors have chosen to transliterate their name in Western form (i.e. surname last). This general rule of thumb encompasses the presentation of Chinese and Japanese names as well.

REFERENCES

Berry, Chris (2003) ' "What's Big About the Big Film?": "De-Westernizing" the Blockbuster in Korea and China', in Julian Stringer (ed.), *Movie Blockbusters*, London: Routledge: 217–29.

Gateward, Frances (2003) 'Youth in Crisis: National and Cultural Identity in New South Korean Cinema', in Jenny Kwok Wah Lau (ed.), *Multiple Modernities: Cinemas and Popular Media in Transcultural East Asia*, Philadelphia: Temple University Press: 114–27.

Im, Yung-Ho (1998) 'The Media, Civil Society and New Social Movements in Korea, 1985–93', in Kuan-Hsing Chen (ed.), *Trajectories: Inter-Asia Cultural Studies*, London: Routledge: 330–45.

James, David E. (2002) 'Preface', in James and Kim 2002: 9–17.

James, David E., and Kim, Kyung Hyun (eds) (2002) *Im Kwon-Taek: The Making of a Korean National Cinema*, Detroit: Wayne State University Press.

Kim, Kyung Hyun (1996) 'The Fractured Cinema of North Korea: The Discourse of the Nation in *Sea of Blood*', in Xiaobing Tang and Stephen Snyder (eds), *In Pursuit of Contemporary East Asia*, Boulder: Westview Press: 85–106.

——(2004) *The Remasculinization of Korean Cinema*, Durham, NC: Duke University Press.

Ko, Mika (2004) 'The Break-Up of the National Body: Cosmetic Multiculturalism and Films of Miike Takashi', *New Cinemas*, 2, 1: 29–39.

Lee, Hyangjin (2000) *Contemporary Korean Cinema: Identity, Culture, Politics*, Manchester: Manchester University Press.

Leong, Anthony C. Y. (2003) *Korean Cinema: The New Hong Kong: A Guidebook for the Latest Korean New Wave*, Victoria: Trafford Publishing.

Park, Seung Hyun (2000) *A Cultural Interpretation of Korean Cinema, 1988–1997*. Unpublished doctoral dissertation, Indiana University.

Schönherr, Johannes (2004) 'Permanent State of War: A Short History of North Korean Cinema', *Film International*, 8: 24–33.

Sherzer, Dina (2001) 'Gender and Sexuality in New New Wave Cinema', in Alex Hughes and James S. Williams (eds), *Gender and French Cinema*, Oxford: Berg: 227–39.

Standish, Isolde (1994) 'Korean Cinema and the New Realism: Text and Context', in Wimal Dissanayake (ed.), *Colonialism and Nationalism in Asian Cinema*, Bloomington: Indiana University Press: 65–89.

Zhang, Yingjin (2002) *Screening China: Critical Interventions, Cinematic Reconfigurations, and the Transnational Imaginary*, Ann Arbor, University of Michigan: Center for Chinese Studies.

NOTES

1. A Bibliography of Works on Korean Cinema, compiled by SooJeong Ahn, may be found at the end of the present volume. At the time of going to press, Kyung Hyun Kim's *The Remasculinization of Korean Cinema* (2004) is the most recently published work on the subject. An ambitious and intellectually impressive achievement, Kim's book may be said to mark the moment when English-language Korean Film Studies finally came of age. Numerous other books by various authors are forthcoming.
2. For a useful discussion of North Korean cinema, see Lee (2000). See also Kim (1996) and Schönherr (2004).
3. Yung-Ho Im (1998: 300) points out that on 'the theoretical level, the notions of civil society and new social movements became hot issues among social theorists in Korea' from the late 1980s onwards.
4. Confirmation of the contemporary cultural significance of this term is provided by the fact that there now exists an academic journal entitled *New Cinemas*.
5. This murky situation is explicitly acknowledged in the awkward and bizarre title of Anthony C. Y. Leong's book *Korean Cinema: The New Hong Kong: A Guidebook for the Latest Korean New Wave* (Leong 2003). Similar dilemmas confront scholars of other national cinemas. For instance, Sherzer (2001) draws attention to the unprepossessing neologism 'French New New Wave Cinema'. Similarly, Ko (2004: 30) discusses use of the label 'new Japanese New Wave' attached by some journalists to the films of contemporary directors such as Miike Takashi.
6. For a discussion of the Korean blockbuster, see Berry 2003.
7. For example, Michael Robinson's opening survey chapter argues the need to consider 1988 as the date during which the most important social changes in contemporary Korean society manifested themselves. Conversely, Darcy Paquet's subsequent chapter identifies key structural changes as occurring within the relative autonomy of the Korean film industry at a later moment, namely 1992. Such differing perceptions concerning timelines and the pace of change should not be viewed as conceptual weaknesses, but rather as one of the strengths and main intellectual preoccupations of this volume.

PART I

FORGING A NEW CINEMA

1. CONTEMPORARY CULTURAL PRODUCTION IN SOUTH KOREA: VANISHING META-NARRATIVES OF NATION

Michael Robinson

No discussion of Korean film or culture is meaningful without considering its production within, until recently, an extraordinarily unstable political context. While a halting transition to constitutional rule since 1988 has tempered the violent ups and downs of South Korean politics, it is still a society in which cultural production free from the stultifying influence of governmental controls or political passions is a relatively new experience. Recent global recognition and fascination with Korean film gloss over the complex experience that underlies the evolution of this now vital, innovative and regionally influential industry. The critical emphasis on its freshness, innovation and daringness is particularly ironic in the light of the recent history of South Korean cultural production. Until recently the Korean film industry was in decline and its production, with notable exceptions, focused on generic melodramas (often of poor quality) made expressly for the purposes of gaining licences to screen more profitable Hollywood exports. The shift is a direct result of political changes in South Korea. It also heralds the emergence of a new generation of Korean artists in all fields whose creative energies are free from overt control by the state and, more importantly, the restricting political, cultural and social obsessions that dominated Korean society between its liberation from colonial rule in 1945 until the advent of real civilian democratic politics after 1988.

The year 1988 is generally accepted as a watershed between a long period of military intrusion in South Korean politics and a shift towards more open, liberal democratic governance. From the time of the military coup of Park

Chung Hee (Pak Chŏng-hŭi) in 1961 to the end of Chun Doo Hwan's (Chŏn Du-hwan) Sixth Republic, also begun by a military coup in 1980, Korean politics were dominated by generals turned politicians. Their use of legal and extra-legal power to repress dissent, cow the national assembly and concentrate power in a highly centralised administrative structure made a mockery of South Korea's formal constitutional structure. Such power extended to the control of cultural life in South Korea as well. Every major regime change from 1960 until 1988 was accomplished only by major upheavals from below or military coups from above. After 1960, however, twenty-five years of economic development led to structural changes in South Korea that made the continued insistence of its military leaders on discipline and unity in the name of development and military security increasingly meaningless. By the mid-1980s, a coalition of student activists and labour was joined by the urban middle class in massive demonstrations demanding democratic reforms that culminated in the summer of 1987. Thereafter, the government promulgated a new direct election law, a new press law guaranteeing free speech, and a number of other concessions. The elections of a new government in 1988 marked the first peaceful transfer of power in South Korean history. This transfer of power marked the rapid evolution of a more open public sphere that created a space for more diverse and creative cultural production in Korea.

To appreciate Korean film at the beginning of the twenty-first century requires at least a passing understanding of the political, cultural and social obsessions that dominated South Korea over the last half of the last century and, for the most part, supported authoritarian rule until the late 1980s. First and foremost among them is the fact of political division (Paik 1993a: 574–5).[1] The situation in which North and South Korean states currently divide the peninsula, each claiming to be the legitimate political expression of the Korean people, is an artefact of the Cold War and bipolar world order that has only recently faded away. The artificial division of Korea lies directly across the fault lines of this global rift enforced by the mutual antagonisms of the United States and Soviet Union in the aftermath of World War II. Furthermore, this division was hardened by the catastrophic Korean War (1950–53). The war desolated both Koreas. It left a legacy of separated families, millions of deaths, atrocities on both sides, the physical destruction of Seoul in the South, the virtual levelling of the North by US bombing, and psychologically traumatised several generations of Koreans. As a result, both Koreas rebuilt their societies in an atmosphere of security paranoia (the North focused on the threat from the United States and the South on another invasion from the North). Thereafter, security concerns legitimated extraordinary state control and the militarisation of their respective societies.

The two Koreas also became proxies for the ideological split between socialism and capitalism that underlaid the Cold War. Fiercely antagonistic, both Korean states developed political cultures that were narrowly defined by their primary Other: the South's virulent anti-Communism in response to the North, and the North's unique brand of socialist self-reliance and enmity toward the South as a dependency of global capitalism. After the Korean War, the political culture of North Korea evolved around the Great Leader's (Kim Il-sŏng) solipsistic and highly nationalistic *chuch'e* (self-reliance) ideology to the exclusion of all other ideas. By the time of his death in 1995 and the emergence of his son, Kim Chŏng-il, to leadership, North Korea had developed into a hermetically sealed society with a totally self-referential culture – a culture hardly conducive of creativity and diversity (Cumings 1997: 394–433). Thus, post-Korean War North Korean cultural production is a total creature of the state; all culture must be based on the essence of *chuch'e* ideology.

For its part, South Korea developed after the Korean War as one of the most militantly anti-Communist societies in the world. The South's first President (1948–60), Syngman Rhee (Yi Sŭng-man) based his rise to power on his intransigent anti-Communist and nationalist credentials. While South Korea was in name a constitutional republic, Rhee's presidency continued the repressive emergency powers that had evolved during the war years; and he added a National Security Law (NSL) that allowed the police wide latitude to arrest people for their political views. Indeed, a modified version of the NSL remains embedded in Korean law even after the post-1988 democratisation. To many conservative Koreans and to most post-Korean War regimes, something like the NSL remains an important weapon against Communist subversion from the North no matter how blatantly it contradicts the constitutional rights of free speech and assembly. To be charged as a Communist or Communist sympathiser was an oft-used technique of the Rhee government to silence and eliminate its enemies. Later leaders such as Park Chung Hee (1961–79) and Chun Doo Hwan (1980–88) perfected its use against their political opponents. Security paranoia and the perceived threat of Communist subversion also led to the creation under Park Chung Hee of a large, draconian secret police force, the notorious Korean Central Intelligence Agency (KCIA). The KCIA was a spectre in political life throughout the 1960s, 1970s, and 1980s, and its nefarious activities extended into the realm of cultural production as well.

Compared to its Northern neighbour, South Korean society has always been more open, even in the era of tightest authoritarian controls during the years of Park Chung Hee's *Yushin* Constitution (1972–79) and Chun Doo Hwan's Fifth Republic (1981–87).[2] But this should not lead us to think that repression was limited to the political realm. Cultural production had always to confront government controls whether in the form of licences, registration systems, overt censorship, or just the chilling effects of intimidation leading to perhaps the worst outrage of all, self-censorship (Robinson 1984: 312–46). It was not only the case that journalism and creative writing had to cleave to a neutral political line, censorship intruded into the visual arts as well.[3] Any treatment in the arts that could be considered as either critical, whether directly or indirectly, of the current regime, or worse yet, supportive of socialism in general and/or the North Korean regime in particular, would draw the state's attention. Even academic research came under government scrutiny, and some professors who dared to recognise the Korean Communist movement during the colonial period as an integral part of modern Korean history lost their jobs in the 1970s as a result.

Anti-Communism in the South and the exclusive focus on *chuch'e* ideology in the North was augmented by the second widespread preoccupation, a strong, almost obsessive, nationalism. As noted above, *chuch'e* ideology defines the nation as totally self-reliant, counterpoised against all others including their Southern brethren who, in Northern nationalist discourse, are simply lackeys of American-led global capitalism. So unitary is its logic that, in its name, North Korea has become perhaps the most isolated nation-state in the world today. Nationalism in South Korea is more complicated: first, because it has always viewed itself as part of the world system; second, because as a more open society it tolerates a broader spectrum of what might define the nation; and finally because in the past the Republic of Korea (ROK) state has had to defend itself against charges from the North, and at times its own political opposition, of the collaborationist (with Japanese colonialism therefore non-nationalist) nature of its founding élites (Robinson 1993: 183). With different emphases, the North and South Korean states each imposes its own narrative of national becoming that legitimates its claims to be the single true political expression of the Korean people. The means at hand for doing this lies in the cultural realm. Like all other states, North and South Korea each favours a specific historical narrative of nation within the curriculum of its very centralised educational system. In their early decades each state spent precious resources to codify the architectural, iconographic, artistic and literary expressions of the nation, past and present. These activities led to interesting bifurcations of Korean history and its traditional cultural legacy.

The North focused its historical and cultural lineage on the northernmost of three ancient kingdoms extant on the peninsula between the fourth and seventh centuries. This kingdom, Koguryŏ, was, interestingly, a trans-Yalu state that held sovereignty at one time over parts of Manchuria and Liaotung; it was also militarily the most powerful. The South, however, stresses a lineage that, while including Koguryŏ, features more prominently the southernmost Silla kingdom, the kingdom that first unified the peninsula in the later part of the seventh century. The territorial logic is obvious, and each state works with the historical traces it controls but, over time, such practices skew the study of the entire history of the peninsula and its environs, not to mention the story as it might unfold in their respective middle-school textbooks. In fact, this war over different aspects of the historical past in north-east Asia is a wider conflict that draws in the Japanese and Chinese. Currently the Chinese are pushing to have the tombs of the ancient Koguryŏ monarchs designated by UNESCO as World Heritage Sites, claiming them as a part of Chinese history to the distraction of both the North and South Koreans.[4] From the late nineteenth century, and during its colonial domination of Korea (1910–45), Japan worked assiduously to create a history of north-east Asia that would place itself at

isolated North

its centre, thus legitimising its colonisation of Korea and later seizure of Manchuria in 1931 (Pai 2000). Because of this *ex post facto* nationalist, historiographical warfare, the archaeology and early history of the region remain a highly contested project.

A third obsession that has affected cultural production in Korea in the postwar era is the memory of colonialism. As in many non-Western societies, the failure of the ancient regime, in Korea's case the Chosŏn dynasty (1392–1910), to defend its sovereignty against the Western and Japanese imperialist onslaught in the late nineteenth century cast a pall over its entry into the modern world system. In Korea, reformers and modernisers, in and out of government, fought a losing battle with an intransigently conservative élite to carry out the radical social and political changes that would have been necessary for the preservation of Chosŏn sovereignty. In the end, the progressives were caught in a dilemma that informed cultural development in Korea for the better part of the 1900s. That is, modernisers in Korea took their inspiration from the very forces (most notably the Japanese) that threatened the political and cultural autonomy of what they hoped might become a modern Korean nation. By doing this, early Korean nationalist intellectuals placed themselves in a position that was critical of the Korean tradition (weak, backward, unscientific, superstitious) and that supported a modernity dominated by the future colonial ruler of Korea (Schmid 2002: 101–38). From its beginnings Korean nationalism was a project to create a modern Korean nationalist culture while jettisoning what it viewed as the sources of weakness and corruption in the tradition that left Korean society prostrate in the face of Japanese power by the turn of the century. This placed them in conflict with their own tradition, the usual repository of symbols from which the content of any national identity is formed.

The advent of Japanese colonial rule in 1910 transformed Korean nationalism into an independence movement. Unfortunately, a unified and purposeful movement to regain political independence was repressed effectively by Japanese power; only with Japan's defeat in 1945 did Korea regain its independence, but no one leader or group within the fragmented nationalist movement could claim credit for the Japanese defeat. And within a month of liberation, the United States and Soviet Union had imposed a joint occupation setting the stage for the division of Korea and the continuing nationalist conflict that is now organised around two opposing political systems, each claiming leadership of the nation. What is important for the purposes of this chapter, however, is the cultural experience under Japanese rule and its lingering effects on cultural production in post-liberation Korea. The Japanese annexed Korea with the long-range intention of assimilating Korea into Japanese society. The ultimate logic of such an ideology meant the destruction of native Korean culture, its language, mores, customs, in short all those things that made Koreans culturally distinct from Japanese. This appallingly arrogant policy emerged from the Japanese belief in a historical, cultural affinity between Japan and Korea, the proximity of its colony to the metropole, and a general cultural hubris of the Japanese themselves in the early twentieth century – a product of their own successful modernisation and their enthusiasm for technocratic, social engineering.

While the political movement to regain independence was crushed within Korea and fragmented into internecine factional struggle in exile, nationalist intellectuals carried out a valiant effort to create a high modern national culture. This was a movement to define the Korean nation, codify the Korean language, create a modern literature, and write a national history. In short, Korean intellectuals conceived most cultural production as part of a struggle to define and preserve a Korean cultural identity in the face of Japanese cultural domination. The battle played out, however, within the limits defined by Japanese colonial authorities. After an initial decade of total repression within the cultural realm, the Japanese tolerated a limited range of nationalist cultural expression within a native press, publishing industry, film, visual arts, dance and theatre, and music. As long as Koreans did not overtly challenge Japanese political authority, they could write their histories and do their linguistic studies. But any criticism of Japanese, in short any *lèse-majesté*, was subject to censorship just as overt political resistance, especially that emanating from the left, was severely repressed. This truncated the cultural world of the Korean colony by forcing Korean cultural production into safe areas of discourse.

After all, the Japanese had the resources of the state at their disposal, and they devoted tremendous energy to reinterpreting the Korean cultural heritage as a part of the larger evolution of Japanese culture. This meant organising an enormous historical and archaeological project to rewrite the entire history of north-east Asia and create texts that explained this new interpretation of Korea in the expanding public school system. The Japanese controlled the entirety of Korean space, ruins, archaeological sites, temples, extant art and physical objects. From the late nineteenth century Japanese collectors and archaeologists had swooped down to remove to Japan the most prized objects representing the Korean past. Together, the state projects to museumify the Korean tradition and interpret it as part of Japanese history, along with the considerable publishing done within Japanese academe, represented a colossal challenge to private Korean researchers and intellectuals who attempted to counter what they rightly saw as a mutilation of their national heritage (Pai 2000).

Perhaps a more telling structural problem affecting the creation of a Korean national culture was the cultural and economic dominance of Japan. Japanese culture defined the modern sphere in Korea. The best jobs and opportunities for the educated Korean middle class lay in the colonial bureaucracy or Japanese-dominated semi-governmental corporations or private companies. Over time, particularly by the 1930s when it appeared Korean political resistance was a dead letter, the very people who might have been the leaders of a vital Korean nationalist cultural/political movement were gradually co-opted by their participation in the modern life of the colony (Shin and Robinson

1999: 1–18). They were co-opted in the sense that, to be successful and upwardly mobile, they had to emphasise the Japanese side of a hybrid identity they had developed as colonial subjects. To be sure, Koreans never abandoned their ethnic identity *in toto* – colonialism encourages adoption of the cultural norms of the coloniser while continuing to discriminate on the basis of the great ethnic divide between ruler and subject. And the success of the Japanese in garnering the participation of middle-class Koreans in colonial life did not stop the creation of a significant body of Korean nationalist cultural formation. But, after the sudden demise of Japanese rule, some aspects of colonial cultural production became suspect.

The last decade of Japanese rule roughly coincided with World War II in Asia. We must remember that the war started in Asia with the Japanese invasion of China in 1937. As Japan's aggression in China morphed into an attempt to dominate not just China but south-east Asia and Indonesia, it evolved a policy of total war mobilisation at home and in its older colonies. In Korea, a policy of forced cultural assimilation accompanied the economic and political mobilisation for total war. By the time of Hitler's invasion of Poland in 1939, the Japanese had banned Korean language use in colonial schools and required that Japanese be used in all public and semi-governmental offices. A collection of mass associations of writers, film-makers and artists was organised to mobilise cultural production in the service of war propaganda. These leagues were cultural expressions of a myriad of other leagues that organised all natural groupings (youths, women, labourers, government employees etc.) for collective action in the service of the war. By the time of Pearl Harbor in 1941, the Japanese had banned Korean-language publications. They even forced Koreans to change their names to Japanese surnames in order to advance the fiction that their largest and most populous colony was not a colony at all but part of the 'inner lands' of Japan proper.

I am convinced that the Japanese cultural assimilation failed dismally. They could never have hoped to efface a cultural identity of 25 million Koreans that had been several millenniums in the making. But the fact that they tried is crucial to understanding post-war Korean assumptions about their national culture and why Koreans have nurtured this memory and even projected it backwards to encompass the total reality of their colonial experience. This is because the cultural assimilation programmes, in hindsight laughable, came in conjunction with the worst depredations of colonial rule between 1937 and 1945. The memory of these cultural outrages was, therefore, intensified accordingly. During the war the Japanese progressively squeezed the Korean population of their lucre and labour in unimaginably brutal ways. By 1945 perhaps as many as 3.5 million Koreans were abroad, in Japan, Manchuria, Sakhalin, China and south-east Asia, working in the worst jobs in mines and factories or serving as labour and cannon-fodder for the Japanese military. Those left at home were working flat out in war industry and being forced to contribute their rice and precious metals to the Japanese war effort. Lucky families were able

to hide their draft-age children in the countryside, but so many found themselves caught up in the maw of the Japanese military. Perhaps the most brutal
memory revolves around the tens of thousands of Korean women who were
lured or conscripted outright into the so-called *wianbu* (Comfort Corps), a
system of forced prostitution that serviced the sexual needs of the Japanese military in China and south-east Asia.[5] It is small wonder then that the Koreans cul-
tivated a hatred for the very mention of the period of Japanese rule in the
post-war era. And even a half a century removed in time, these wounds, cultural, spiritual and physical, remain only partially dormant and liable to painful
reopening at the least provocation.

The background sketched above is offered in order to create a context for
post-war cultural formation in South Korea. The politics of authoritarian governments and their sensitivity to anything that might be construed as pro-
Communist or in any manner deleterious to the legitimacy of these regimes led
to the creation of both informal and formal censorship systems. This narrowed
the range of acceptable topics for publishing or film-making on political
grounds. More broadly and until recently, South Korean regimes' sensitivity to
world opinion and its own domestic propaganda bent on disciplining the population for continuing hardships in the name of economic development constrained portrayals of poverty, miserable working conditions, class or gender,
and urban squalor. Such expression could be conceived as criticism of the
regime itself. This was especially the case during the later part of the presidency
of Park Chung Hee as well as the Fifth Republic of Chun Doo Hwan. The emergency decrees were vaguely worded prohibitions on any criticism of the person
of the president or the *Yushin* Constitution itself. As such, they gave censors the
power to consider even portrayals of poverty or social injustice as direct
'criticism' of the *Yushin* system and thus damaging to social and political
harmony. This is to not overstate the case of formal censorship. The main
problem in the cultural arena was the possibility of drawing the attention of the
authorities to one's work. Once flagged as either politically suspect or socially
'unhealthy' any number of bad things could happen given the oppressive
scrutiny maintained by the state.

Park Chung Hee was also the president who most directly mobilised the
power of the state in the service of nationalist cultural construction. Park
mobilised nationalism and patriotism to support the legitimacy of the state; his
regime also mobilised nationalism in the service of economic development (see
Park 1962).[6] Under Park the first cultural preservation acts were passed in
1961. Thereafter, the ROK created a system that inventoried, classified and pro-
tected National Cultural Properties such as ruins, temples, art objects and crafts
on the basis of their cultural and historical significance.[7] More interestingly, the
1961 law created a system for the identification and support of Intangible
Cultural Assets. Intangible Cultural Assets were artists, craft-workers and performers of traditional arts who were given stipends by the government to pass
on their knowledge to future generations in order to preserve those arts that

were in danger of extinction. Such a system placed traditional arts in a cocoon, behind glass as in a museum diorama. It also politicised the traditional arts because it immediately encouraged proponents of various schools of dance, song and crafts, among others, to lobby government committees in order to legitimise their respective traditions and to obtain the state stipends that came with being chosen as an intangible cultural property.

State support of museums, academies for traditional arts, and reconstruction of ancient palaces, tombs, temples, and other architectural sites reached its height during the presidency of Chun Doo Hwan. Chun was feared because of his ruthlessness, but he was uniformly loathed. He had seized power in the aftermath of the bloody suppression in May 1980 of a popular uprising in the south-west city of Kwangju (Gwangju), a traditional stronghold of political opposition (Lewis 2002). The nationwide movement that spawned the Kwangju rebellion initially had been in protest to continuing martial law and the refusal of the government to institute democratic reforms in the aftermath of Park Chung Hee's assassination the year before. Chun's emergence as a new dictator at this moment destroyed the hope for an opening towards a more liberal political climate and fatally compromised his legitimacy as a ruler. In order to redress his legitimacy problems Chun lavished support on the traditional arts. As a result, Korean people got new museums and new performance venues, but Chun never overcame the loathing of the citizenry.[8]

There is another issue that clouds cultural production in Korea and that is related to the obsession with traditional roots of national identity. This is the particular ambivalence with which post-war Koreans have embraced Western popular culture. South Korea's startling evolution from dirt-poor 'third world nation' to middle-class industrial and global trading power between 1960 and 1985 has been well documented. Less understood is the effect of this telescoped development on Korean culture and society. Over the space of twenty-five years, hyperdevelopment transformed Korea from a rural agrarian country into an urban, industrialised and consumer-oriented society (see Amsden 1989; Lie 1998).[9] The astounding growth rates brought equally dramatic changes in Korean society. General living patterns, work-places, family structure and social values were all transformed by the rapid structural change that accompanied this growth. Social and cultural critics decried the loss of traditional values and customs in the rush not to be left behind during this unprecedented period of social and economic mobility. Moreover, state officials also feared that traditional patterns of authority and idealised values of sobriety, frugality and hard work stressed within their idea of Korea's Confucian tradition were being trampled in rapid transition to a consumer-oriented society. Ironically, government newsreels enjoined people to save money by simplifying traditional ancestor rites and burial customs, such propaganda clashing with their own worries that important traditions were rapidly being lost. During the 1970s sumptuary legislation prohibited (with little effect) the use of foreign languages in commercial signage and 'long-haired' youths were accosted by the police and in some cases had their locks forcibly shorn to comply with school regulations.

The imperatives of Cold War ideology, national identity struggles, and the concern for the corrosive effects of Western capitalist culture on traditional values have weighed down (with seriousness) cultural and artistic production in post-war South Korea. My choice of the metaphor of weight is deliberate. Milan Kundera depicted its antithesis in his famous novel, *The Unbearable Lightness of Being*; in this work lightness evoked the existential difficulties that followed political change (Kundera 1991). In this case, the spiritual crisis described was the fall of Communism in Czechoslovakia and a shift from the heaviness of political burden (the struggle for democracy) to the lightness of Western consumerism and the absence of struggle.[10] I submit that a similar dynamic was (and remains) at play in South Korea in the aftermath of the successful democratisation movement of the late 1980s. For forty years cultural life and production had been weighed down by the heavy responsibilities of national cultural preservation, resistance to authoritarian politics, and the ambivalent discourse centred on the debate about a true Korean culture and the assault of Western popular mass culture.

Perhaps this was most true of the 1980s, the period when the combined weight of these movements pressed down the hardest on the Korean people. Those that bore the brunt of this weight were referred to as the 3-8-6 generation. These were Koreans in their thirties, attending college in the 1980s, and who were born in the 1960s. By the 1980s the student movement in Korea had become thoroughly institutionalised. Freshmen who entered college in the 1980s were pressured into study clubs where seniors indoctrinated them into the intricacies of opposition ideology by reading underground classics of Marxist theory. Student life was saturated with political activities that included on-campus as well as more dangerous off-campus demonstrations. There was little room not to be political. The college student mass and their leaders are generally credited with leading the successful democratisation movement that peaked in 1987. In the summer of 1987, demonstrating students and wildcat labour strikes were joined in a series of massive citizen demonstrations by what had heretofore been a quiescent urban middle class. The demonstrations forced the government to announce a number of important reforms, including: a new election law providing for direct presidential elections; guarantees for a free press; and provisions for the election of local officials and other serious concessions. This augured the end of military intrusion in politics and led, ultimately, to the election of the first non-military politician as president in 1992.

While the struggles of the 1980s led to the beginning of democratisation and true civilian governance, cultural life thereafter seemed vacuous and purposeless to many who had devoted their life's work to opposing authoritarian rule. Some artists who expressed their sense of detachment in the new era of apolitical cultural life were roundly criticised as somehow giving up. Yet, such expressions captured what many felt was the existential crisis that had beset

Korean culture in the 1990s. Kim Chi-ha, whose work in the 1960s and 1970s pioneered open criticism of authoritarianism, is representative of a new detachment from politics. His most recent collection of poetry, *Hwagae* (*A Flowering*), seems to evoke the desencanto of the post-democratisation era. His disorientation is directly a result of his freedom. In a poem entitled 'The Aloneness of Freedom' he writes:

> The iron shackles are broken,
> In the aloneness of freedom
> I long for your order of oppression.
>
> I shall have no dreams;
> I will not stop this business of
> Bearing pain with dreams.
>
> I will live from day to day without feeling
> This life I cannot bear.[11]

The evolution of Korean democracy since 1987 has been slow and painful. For the arts, however, democratisation has provided unprecedented freedom of expression. And the 1990s witnessed a remarkable renaissance for film, literature and theatre. Suddenly, artists were free to comment on the political repression of the past. Moreover, novelists and film-makers could explore the issue of a divided Korea virtually free from censorship. By the mid-1990s the fear of North Korean Communism had also abated. While the National Security Law that prohibited outright praise of North Korea remained, one anomalous feature of the imperfect democratisation, namely a spate of television dramas, films and novels, examined the painful social and political contradictions of authoritarian rule over the past twenty years. One particularly influential television series, *Moraesigye* (*Hourglass*, 1995), provided in melodramatic form a reckoning of social and political fissures in 1980s Korea. Its characters represented enmeshed archetypes, including student activists, salarymen, government officials, business tycoons, police, and labourers – all the antagonists in the political drama of post-war Korea. Normal activity virtually stopped during the hours of the television series as people tuned in for the latest episode. It was a national purging of the past; finally, there opened a direct discussion of the trials, tribulations, pain and suffering caused by repressive politics and the inequities and uncertainties in Korea's rapidly changing society in the 1970s and 1980s.

Nowhere has this new freedom of expression been more obvious than in the arena of film. Indeed, I would submit that the so-called 'Korean Wave' (*Hanryu*) of successful recent media products is one direct example of the new energies loosed in the 'apolitical' post-democratisation era. It was only in the 1990s that the government began to pull back from what had been almost thirty years of intrusion into all aspects of film production. As Darcy Paquet's chapter in this volume makes clear, direct censorship, quota systems, licensing manipulation, direct investment and the creation of a standards bureau were features of this intervention in the film industry. Indeed, the entire history of Korean film has been marked by government interference. From its beginning in the colonial period, film-makers were damned if they did or did not; namely, they suffered censorship if they pushed the margins politically or severe criticism from contemporary nationalist élites at the time if they sought refuge in the creation of escapist melodramas. Either way, colonial cultural repression, whether by colonialists or by élitist Korean intellectuals, constrained creativity. Moreover, with hindsight post-liberation nationalist intellectuals criticise Korean films of this era for having to rely on Japanese financing or for being made as propaganda for the colonial regime. But for film-makers of that era, to make movies meant working within the system. Even famous *auteur* directors such as Na Un-gyu ended up working within the state-controlled film industry of the late colonial period.[12]

Interestingly, post-liberation cinema had to endure many of the same structural constraints that the film industry suffered during the colonial era. Film-makers had to compete with much more popular Hollywood films, lacked indigenous sources of finance, and had to manoeuvre within a strict regime of censorship. Korean directors made some very good films, but such films never caught on with the Korean public whose appetite for Hollywood blockbusters seemed insatiable; or, if they were not sufficiently 'engaged' politically, film-makers were trivialised by Korean critics. Only in the 1980s did Korean films gain recognition at the level of international film festivals, but even prize-winning films such as Im Kwon-Taek's (Im Kwŏn-t'aek) *Mandala* (*Mandara*, 1981) failed to capture a broad Korean audience. Moreover, the films of the 1980s continued to harp on heavy topics such as the materialism and moral decay of post-development Korea, the agony of division, or paeans to nation and to lost traditions.

This string of artistically successful, politically engaged, but commercially unviable films ended as the post-democratisation era deepened. One film marked both an end and a beginning within the field of Korean cinema in the early 1990s. Im Kwon-Taek's *Sopyonje* (*Sŏp'yŏnje*, 1992) broke ground as the largest grossing, up to that time, Korean film in the post-war era. It marked a beginning in the sense that it anticipated the commercial successes of a number of smash hits that have brought Korean audiences back to the theatres and, more importantly, back to Korean films since the mid to late 1990s. More significantly, perhaps, *Sopyonje* represented a culmination (an ending?) of post-war angst – the smouldering resentments, grief and tragedy borne by Koreans through decades of division, political repression, and social and political turmoil. Its tale of itinerant *p'ansori* singers struggling to keep alive a dying tradition of sung oral narrative captured Korean audiences at several levels.[13] The theme of lost traditions and the powerful evocation of core Korean feeling in song provoked an outpouring of discussion about the future of Korean

Figure 5 A beginning and an end for South Korean cinema: *Sopyonje* (1992).

society and the dangers of losing its cultural roots. This film catapulted *p'ansori* into a status as the iconic folk art form that singularly expressed Korean national feeling. Moreover, one of the film's main plot lines in which the student-daughter in the fictive family of singers is blinded by the father so that she might gain the *han* necessary for her singing to reach its ultimate power in some way seemed to sublimate the collective *han* in 1990s Korea itself. The Korean word *han* carries a broad sense of a deeply seeded Korean experience of oppression and unrequited resentment borne of generations of struggle. It was as if *Sopyonje*'s evocation of *han* at this particular moment in contemporary Korean history tapped into a strong desire of Koreans at all levels of society to remember their sufferings but to move on. I do not want to carry this analogy too far. To my mind, however, this marks a lifting away of the ponderous weight of social and political activism within the culture industry of Korea, a liberation, if you like, from the imperatives of the master narratives of nation, anti-Communism, and lament over modernisation's assault upon traditional Korean culture and memory.

From the late 1990s this liberation has been particularly obvious in the arena of film. The blockbuster *Shiri* (*Swiri*, 1999) out-grossed *Titanic* (US, 1997) in Korea, no mean achievement given that *Titanic* earned the most money worldwide of any film ever. More significantly, it treated the theme of division in

Figure 6 North Korean as human being: the blockbuster *Shiri* (1999).

unprecedented ways. For the first time, North Koreans were presented as human beings – this a huge first step away from the master narrative of the Cold War and the demonisation of the South's Northern brethren. Another hugely successful film, *Joint Security Area* (*Kongdong gyŏngbiguyŏk JSA*, 2000), moves this normalisation of North Koreans further with its love story between North and South Korean protagonists. Even the perennial trope of evil Japanese colonists was blown open by *Lost Memories 2009* (*2009 Losŭt'ŭ memorijŭ*, 2002) where its unprecedented plot device that posits a continued Japanese occupation of Korea in the year 2009 and time-travel underlay its box-office success. Suddenly, directors are using politically or culturally charged themes as simple plot elements or settings in their scenarios for their dramatic effect, not to make a political point. And Korean audiences seem also to have lost their self-consciousness about such themes.

Something has clearly changed within the culture industry in South Korea. The failing grip of the old master narratives has loosed new energies and made new synergies possible. And it is these synergies that now command the attention of an increasingly large foreign audience for recent Korean film, captivated as they are with its freshness, technical virtuosity and startling candour. As Nancy Abelmann and Jung-ah Choi ask in this volume, how can a film like *Attack the Gas Station* (*Juyoso sŭpgyŏksagŏn*, 1999) featuring as it does liberal doses of violence, fierce cultural iconoclasm and scathing social commentary, be a comedy? Part of their answer parallels this chapter's contention that Koreans, now revelling in the lightness of liberation from the master narratives

Figure 7 Love shared between North Koreans and South Koreans: *Joint Security Area* (2000).

of their past, are now willing to laugh both with and at themselves. Perhaps this joy is taken for granted by Koreans under the age of forty but, for their elders, this must still feel strange – a strangeness borne of finally receiving permission to view the past without regret and banish its pain from the present.

REFERENCES AND BIBLIOGRAPHY

Amsden, Alice (1989) *Asia's Next Giant: South Korea and Late Industrialization*, Oxford: Oxford University Press.

Cumings, Bruce (1980, 1990) *The Origins of the Korean War*, Volumes I and II, Princeton: Princeton University Press.

——(1997) *Korea's Place in the Sun: A Modern History*, New York: W. W. Norton.

Howard, Keith (ed.) (1995) *True Stories of the Korean Comfort Women*, London: Cassell.

Kim, Uchang (1993) 'The Agony of Cultural Construction: Politics and Culture in Modern Korea', in Hagen Koo (ed.), *State and Society in Contemporary Korea*, Ithaca: Cornell University Press: 163–96.

——(2003) 'Poetics of Presence: Korean Writing in the Post-Democracy Movement Era'. Unpublished manuscript given as Patten Lecture at Indiana University, March 2003.

Kundera, Milan (1991) *The Unbearable Lightness of Being*, New York: Harper Publishers.

Lee, Hyangjin (2000) *Contemporary Korean Cinema: Identity, Culture, and Politics*, Manchester: Manchester University Press.

Lewis, Linda (2002) *Laying Claim to the Memory of May: A Look Back at the 1980 Kwangju Uprising*, Honolulu: University of Hawai'i Press.

Lie, John (1998) *Han Unbound: The Political Economy of South Korea*, Stanford: Stanford University Press.

Pai, Hyung-il (2000) *Constructing 'Korean' Origins: A Critical Review of the*

Archaeology, Historiography, and Racial Myth in Korean State-Formation Theories, Cambridge, MA: Harvard University Asia Center.

Paik, Nak-Chung (1993a) 'The Idea of Korean Literature Then and Now', *Positions* 3, 1 (January): 574–85.

—— (1993b) 'South Korea: Unification and the Democratic Challenge', *New Left Review* 197 (January–February): 67–84.

Park, Chung Hee (1962) *Our Nation's Path*, Seoul: Republic of Korea, Ministry of Culture and Information.

Pihl, Marshall R. (1994) *The Korean Singer of Tales*, Cambridge, MA: Council on East Asian Studies Publications.

Robinson, Michael (1984) 'Colonial Publication Policy and the Korean Nationalist Movement', in Ramon H. Myers and Mark R. Peattie (eds), *The Japanese Colonial Empire 1895–1945*, Princeton: Princeton University Press: 312–46.

—— (1993) 'Enduring Anxieties: Cultural Nationalism and Modern East Asia', in Harumi Befu (ed.), *Cultural Nationalism in East Asia: Representation and Identity*, Berkeley: Institute of East Asian Studies, University of California Press: 167–87.

—— (1994) 'Narrative Politics, Nationalism and Korean History', *Papers of the British Association for Korean Studies* 6: 26–40.

Schmid, Andre (2002) *Korea Between Empires 1895–1919*, New York: Columbia University Press.

Shin, Gi-Wook and Robinson, Michael (1999) 'Introduction: Rethinking Colonial Korea', in Gi-Wook Shin and Michael Robinson (eds), *Colonial Modernity in Korea*, Cambridge, MA: Harvard University Asia Center, Harvard University Press: 1–18.

Shin, Gi-Wook and Hwang, Kyung Moon (eds) (2003) *Contentious Kwangju: The May 18 Uprisings in Korea's Past and Present*, New York: Rowman and Littlefield Publishers, Inc.

NOTES

1. Paik's point here is that the fact of division expands beyond the mere issue of political separation to encompass every facet of South Korean life: social, cultural, economic and political. To Paik, division is both a structural condition and a mentality in contemporary Korean life.
2. The *Yushin* Constitution created the Fourth Republic and provided for an indirect election of the president virtually guaranteeing Park Chung Hee presidency for life. The constitution was supported by a series of emergency measures that made illegal even vague criticism of the president or the constitution itself, thus providing wide censorial power to the police. All publications, newspapers, and other public forms of expression – including films – were covered by these laws.
3. Post-war censorship was perhaps more effective than the Japanese system where language issues often hampered colonial efforts to monitor the publishing industry.
4. In the winter of 2004, private historical associations co-ordinated a global e-mail offensive using Korean middle- and high-school students to alert historians of East Asia and other interested parties to the Chinese application for World Heritage Status for the Koguryŏ tombs in China's north-eastern provinces.
5. For direct testimony of these women, see Howard 1995.
6. Park's speeches brought together in this collection focus on aspects of the 'national' tradition that most served the need of his government to promote loyalty to the state and frugality in economic matters. Hence, Park evoked a return to Confucian values of duty, loyalty and propriety.
7. There was a clear hierarchy to classification with the top designation being 'National Treasure' and less-important properties simply denoted as 'National Cultural Properties'.

8. Chun was later imprisoned for massive fraud after the discovery of an illegal political slush fund of hundreds of millions of dollars that had been commandeered from major industrialists as well as directly stolen from government coffers.

9. Between 1960 and 1985 South Korea's 80:20 ratio of rural to urban population had inverted. Over 80 per cent of South Koreans lived in cities of 10,000 or more in 1985. Moreover, in the same time-frame the per capita income of Korea went from 80 to 4,500 dollars per year.

10. I borrow this metaphor from Kim (2003).

11. This translation is by Uchang Kim. I am indebted to him for using this example for a similar point made in his unpublished paper given as a Patten Lecture at Indiana University, March 2003 (Kim 2003).

12. Na Un-gyu burst upon the early Korean film scene as director of and actor in *Arirang* (1926), perhaps the most famous Korean silent film ever made. It has always been read as an allegory of Korean resistance to Japanese rule.

13. *P'ansori* is a folk tradition of sung oral narrative. The singer alternately sings and declaims while accompanied by a drummer. Sung by itinerant performers moving from market to market, performances could last up to eight hours requiring enormous stamina and skill by the singer. Modern performances are usually based only on portions of the traditional texts. For more on *p'ansori*, see Pihl (1994).

2. THE KOREAN FILM INDUSTRY: 1992 TO THE PRESENT

Darcy Paquet

In 1992, as South Koreans looked towards a new future without their hated military government, the local film industry found itself at a similar crossroads. On the one hand, changes in the political sector were promising the birth of a freer society. For socially conscious film-makers, such as Jang Sun-woo (Chang Sŏn-u), Park Kwang-su (Pak Kwang-su) and Im Kwon-Taek (Im Kwŏn-t'aek), this meant a new-found freedom to explore themes and ideas that had been banned for decades. In the coming years, films such as Park Kwang-su's *To the Starry Island* (*Kŭ sŏme kago ship'da*, 1993), which touched on atrocities committed during the Korean War (1950–53), and Jang Sun-woo's *A Petal* (*Kkonnip*, 1996), concerning the 1980 Kwangju massacre, would put a new perspective on Korean history and society.

Nonetheless, in 1992 film producers and investors housed in the offices of *Ch'ungmuro* (a street which formed the Korean film industry's traditional hub, and a byword for the industry) were gripped with the fear that local cinema was about to vanish. Many film companies were going out of business. The percentage of ticket sales accounted for by local films was reaching all-time lows (18.5 per cent in 1992, and 15.9 per cent in 1993). A lack of investors meant that fewer and fewer movies were being made. Most ominously, the local film market which, like that of China, had long enacted strong barriers to foreign imports, had just been forced open. Hollywood studios had established branch offices on Korean soil for the first time, and the spectre of unrestricted competition with the Hollywood majors looked likely to drive Korean cinema into a small corner of the overall market. A quotation from the introduction to *Korea Cinema 93*, an annual publication by the Korean Motion Picture Promotion Corporation (since renamed the Korean Film Commission), illustrates the level of concern in the industry:

> The state of affairs of the Korean film industry in 1993 [is] more than just a depression. Its slump is so serious that the industry may collapse completely . . . the Korean film industry [has been brought] to the edge of a cliff, where it is about to fall. ('Films in 1993': 3)

Korea's ultimate response to this dilemma was to pursue a newly invigorated drive towards commercial cinema. In using the term 'commercial cinema' I do not intend to invoke a dichotomy between 'artistic cinema' on the one hand – praised by critics and screened at prestigious film festivals – and simplistic works which are supposedly more popular with the general public. This distinction is shown to be problematic when we note that Korean audiences have turned such challenging and complex works as *Oasis* (*Oasisŭ*, 2002), *Memories of Murder* (*Sarin-ŭi ch'uŏk*, 2003), *A Good Lawyer's Wife* (*Baramnan kajŏk*, 2003), and *Old Boy* (*Oldŭ boi*, 2003) into number-one box-office hits.

Instead, commercial cinema refers to the ability of films to recoup their budget – large or small – at the box-office or through other means such as video or international sales. The new generation of producers who gained prominence in the early 1990s – and who would ultimately transform the industry – placed a strong focus on the profitability and self-sufficiency of films. Henceforth, even acclaimed directors would be given intensified pressure not only to make good films, but to make films that would not lose money.

There was also a simultaneous push by the government and the film industry to build a stronger industrial base for film-making. This involved forming larger and more powerful film companies, building more technically advanced infrastructure, opening film schools to provide better training, and searching for new sources of finance for the making of films. The new generation of producers would make full use of Korea's *chaebŏl* (large conglomerates), venture-capital companies, and generous government funding to bring this about.

By 2001, South Korea possessed one of the strongest commercial industries in the world outside of the United States or India, with local cinema accounting for 45 to 50 per cent of overall ticket sales, and individual films outperforming even the biggest Hollywood blockbusters. The commercial success of local cinema also helped to give an unusually large number of new directors an opportunity to make their début.

This chapter aims to chart how the structure of the Korean film industry has changed since 1992, focusing particularly on governmental policy, sources of film finance, and evolving standards of production. While recognising the drawbacks and new problems caused by the Korean film industry's push towards industrialisation, I contend that overall it was a positive development. Many of the lauded film movements of the past, such as 1910s German Expressionism or Italy's 'Young Cinema' of the late 1950s and early 1960s, took place within the context of a strong and popular local industry. In similar fashion, New Korean Cinema owes much of its robustness and diversity to fundamental changes in the film industry that were carried out in the 1990s.

Film Policy and the Opening of the Korean Film Market

Before the rapid development of the 1990s, some key changes in governmental policy in the mid-1980s set the stage for the industry's later transformation. For decades, Korea's film sector had operated under a piece of legislation called the Motion Picture Law (*Yŏnghwa bŏp*), introduced under military dictator Park Chung Hee in January 1962. Designed more than anything else to restrict and control the development of the film industry, the Motion Picture Law employed various tools to enact strict censorship, limit imports and to consolidate the industry into a handful of large companies which could then more easily be controlled by the government.

Under this policy, production companies were required to hold a licence from the government in order to make films, and so independent production was banned. To receive a licence, film production companies were required to own their own studios and film equipment, to have a certain number of crew members or actors under contract, to own a large amount of capital, and to produce a minimum number of films per year. Under such restrictive requirements – designed to force smaller companies out of business – the number of film companies in Korea quickly plunged after the law was introduced, and it remained at a low level until the 1980s. Meanwhile, the law limited imports by means of a quota, which stipulated that companies could import foreign titles only after producing a given number of local films.

The government also exercised strong censorship through a Public Ethics Committee which had the power to censor or to modify films as it wished. Any hint of questioning or criticising the government's ideology would result in cuts, an outright ban or worse: for example, directors Yi Man-hŭi and Yu Hyŏn-mok were both briefly arrested in the 1960s for making films judged to be sympathetic to Communism. Even seemingly innocuous material was often removed for reasons that remain mysterious. Perhaps the most thoughtful examination of this issue can be found in Kim Hong-jun's video essay *My Korean Cinema* (*Na-ŭi hanguk yŏnghwa*, 2003), which contains a section detailing the cuts made to Ha Kil-jong's coming-of-age classic *March of Fools* (*Babodŭl-ŭi haengjin*, 1976).

In the decade since its adoption, the Motion Picture Law was revised four times (in 1963, 1966, 1970 and 1973) but it continued to function primarily as a means of controlling and regulating Korean cinema rather than promoting it. Frequent changes to lower-level regulations and the irregular enforcement of rules made for considerable chaos within the industry. The typical company that emerged under such policy was a capital-rich, commercially oriented firm based in Seoul that produced Korean films quickly, cheaply and in large quantities in order to obtain permission to import more profitable foreign titles.

The fifth and sixth revisions to the Motion Picture Law, enacted in December 1984 and December 1986, would usher in the most far-reaching changes to film policy until the Motion Picture Law was replaced by a Film Promotion Law in 1996. The fifth revision brought about three major changes: 1. the licensing system for film companies was replaced with a simple registration system whereby film companies would submit a form and a cash deposit to the Ministry of Culture and Information; 2. an independent producer system was established whereby companies or individuals not registered with the Ministry of Culture and Information could legally produce one film per year, provided they submitted a copy of the film to the Ministry; 3. production companies and import companies were henceforth divided into separate legal entities.

The most immediate effect of this revision was the proliferation of production companies, from twenty in 1984 to 104 by 1988. In most cases, the new additions were headed by younger producers who had been unable to launch their own companies under the old policy. Although censorship remained strict and the newer producers relied on many of the same sources of finance as the more established companies (i.e. foreign imports and the sale of theatrical rights to regional distribution networks outside of Seoul), these younger producers would later assume a leading role in introducing new practices in the production of feature films (Hwang 2001: 23).

The sixth revision, in contrast, was a product of outside pressure rather than a reform propagated from within. In 1985, the Motion Picture Export Association of America (MPEAA) issued a strong complaint to the South Korean government with regard to the country's various restrictions on film imports and, after subsequent negotiations between the two governments, a Korea–US Film Agreement was signed later that year.

The content of the agreement was incorporated into the sixth revision of the Motion Picture Law, and consisted of the following: 1. foreign-owned film companies were now allowed to operate on Korean soil; 2. import quotas for foreign films would be abolished, as well as a mandatory ceiling on prices paid for imports; 3. the 100 million won tax ($85,000 at 1986 exchange rates) levied on each imported film – which formerly went into a film-promotion fund – would be abolished. To compensate for these changes, the Screen Quota system, which stipulated that theatres must screen Korean films for a minimum number of days per year (106 to 146, depending on various factors), was retained and the government pledged more fully to enforce it.

Following the sixth revision, the number of foreign films imported into Korea each year jumped almost tenfold, from twenty-seven in 1985 to 264 in 1989. Most significantly, the revision also paved the way for Hollywood studios to set up their own branch offices within Korea. UIP was the first to register in March 1988, with four others to follow: Twentieth Century Fox in August 1988, Warner Bros. in December 1989, Columbia Tristar in October 1990, and Disney (Buena Vista International) in January 1993.

These developments were met with fierce protests by the Korean film community, which warned that Hollywood branch offices would swiftly come to dominate the market with their marketing power, strong content, and the financial backing of their parent companies. When UIP released its first title, *Fatal Attraction* (US, 1987), in 1988, a group of protesters sparked a media frenzy by releasing live snakes into a theatre screening the film.

By 1992, the Hollywood branch offices had not only taken over a significant share of the local market but they had brought about changes to the distribution system which left Korean film companies in a state of crisis. The chain reaction that was created deprived local producers of one of their prime sources of production finance.

Ever since the early 1960s, the Korean distribution sector had been divided into six regional markets, centred around Seoul, Greater Seoul, Pusan, Taegu, Kwangju and Taejon. Before making a film, Seoul-based production companies would obtain financing by pre-selling release rights to regional distributors. Once the film was completed, the production company would book the film directly into a major Seoul theatre, while regional distributors would release the film in their own territories, taking whatever profit was created for themselves. Such a system made it possible for a production company to make a film with a comparatively small amount of money, and for risk to be shared among various distributors throughout the country. At this time, however, Hollywood branch offices (UIP in particular) were pioneering nationwide direct distribution in which a Seoul office would bypass regional distributors and book films directly into theatres across the nation. Less concerned about spreading risk, the branch offices could receive a much higher profit margin from such an arrangement. Gradually, regional distributors lost their influence and sources of revenue and, by 1992, it was clear that South Korea was becoming a single market. For many Korean film companies, this posed a grave threat.

THE *CHAEBŎL* ENTER THE FILM INDUSTRY

In many ways a new era began for the Korean film industry with the release of director Kim Ŭi-sŏk's *Marriage Story* (*Kyŏrhon iyagi*) on 4 July 1992. The film, a comedy about a newly-wed couple whose marriage begins to suffer as the wife's career takes off, was a smash hit at the box-office, drawing 526,000 admissions in Seoul alone. At the time, it was the third-highest-grossing Korean film of all time, after Im Kwon-Taek's *Son of a General* (*Changgun-ŭi adŭl*, 1990: 679,000 admissions) and Kim Ho-sŏn's *Winter Woman* (*Kyŏul yŏja*, 1977: 586,000 admissions).

Marriage Story marked the first major success of so-called 'planned films' (*kihoek yŏnghwa*), a new method of conceiving and producing movies which was championed by a younger generation of producers. Notably, the film was also 25 per cent financed by Samsung, the first of Korea's *chaebŏl* to make a decisive move into the film industry. Other *chaebŏl* would quickly follow suit,

Figure 8 A planned film: *Marriage Story* (1992).

and soon these conglomerates would become the Korean film industry's most important source of finance.

The *chaebŏl*'s decision to enter the film industry was influenced by several factors, particularly the video market. Three of the largest *chaebŏl* – Samsung, Daewoo and LG – not only manufactured VCRs for domestic and international markets, but also operated video divisions to provide content for this lucrative industry. Video-cassette rentals and sales became an increasingly large and profitable industry since its launch in the mid-1980s. In 1991, however, Hollywood branch offices such as Twentieth Century Fox started their own video labels within Korea. With many of the biggest Hollywood films now taken by the branch offices, increased competition for the films which remained led to a sharp rise in the prices paid for video rights, Korean films included. Korean films at this time cost on average only 500 to 600 million won ($560,000 to $670,000 at 1992 exchange rates) to produce and, by 1992, the video rights to more-successful Korean titles were selling for more than it cost to make the film. Given this situation, conglomerates such as Samsung and Daewoo found that, by investing in films at the production stage (and sharing some of the project's risk), video rights could be obtained much more cheaply. Similarly, the scheduled launch of cable television in South Korea in 1995 promised another opportunity to earn profits from film-making. Both Daewoo and Samsung would eventually launch their own movie channels.

The other major factor that induced the *chaebŏl* to enter the film industry was the increasingly influential group of young producers who had entered the film industry in the mid-1980s. These producers, who were pushing for a 'rationalisation' of the film-making process, proved to be good partners for the *chaebŏl*, who wished to introduce their business practices into the industry. Without this confluence of attitudes and ideals on the part of film producers and investors, it is unlikely that the *chaebŏl* would have become so involved in the film business.

As time passed, the conglomerates expanded their activities in the film industry. Whereas initially they engaged in partial financing, by 1995 most *chaebŏl* would fully finance a film's budget in return for all rights to a film, including theatrical release, video and cable television. *Millions in My Account* (*Tonŭl katko ttwiŏra* – Samsung, 1995), *A Hot Roof* (*Kae gat'ŭn nal-ŭi ohu* – Samsung, 1995), *Three Friends* (*Se ch'in'gu* – Samsung, 1996), *A Single Spark* (*Arŭmdaun ch'ŏngnyŏn Chŏn T'ae-il* – Daewoo, 1995), *Their Last Love Affair* (*Chidokhan sarang* – Daewoo, 1996), *Hairdresser* (*Heŏ dŭresŏ* – Haitai, 1995), *Farewell My Darling* (*Haksaeng bugun shinwi* – Jinro G-TV, 1996) and *The Adventures of Mrs. Park* (*Pak Pong-gon kach'ulsagŏn* – SKC, 1996) are all examples of films that were fully financed by conglomerates.

Figure 9 Funded by conglomerate Daewoo: the politically incendiary *A Single Spark* (1995).

Many of the *chaebŏl* also drew up exclusive contracts with production companies, providing financial support in return for the rights to their films. Examples of this include Daewoo with Cine2000, Samsung with Uno Films (later renamed Sidus), Myung Films and Cinema Service, and SKC with Ahn's World Productions. In so doing, the *chaebŏl* could assure themselves of a steady stream of content, while gaining more influence over the production process.

The *chaebŏl* moved to fill gaps in the distribution market following the collapse of regional distributors. Although a few Seoul-based firms such as Hapdong Films and Taehung Pictures had made an effort to forge nationwide distribution chains in the early 1990s, the *chaebŏl* used their financial strength to buy or rent theatres in regional areas outside of Seoul so that they could distribute their films directly throughout the country. Samsung Entertainment was established as an investment/distribution company in 1995, while Daewoo, which had established a small distribution operation earlier, stepped up its activities. The *chaebŏl* therefore succeeded in creating powerful, vertically integrated film companies that could control the making and exploitation of a film from the pre-production and financing stage through production, distribution, exhibition and its release in ancillary markets such as video and cable television.

The *chaebŏl* had considerable influence on the film-making process in Korea and, although major companies such as Samsung, Daewoo, and SKC would all be gone from the industry by 1999, the changes they brought about would remain in place long after their departure. The first noticeable effect of the *chaebŏl*'s entry was a rise in budgets. With large amounts of capital available, budgets rose from an average of 500 to 600 million won in 1992 to 1.5 to 2 billion won four years later. At the same time (due partly to the difficulties faced by companies which did not work with the *chaebŏl*), the overall quantity of production would fall from a pre-1991 average of over 100 films per year to about sixty by 1993 – an average that would hold for the next decade.

The *chaebŏl* also brought about a new emphasis on accounting, or at least the handling of money. A large difference could be seen in the more corporate approach of the *chaebŏl* and the money-handling skills (derogatively referred to as 'finger counting') employed by Korea's older film companies (Hwang 2001: 29). A new emphasis was placed on drawing up detailed budgets in advance and taking steps to encourage efficiency in film-making though the *chaebŏl*, too, would draw criticism from industry observers for a lack of transparency.

In their preference for using well-known actors as a means of reducing a project's risk, the *chaebŏl* also magnified the influence of the local star system. Salaries for the most famous stars, such as Han Sŏk-kyu or Shim Ŭn-ha, rose accordingly, gradually outdistancing the amounts paid to stars in Japan, for example. This not only encouraged the further rise of budgets, but also created a further predisposition towards narratives with one or two strong central characters that could effectively highlight a major star.

A comparatively conservative approach to investing would also push Korean cinema towards the mainstream. The *chaebŏl* generally preferred clearly specified genres, believing them to have a better chance of box-office success. The appearance of new genres, such as the sex-war comedy, was encouraged as a means of competing with Hollywood cinema. At times, however, an overly formulaic approach may have weakened, rather than strengthened, the competitiveness of local cinema. Hit films, when they appeared, tended to produce a string of imitations because they were easy to pitch to investors. Audiences often tired of such repetition, however, and the *chaebŏl* sometimes faced criticism from film-makers and critics for their preference for the familiar over the innovative. One major downside of the *chaebŏl*'s approach is that it failed to encourage more diverse styles of film-making.

The most influential (and beneficial) aspect of the *chaebŏl*'s business activities, however, was their investment in local infrastructure. Many of the leading production companies that emerged in the late 1990s were able to produce their first films with the financial support of the *chaebŏl*. The distribution networks set up by the *chaebŏl* put a check on the growth of the Hollywood branch offices, and gave local films a better chance to remain in theatres and so maximise their box-office potential. Films such as *The Fox Of Nine Tails* (*Kumiho*, 1994) pioneered the use of computerised special effects, helping to build a special-effects industry that, by 2001, would rank among Asia's strongest. The sheer size of the conglomerates and the amounts of money they spent gave a significant boost to Korea's film infrastructure.

The vertically integrated structure of the *chaebŏl*'s film divisions, which were involved in film finance, production, distribution, exhibition, and video markets, also served as a model for the major companies of the future, such as Cinema Service and CJ Entertainment. In their efforts to compete directly with the Hollywood majors by creating large, powerful film businesses, the *chaebŏl* kept Korean cinema firmly rooted in commercial cinema.

By contrast, one can easily imagine an alternative scenario that might have happened, under which film-makers would come to depend on government support for making films that stood little chance of recouping their budgets at the box-office. (Taiwan in the late 1990s might serve as an example.) Such a system might provide some real advantages in that film-makers would enjoy greater creative freedom without interference from investors. It also could make it easier for marginalised voices to find expression through cinema without the pressure to appeal to a wide spectrum of viewers.

Over the long term, however, such film-making environments usually lead to a shrinking of the film industry, and film-makers become vulnerable to their government's commitment to (or disinterest in) local cinema. Tickets sold to local films in Taiwan accounted for an all-time low of 0.1 per cent in 2001 and, apart from established directors like Hou Hsiao-hsien and Tsai Ming-liang (who, with their international reputations, often draw investment from overseas and stand a greater chance of earning a profit through international sales), few film-makers saw the opportunity to make films.

THE INTRODUCTION OF PLANNED FILMS

Many of the changes that took place in the industry in the early and mid-1990s were brought about not only by the *chaebŏl*, but by the group of young producers who formed alliances with them in a bid to develop the industry. Highly critical of the production methods that were prevalent at older film companies, these individuals pushed for a rationalisation of the film-making process through the introduction of so-called 'planned films'.

Prior to the fifth revision of the Motion Picture Law, there was very little internal pressure to change or to develop the production system used by major film companies. Local film production took place in separate divisions within larger companies that earned most of their profits from importing Hollywood or Hong Kong films. Korean films were generally not expected to make money on their own. Often, little time was spent developing a film before shooting began. Plots were usually adapted from well-known novels or stories, or else drawn up by respected directors or screenwriters. After the screenwriter produced a script, a lone producer in charge of the film would edit it personally before submitting it to regional distributors outside of Seoul. After incorporating any changes requested by the regional distributors, the producer would receive financing from them and the film would enter production immediately. (This practice was derogatively called *ipdosŏnmae*, or the 'pre-harvest sale of rice'. See Ch'oe 1993: 243–4.) After production was legally separated from imports in the Motion Picture Law's fifth revision, there gradually appeared a new emphasis on making local movies profitable, particularly by the young producers who were gaining their first experience in film-making. Having received much of their film education at a series of lectures and workshops held at the German and French cultural centres in Seoul in the 1970s and 1980s (some refer to this group as the 'Cultural Centre Generation'), their approach to the film business contrasted sharply with that of older producers.

The planned film essentially involved pre-selecting a target audience and marketing strategy, and using a long period of script development to improve chances of success at the box-office. Apart from the producer, a separate person would be placed in charge of 'planning' (*kihoek*) to ensure a more thoroughly developed film. Planned films also introduced market surveys into Korean film-making. In the development stage of film-making, a target audience of a certain age group or sex was chosen, and then surveys and market research would be used to determine themes or actors who would be most likely to appeal to the chosen group (Hwang 2001: 47). Proponents of planned films were also heavily involved in film promotion. Following the example of the Hollywood branch offices, they introduced pre-release marketing, whereby advertising for a film would appear weeks or months in advance of its release. Again, market analysis was used to direct advertisements to the film's target audience.

Marriage Story, for which Shin Ch'ŏl and Yu In-t'aek are credited with planning, remains the most widely cited example of a planned film. Setting out in the fall of 1989 to make a movie about married life, the production staff conducted large numbers of interviews with young married couples and office workers to provide material for the film's plot. The writing of the screenplay involved eight authors and sixteen rewrites. Throughout the development and pre-production process, meetings were held frequently to discuss changes in the script and strategies for marketing the film.

Marriage Story's success at the box-office set a strong example, and many future productions would adopt a similar system, including *Mister Mama* (*Misŭt'ŏ Mamma*, 1992), *That Man, That Woman* (*Kŭ yŏja kŭ namja*, 1993), *The 101st Proposal* (*Baekhan bŏntchae p'ŭrop'ojŭ*, 1993), *Two Cops* (*T'u k'apsŭ*, 1994) and *Out to the World* (*Sesang pakkŭro*, 1994). Although the concept of the planned film was never universally adopted throughout the industry (and is not in common use today), it would exert a strong influence on film-making until the adoption of a producer system which more closely resembled that of Hollywood in the mid-1990s.

It is worth noting that many of the producers credited with planning on these early 1990s films went on to create some of the best-known contemporary films in Korean cinema. Shin Ch'ŏl and his production company, Shincine, would produce *The Letter* (*P'yŏnji*, 1997), *A Promise* (*Yaksok*, 1998), *Lies* (*Kŏjinmal*, 1999) and *My Sassy Girl* (*Yŏpkijŏgin kŭnyŏ*, 2001). Yu In-t'aek's company, Keyweck Shidae (literally 'Age of Planning'), would produce *A Single Spark* (*Arŭmdaun ch'ŏngnyŏn Chŏn T'ae-il*, 1995), *The Uprising* (*Yi Jae-su-ŭi nan*, 1999) and *Resurrection of the Little Match Girl* (*Sŏngnyangp'ari sonyŏ-ŭi chaerim*, 2002). Shim Chae-myŏng of *That Man, That Woman* and Oh Chŏng-wŏn of *The 101st Proposal* set a strong example for women producers, with Shim forming Myung Films and producing *The Contact* (*Chŏpsok*, 1997), *Happy End* (*Haep'i endŭ*, 1999), *The Isle* (*Sŏm*, 2000), *Joint Security Area* (*Kongdong kyŏngbi kuyŏk JSA*, 2000) and *A Good Lawyer's Wife* (*Paramnan kajŏk*, 2003), while Oh formed b.o.m. Film Productions and produced *The Foul King* (*Panch'ik wang*, 2000), *Tears* (*Nunmul*, 2001), *A Tale of Two Sisters* (*Chang-hwa, Hong-ryŏn*, 2003) and *Untold Scandal* (*Sŭk'aendŭl – Chosŏn namnyŏ sangyŏljisa*, 2003).

THE CHAEBŎL'S EXIT AND THE ARRIVAL OF VENTURE CAPITAL

The *chaebŏl*'s exit from the film industry in the late 1990s is often interpreted as a side-effect of the financial crisis that swept much of Asia in 1997. In South Korea, which was forced to turn to the International Monetary Fund and others for a $58 billion rescue package, the *chaebŏl* came under strong economic and political pressure to concentrate on core businesses and dispose of unneeded subsidiaries. Such pressures may indeed have come into play regarding the closure of the *chaebŏl*'s film divisions, particularly in the case of Samsung. Nonetheless, to some extent the *chaebŏl*'s exit from the film industry may have been predetermined. Profits proved to be not as high as expected, and the box-office failure of several expensive films, such as *Inch'Alla* (*Insyalla*, 1996), caused some companies to adopt a much more conservative investment stance. Competition and the collapse of the local currency also pushed up prices for imported films, turning a formerly profitable business activity into a loss-maker. Finally, cable television produced far less money than hoped for, leaving many of the *chaebŏl* looking for the opportunity to make a graceful exit.

In January 1998, SKC closed its video and film divisions and then, in January 1999, Daewoo also dismantled its film, video and music operations. Samsung followed in May 1999, selling its cable television and theatrical venues to the Dongyang Group and closing its distribution arm after the release of *Shiri* (*Swiri*, 1999) and *Mystery of the Cube* (*Kŏnch'ukmuhan yungmyŏn'gakch'e-ŭi bimil*, 1999). It is worth noting, however, that, although the initial group of *chaebŏl* who had entered the film industry in pursuit of video rights had all made their exit, several mid-sized *chaebŏl*, such as Cheil Jedang (CJ Entertainment) and the Dongyang Group (Showbox), would remain in the industry and eventually play a major role.

Roughly simultaneous to the *chaebŏl*'s withdrawal was the appearance of another major source of film finance in venture-capital companies. Although Ilshin Investment had made an early and aggressive push into the film industry in 1995 by financing Kang Che-gyu's (Kang Jae-gyu) box-office hit *The Gingko Bed* (*Ŭnhaengnamu ch'imdae*, 1996) and setting up its own major distribution chain, other venture-capital companies would not make a fully fledged entry into the business until 1998.

Several factors led venture-capital companies to take an interest in the film industry. A boom in the local KOSDAQ stock market left many of the companies with excess capital to invest. Compared to other forms of venture-capital investment which, typically, take four or five years before producing any monetary return, film offered the opportunity to earn back profit on an investment in about a year. Cinema was also considered a growth industry, particularly after the emergence of blockbusters such as *Shiri*, *Joint Security Area* and *Friend* (*Ch'in'gu*, 2001). Finally, governmental policy under President Kim Dae Jung (1998–2003) encouraged venture-capital companies to set up special funds to be used for film production. These funds were attractive as a means of diversifying an investment and spreading risk (the typical fund invested in a wide range of films over the length of its term) while the Korean Film Commission and the state-run Small Business Corporation further encouraged investors by contributing to many of the funds themselves.

The business activities of the venture-capital companies formed a stark contrast to those of the *chaebŏl*. Most avoided investing in movie theatres, cable television and other film-related businesses, instead focusing solely on film finance. Generally they remained as minority investors rather than funding a film's entire budget, preferring to spread their investment in a portfolio of titles. Venture-capital companies also had far fewer people working in their film divisions. They were less inclined to become directly involved in the film-making process, and so decision-making was not as bureaucratic as under the *chaebŏl*. Producers and directors found themselves with comparatively more artistic freedom. Under venture-capital, the title of executive producer (*chejakt'uja* or *chejakja*) replaced the figure in charge of planning. Less concerned about the intensive development of a film, venture-capital companies demanded more careful accounting of costs so as to make production as efficient as possible, particularly during shooting. Often charged with more financial responsibilities than in the Hollywood system, the executive producer would oversee all money-related matters in a production, becoming newly influential in the film-making process.

In the years following 1999 when Korean cinema entered its boom period, venture capital emerged as the film industry's primary source of production finance. What began as a steady stream of investment turned into a torrent by 2001, when more and more venture capitalists invested in films, lured by the success of local hits like *Friend*, and rumours that cinema could guarantee double-digit returns. A bubble of sorts was created in film finance, and the free availability of money would encourage the rise of budgets and salaries, and a willingness to attempt expensive genre pictures that had never before been produced in Korean cinema, such as science-fiction titles *2009 Lost Memories* (*Ich'ŏngu losŭt'ŭ memorijŭ*, 2002) and *Natural City* (*Naech'yurŏl sit'i*, 2003).

FILM POLICY IN THE 1990S

The major shifts that occurred throughout the 1990s in film finance and standards of production took place at the same time as the government's rewriting of film policy. With a democratically elected government in office, and given the new challenges faced by the film industry after the market's opening to foreign competition, a consensus emerged that a new film policy should be drafted to assist and promote, rather than to regulate, the film industry.

In 1995, a Basic Film Promotion Law (*Yŏngsang chinhŭng kibon bŏp*) was passed which stated the government's intention to promote the industry but, lacking any practical measures, the law served mainly an idealistic function. Then, in December, a Film Promotion Law (*Yŏnghwa chinhŭng bŏp*) was drawn up to modify and take the place of the Motion Picture Law, going into effect in July 1996. Among the measures introduced was the creation of a Film Promotion Fund to support local cinema.

Although by 1996 many of the restrictions which had formerly hampered the film industry had now been repealed, one aspect of government policy continued to draw controversy and criticism from inside and from outside the industry: film censorship. The Public Performance Ethics Committee, a government board charged with the pre-screening and censoring of films, continued to operate after the end of military rule, even if standards had relaxed greatly. In early 1996 it blocked the release of the film *He Asked Me If I Know Zita* (*Kŭnŭn naege jit'arŭl anŭnyago murŏtta*, 1997) for its ridiculing of the country's president while, in July of the same year, it held up the release of Jang Sun-woo's

Timeless, Bottomless, Bad Movie (*Nappŭn yŏnghwa*, 1998) for strong sexual content.

In October 1996, however, Korea's Constitutional Court ruled that governmental pre-censorship of films was in violation of the constitution. This landmark victory for free expression resulted in a first revision of the Film Promotion Law the following year, under which the Public Performance Ethics Committee was replaced with a civilian board which would assign ratings, rather than directly censor films. Nonetheless, controversy arose when the law was written to allow the board to assign a 'Deferred' rating to works considered inappropriate for public viewing. Kim Yu-min's *Yellow Hair* (*Norang mŏri*, 1999) became the first film to receive such a rating when it was delayed for three months because of a sexually explicit scene which was later digitally darkened before release.

A second revision of the Film Promotion Law, which took place in 1999, reorganised the ratings committee into the Korea Media Ratings Board but censorship continued to be an issue, as Jang Sun-woo's *Lies* and other films were given Deferred ratings because of their sexual content. Although the Constitutional Court would judge the Deferred rating to be unconstitutional in September 2001, the Media Ratings Board managed to block the release of Park Jin-p'yo's independent film *Too Young To Die* (*Chugŏdo choa*) in 2002 by assigning the film a 'Restricted' rating which prevented it from being screened in ordinary theatres. After several months of debate, the film was approved for release with the problematic scenes darkened.

Such censorship as practised by the Media Ratings Board remains a key example of outside bureaucratic control over film-makers, even though the

Figure 10 Pushing the limits of censorship: sexually explicit *Lies* (1999).

range of what is allowed to be shown in Korean theatres is much wider than it was even a few years ago. In general, however, the reform of film policy throughout the 1980s and 1990s has resulted in much less direct bureaucratic and governmental interference in the film industry.

At the same time, government policy now allows for significantly greater economic pressures to enter the film-making process. From the opening of the Korean market to the Hollywood majors to the abolition of the import quota, directors and producers now face a working environment which is considerably hostile to films that do not turn a profit. Promotional bodies like the Korean Film Commission try to compensate for this by providing financial support to independent, low-budget or so-called 'art-house' cinema. Nonetheless, the general trend from the bureaucratic interference of pre-1992 to heightened economic pressures in the 1990s – and Korean companies' success in dealing with these changes – has had a very strong influence on Korean cinema's development. One might reasonably ask, therefore, whether Korean film, in its focus on commercial cinema and the industrialisation of its film sector, has adopted a 'Hollywood model' of film-making (for an in-depth consideration of this topic, see Berry 2003). In answering this question we should perhaps distinguish between the structure of the industry on the one hand, and the aesthetic or creative character of Korean versus Hollywood cinema on the other.

In terms of industry, it is true that the presence of the Hollywood branch offices in Korea has sometimes set an example that local companies have followed. Instances of this might include the move to nationwide distribution, marketing techniques, and the model of the vertically integrated film company that rose to prominence from the early days of Hollywood. Korea's producer system has also gravitated towards that of Hollywood, though significant differences remain. Hollywood is not the only example of a film industry that embraces commercial cinema, however. Among other recent studies on the subject, David Bordwell's book *Planet Hong Kong* (Bordwell 2000) provides an in-depth look at how Hong Kong film-makers created a thriving commercial industry that differs significantly from that of Hollywood – and one should not forget that India produces more movies and sells more tickets per year than any other industry.

Korean distribution remains profoundly different from that of Hollywood in that Korea has a small local market, and cannot rely on a vast international network to recoup costs. Hollywood companies also make use of complex financing tools that Korean banks do not provide, and so Korean film companies often take on far more financial risk for a project's success or failure. In terms of film-making practices, profound differences remain in the screenwriting process, as well as in the degree of influence a director holds during the shooting of a film (in Korea it remains much higher).

Although not central to this chapter, key aesthetic differences also exist between the cinemas of Korea and Hollywood, in part due to the differences outlined above and in part to cultural differences. In an essay written for the forthcoming anthology *Seoul Searching: Identity and Cultrue in Korean Cinema* (SUNY Press), I outline some of the aesthetic differences between Korean cinema's and Hollywood's approach to one key genre, namely melodrama.

THE BOOM YEARS

From 1999, Korean cinema has experienced a commercial boom that harkens back to its Golden Age of the 1950s and 1960s. Unprecedented box-office strength (in 2001 the top five grossing films in Korea were all locally made) has translated into a proliferation of film companies and increasing success in exporting Korean films to other Asian countries and the rest of the world.

Apart from the three major elements (film finance, standards of production, and film policy) covered in this chapter, the distribution and exhibition sectors have evolved in ways that have contributed to or affected the boom in some way. Korea's first multiplex, CGV Kangbyŏn, was built in 1998 and, since then, aggressive construction of new theatres has pushed the country's total number of screens from 497 in 1997 to over 1,000 in 2002, according to the Korean Film Commission. The arrival of modern theatres and the renovation of older ones are often given credit for unleashing a boom in cinema attendance among young people: yearly admissions rose from 55 million in 1999 to 107 million in 2002. Release strategies for films have also changed. Wide releases have become the norm, with local blockbusters opening on as many as 250 to 300 screens throughout the country by 2003. At the same time, the amount of money spent on marketing and advertising has surged since the late 1990s.

With Samsung and Daewoo no longer operating in the distribution sector, two powerful local film companies have emerged to take leading roles. CJ Entertainment, a subsidiary of the *chaebŏl* Cheil Jedang, was formed in 1996 as an original shareholder of DreamWorks SKG in Hollywood. It launched what would become Korea's biggest multiplex chain, CGV, in 1998 and several cable channels in the following years, in addition to its film financing, production and distribution operations. Cinema Service was formed in the mid-1990s by Kang U-sŏk, director of hit films such as *Two Cops*. After co-operating closely with the older company Hapdong Films to establish a distribution operation, it has gone on to launch its own multiplex chain, a shooting/post-production studio, a video arm and a film school in addition to being the largest individual financer of Korean films (accounting for twenty local films a year by 2003). From 2001 to 2003, Cinema Service and CJ Entertainment together accounted for about 60 per cent of the total market for Korean films, and also secured distribution rights to many major Hollywood-backed titles, such as the *Lord of the Rings* trilogy (2001/2002/2003).

Some industry trends have affected the character of the films being produced in Korea today. As the market for video shrinks (to date DVD has had only a minor effect on the overall industry), the theatrical run of a film becomes more and more important to its ultimate profitability. Since movie-going audiences are primarily under thirty – compared to a more balanced age distribution for video – the overall trend has been to cater for younger viewers. One example of this move towards younger tastes has been the increasing number of films adapted from internet novels written by teens, such as *My Sassy Girl* (2001), *My Tutor Friend* (*Tonggapnaegi kwaoe hagi*, 2003) and *100 Days With Mr. Arrogant* (*Nae sarang ssagaji*, 2004). Investors in particular have supported the trend, believing that the young authors of internet novels are more in tune with the thinking of the average movie-goer.

Another important trend involves film education. In the 1980s and earlier, most film-makers would learn their craft by serving as an apprentice to more-established directors. Lee Myung-Se (Yi Myŏng-se) made his directorial début in 1988 with *Gagman* (*Gaegŭmaen*) after serving as an assistant director to Pae Ch'ang-ho who, in turn, made his début after serving under Yi Chang-ho in the early 1980s. In the 1990s, however, a proliferation of film schools led to the breakdown of this apprentice system. The new film schools provided fewer barriers to film education, and gave students the opportunity to prove their talent through making short films of their own. Director Yi Chae-yong of *Untold Scandal* maintains that he would not have been given the opportunity to make films in the 1980s when most people believed that masculine, 'macho' personalities were better suited to directing (Paquet 2003: 12).

Greater access to education has also led to far more women directors entering the industry than in past years. In 2002, a record five films directed by women were released: *L'Abri* (*Bŏsŭ chŏngnyujang*) by Yi Mi-yŏn, *The Way Home* (*Chipŭro . . .*) by Yi Chŏng-hyang, *A Perfect Match* (*Choŭn saram issŭmyŏn sogae shik'yŏjwŏ*) by Mo Chi-ŭn, *Popee* (*Ppoppi*) by Kim Ji-hyŏn and *Ardor* (*Mirae*) by Byŏn Yŏng-ju. The coming years look to have significantly greater participation by women directors, although males still make up the vast majority.

Despite the gaudy numbers of the boom years, there remain weaknesses in the system which industry insiders are anxious to address. The distribution market is structured to benefit commercial films that go out on wide release. Even very popular movies often spend only four to five weeks in theatres, and so films that are unable to secure a large number of screens – or to spend large sums on marketing – are unlikely to earn a profit. Low-budget independent and art-house releases, in particular, do not have time to let word of mouth spread among viewers, and so theatrical receipts are often dreadfully low. Efforts by the Korean Film Commission to establish a nationwide chain of theatres specialising in art-house cinema have had limited results to date.

In rare cases, film-makers may find support abroad by pursuing international co-productions. Projects such as Kim Ki-dŏk's *Spring, Summer, Fall, Winter . . . and Spring* (*Pom yŏrŭm kaŭl kyŏul kŭrigo pom*, 2003), Chŏn Su-il's *My Right to Ravage Myself* (*Nanŭn narŭl p'agoehal kwŏlliga itta*, 2003) and Hong Sang-su's

Woman is Man's Future (*Yŏjanŭn namja-ŭi miraeda*, 2004) have all been funded in part by European distributors. The Pusan International Film Festival has aimed to encourage further such co-productions with its Pusan Promotion Plan (PPP), a project market that brings together international film finance companies and selected film-makers. Such routes generally remain open only to those directors who have achieved recognition abroad through international film festivals, however, and so for less-established film-makers it is seldom an option.

The unbalanced structure of the distribution system ultimately limits the aesthetic range of films being released in theatres. Non-commercial films that do not appeal to general tastes are forced severely to reduce costs, to rely on the small sums provided by the Korean Film Commission for production support or else to rely on personal money to reach completion. Distribution of such films is often limited to film festivals rather than commercial theatres. This has negative implications for society because the system encourages the further marginalisation of non-mainstream voices and points of view. Although the emergence of new digital film technology has helped to make film-making more accessible, more government support is needed if non-commercial films are to thrive in Korea alongside their commercial cousins.

Despite the problems that remain in South Korea's film industry, the rapid development of its infrastructure remains a highly unusual case in world cinema. Very few countries around the world possess so many local film companies of the size and strength of those in Korea. The power such companies wield in their home market allows local film-makers to reap many of the advantages of the industry's rapid development whereas, in other countries, Hollywood branch offices might benefit the most.

The industrialisation of the Korean film industry has brought many benefits to film-makers. It has helped to create numerous sources for film finance, without which it would be impossible to maintain the current level of over sixty feature films produced per year. This enabled the discovery of new directors, as many young film-makers have been given the opportunity to make their début. The film industry has also become largely self-sufficient, meaning that it could probably survive a sudden cut in support from the government. The large profits earned by Korean film companies have allowed for new and better facilities to be built, thus expanding the possibilities for film-makers in the realms of sound, cinematography, special effects and *mise-en-scène*. The industry's commercial strength and the arrival of powerful local companies have also encouraged more people to pursue work in the industry, from crew members to cinematographers to sound technicians. An industry which seemed to be on the brink of collapse in 1992 has gained an aura of stability in the eyes of the South Korean public.

Perhaps most crucial to the flowering of New Korean Cinema has been the birth of self-confidence among members of the Korean film industry. This confidence has spawned a drive to expand into new, uncharted territories (in international sales, for example, or a new genre) and a willingness to experiment.

It informs much of the aesthetic as well as the industrial character of Korean film. Although it is too early to predict the end of New Korean Cinema, it is a fair guess to say that it will retain its distinct character for as long as this confidence continues to exist.

REFERENCES

Berry, Chris (2003) ' "What's Big About the Big Film?": "De-Westernizing" the Blockbuster in Korea and China', in Julian Stringer (ed.), *Movie Blockbusters*, London: Routledge: 217–29.

Bordwell, David (2000) *Planet Hong Kong: Popular Cinema and the Art of Entertainment*, Cambridge, Massachusetts: Harvard University Press.

Ch'oe, Il-su (1993) 'Chumŏk kugu ŭi uri yŏnghwa ŭi kihwoek' ('The finger counting of our cinema's planning'), *Yŏnghwa P'yŏngnon*: 242–51.

'Films in 1993', *Korea Cinema 93*, Seoul: Korean Motion Picture Promotion Corporation: 3.

Hwang, Tong-mi (2001) *Hanguk yŏnghwa sanŏp kucho punsŏk (Analysis of the Structure of the Korean Film Industry)*, Seoul: Korean Film Commission.

Paquet, Darcy (2003) 'Dressed for success', *Screen International* 1497 (Oct. 31–Nov. 6): 12.

3. GLOBALISATION AND NEW KOREAN CINEMA

Jeeyoung Shin

South Korean cinema has undergone remarkable growth over the past decade. By substantially improving technical and aesthetic qualities, and by responding to the sensibilities of contemporary Koreans, recent Korean films have distinguished themselves from their predecessors. In so doing, they have rapidly been winning back the hearts of those previously estranged domestic audiences who had once preferred foreign films with better production values, particularly those from Hollywood. With Korean films now capturing almost 50 per cent of domestic market share, and some local hits beating even the most lavish Hollywood blockbusters at the box-office, Korean cinema is currently enjoying unprecedented domestic success.

Equally remarkable is the fast-growing popularity of, and interest in, Korean cinema around the globe. With numerous successes at major overseas film festivals and growing international distribution and consumption, recent years have seen a notable rise in Korean cinema's visibility in the international film world. Yet, while contemporary Korean cinema is rapidly drawing attention around the world, its popular success is perhaps most apparent in neighbouring East Asian countries where there has been a veritable surge of interest in Korean popular culture, including films, television dramas and popular music. Indeed, the revenue from film exports alone has grown tremendously, from $0.21 (US) million in 1995 to $11.25 million in 2001 (Kim and Kim 2002: 15). This is an impressive accomplishment especially when considering that, only a decade ago, the South Korean film industry was in severe decline. The opening of the local film market to foreign distributors in 1987 had inspired a sharp increase in the number of imported films. With local cinema already limited in its box-office appeal, the domestic market share of Korean films then dropped significantly, reaching its lowest point in 1993.

While suggesting a local cinema's triumph over the forces of global media, the recent development of Korean cinema invites a number of questions. What is behind the Korean film industry's astonishing recent growth? How and why has Korean cinema become popular beyond national borders and particularly in East Asia? What implications does the success of Korean cinema at home and abroad have for an understanding of processes of media globalisation? In attempting to answer these questions, this chapter explores the relationship between New Korean Cinema and media globalisation, with a particular focus on the role of Korea's globalisation drive. First, I show how the South Korean government's implementation of a globalisation policy assisted and promoted the growth and internationalisation of Korean cinema. While paying attention to some of the major characteristics of recent Korean films, I then examine further the reasons for Korean cinema's success at home and abroad. My argument is that contemporary Korean cinema is both an effect of and a response to media globalisation, and that localisation, regionalisation and globalisation co-exist in the global media cultural economy.

SEGYEHWA AND THE PROMOTION OF THE CULTURE INDUSTRY

The transformation of Korean cinema over the past decade is closely related to the South Korean government's open-door policy. In retrospect, it is clear that this transformation was prompted by the serious decline of the Korean film industry in the early 1990s. The Korean government had succumbed to Hollywood pressure to remove local barriers to imported films by opening up the domestic market, with the result that Hollywood studios set up branch offices in Korea so that they could distribute their own films directly to the local market. By comparison, Korean films – poorly funded and lacking comparable entertainment values – were totally unprepared for such unmediated competition with Hollywood. A rapid decline in the domestic market share of Korean films created an enormous sense of crisis among the local film community.

The plight of the film industry parallels the overall Korean economic landscape at the time. In the early 1990s, after a long reliance on a regulated market economy, South Korea found itself fighting a losing battle with outside forces trying to open the domestic market. Outside pressures to open up the Korean market had certainly existed before the 1990s. By the end of 1993, however, Korea faced a global push for market liberalisation owing to agreements reached at the Uruguay Round of the General Agreement on Trade and Tariffs.[1] The settlement of the Uruguay Round imposed immense threats to Korea's domestic economy, which was soon to face direct competition from foreign companies.

The Kim Young-sam (Kim Yŏng-sam) government (1993–98), led by the first civilian president in thirty years, was endowed with the thorny task of revitalising the Korean economy by enhancing its international competitiveness, as well as with the mandate of democratic reforms. The ultimate response from the Kim administration was to pursue internationalisation and globalisation armed with competitiveness as a survival strategy in the new world order. Accordingly, the Kim government launched its ambitious top-down drive for globalisation and actively undertook measures for economic liberalisation.

As Samuel S. Kim (2000) notes, no state in the post-Cold War era has embraced globalisation as publicly as South Korea under the Kim Young-sam administration. After a series of initial preparations, President Kim formally announced the *segyehwa* policy in the Sydney speech of 17 November 1994 (Bobrow and Na 1999). Using the Korean term *segyehwa* (*segye* meaning 'world' and *hwa* meaning 'becoming/turning into') for 'globalisation', Kim's *segyehwa* campaign reveals a nationalistic urge for Korea's advancement in a rapidly globalising world. Not discouraged by the poor achievement of Kim Young-sam's *segyehwa*-driven administration, the Kim Dae Jung government (1998–2003) sustained a globalisation drive with greater enthusiasm (Samuel S. Kim 2000: 3).

It is worth noting that Korea's globalisation policy is based on a dual interpretation of globalisation, demanding a parallel development of comprehensive national restructuring and more narrowly focused economic restructuring (Gills and Gills 2000). On the one hand, *segyehwa* was committed to a fulfilment of national advancement, in all aspects, to the level of the world's most developed nations. It thus involved a wide range of reforms, encompassing political, economic, social and cultural restructuring. On the other hand, despite the campaign's emphasis on broad national development, much of its energy was directed toward the rapid internationalisation and globalisation of the Korean economy. This economically oriented globalisation was not simply designed to enhance the Korean economy's international competitiveness by encouraging Korean companies to operate on a global level. Regarding increasing demands for market liberalisation, it was also meant to improve Korean firms' competitiveness with foreign corporations in the domestic market.

The zeal of Korea's economic globalisation also included media and cultural sectors, which were not only facing severe foreign competition at home but also had burgeoning aspirations to the global media market. The Korean government's globalist approach to the media sector was triggered by recognition of culture as an industry that can produce a huge profit. In May 1994, the Presidential Advisory Council on Science and Technology reported to President Kim Young-sam an eye-opening statistic showing that profits from the Hollywood blockbuster *Jurassic Park* (US, 1993) equalled the export revenue of 1.5 million Hyundai cars, and it urged him to promote the high-technology media industry as a strategic national industry (H. Kim 1994). Since Hyundai cars are the symbol of Korea's economic growth, the comparison underscored the need for the active promotion of the culture industry, and thus became a decisive factor in revolutionising the Korean government's approach to the media industries (Shim 2002: 340).

The Kim Young-sam government soon set out its plans to promote and support the media industry as the strategic industry for the twenty-first century (M. B. Kim 1994). The government's efforts to promote the local film industry started with the shift in film policy from control to promotion. Among the earliest major moves was the establishment of the Basic Motion Picture Promotion Law (*Yŏngsang chinhŭng kibon pŏp*) in January 1995. While lacking practical measures, the Law aimed to establish basic conditions to facilitate the advancement of local media culture and the promotion of the media industry by requiring that relevant governmental bodies create conferences, policies and funds for media promotion.[2]

More importantly, after a process of wide consultation, the Film Promotion Law (*Yŏnghwa chinhŭng pŏp*) was established in December 1995 to modify and replace the previous Motion Picture Law (*Yŏnghwa pŏp*) that had long regulated the local film industry. One of the most notable measures introduced in the new law was the establishment of a Film Promotion Fund (*Yŏnghwa chinhŭng kŭmgo*) to support the local film industry. The Film Promotion Law also repealed regulations requiring official approval from the Ministry of Culture and Sports, in advance, for exporting Korean films, and for co-producing films with foreign companies.[3] By making the international co-production and export of Korean films easier, these devices encouraged the globalisation of Korean cinema.

Korea's efforts to promote the film industry also encouraged the entry of large corporations or *chaebŏl* into the film business, and they played an important role in enhancing the infrastructure of the Korean film industry. In 1995, as a means to induce large capital from *chaebŏl*, the government allowed film productions to receive tax breaks previously limited to manufacturers (Chin 1994). In addition, the impressive market success of *Marriage Story* (*Kyŏlhon Iyagi*) in 1992, which was partly financed by Samsung, had a large influence on the *chaebŏl*'s entry into the film industry. By the mid-1990s, large corporations, such as Hyundai, Samsung and Daewoo, actively participated in various aspects of the film business, from production to distribution and exhibition.

Though it was short lived, soon replaced by venture-capital companies after the IMF (International Monetary Fund) crisis in 1997–98, the *chaebŏl*'s involvement had a significant impact on the Korean film industry. By providing large amounts of capital for film-making, the *chaebŏl*'s input helped improve the technical qualities of Korean cinema. In addition, by promoting efficiency, the *chaebŏl* also helped to modernise the film industry. As a result, by boosting local cinema's competitive edge, such contributions enabled the film industry to survive Hollywood competition, and even to outdo the latter's performance at the box-office.

The project of the internationalisation of Korean cinema became more pronounced with the formation of the Pusan International Film Festival in 1996, Korea's first international film festival. Held annually in the south-eastern port city of Pusan, the festival was originally supported by the Pusan city government, but the central government also began supporting it in 1998 (D. Kim 2000: 25–6). With strong support from the Korean government, and with the enthusiastic participation of the Asian film communities, the festival has become a leading film event in Asia.

While serving as a showcase for Asian films, the Pusan International Film Festival has promoted Korean cinema in several ways. First, its 'Korean

Panorama' section has exclusively presented major contemporary Korean films, and its 'Retrospective' section has introduced the work of several senior Korean directors. Second, the festival has acted as a gateway for Korean cinema's advancement abroad (D. Kim 2003). As the number of foreign programmers of major film festivals attending the festival grows, more and more Korean films have also been invited to their festivals. For example, after a retrospective was held on director Kim Ki-yŏng at the second Pusan International Film Festival in 1997, Kim's films were invited to many other film festivals including the 1998 Berlin International Film Festival. Third, through their participation in the festival, local film professionals began targeting overseas markets and actively seeking ways to initiate co-productions with foreign companies (D. Kim 2003).

The globalisation of the Korean film industry continued in the years of Kim Dae Jung's presidency. Responding to culture's economic potential, Kim stressed the promotion of the culture industry as a top priority from the very beginning of his administration. His enthusiastic promotion of the culture industry is clear from the establishment of the Basic Culture Industry Promotion Law (*Munhwa sanŏp chinhŭng kibon pŏp*) in February 1999. Kim's government promoted in particular high-value-added culture industries such as film, animation and multi-media, and it established the Korea Culture and Contents Agency (*Hanguk munhwa k'ŏnt'ench'ŭ chinhŭngwŏn*) in 1999 to support animation, music and video games.

If South Korea's efforts to globalise its film industry had initially focused on the improvement of its competitiveness at home, since the late 1990s the promotional endeavour has increasingly aimed at the elevation of Korean cinema's international profile and the growth of international sales. In February 1999, the Film Promotion Law was revised, including a substantial reorganisation of the Korea Motion Picture Promotion Corporation (KMPPC) (*Hanguk yŏnghwa chinhŭng Kongsa*) as the Korean Film Commission (KOFIC) (*Yŏnghwa chinhŭng Wiwŏnhoe*). KOFIC consists of a government-appointed civilian board. Following the Kim Dae Jung government's 'support without control' guidelines, however, KOFIC has been allowed greater independence and authority in formulating film policies, even though it is funded by the Ministry of Culture and Tourism. While continuing the duties of the KMPPC, KOFIC has strengthened efforts to promote and globalise Korean cinema.

To promote Korean films abroad, KOFIC sets up pavilions at major international film festivals and markets.[4] It also provides translations and prints, and it pays for the production of subtitles for selected films targeting overseas film markets or international film festivals. In addition, KOFIC subsidises travel costs for those film-makers whose films are invited to major film festivals, and it offers cash awards to film professionals who are officially invited to major festival competitions.

As noted above, being a state-led policy, Korea's globalisation drive was motivated by strong nationalist interests. The governmental push to globalise Korea's culture industries was intended not only to improve the competitiveness of the national economy, but also to promote cultural autonomy and integrity. Remarkably, Kim Young-sam's unique vision of Korea's globalisation mandated that globalisation be achieved through Koreanisation. He asserted: 'Globalization must be underpinned by Koreanization. We cannot be global citizens without a good understanding of our own culture and tradition . . . Koreans should march out into the world on the strength of their unique culture and traditional values. Only when we maintain our national identity and uphold our intrinsic national spirit will we be able to successfully globalize' (Y. Kim 1995: 273).

Elsewhere I have noted that this seemingly contradictory demand for simultaneous globalisation/globalism and Koreanisation/nationalism reflects 'the ambivalence of the politics of cultural identity applied to the culture industry'. The concept of globalisation through Koreanisation provides 'a perfect ground for the ongoing commercialization and commodification of "traditional" culture by the culture industry, while claiming to protect cultural identity from the threats of cultural imperialism or homogenization'. (Shin forthcoming) In targeting international markets, including major international film festivals and the art-house circuit, Korean films often employ the strategy of marketing difference based upon a unique identity. The best example of this is the work of Im Kwon-Taek, the most widely known Korean director, who won the Best Director award at the Cannes Film Festival for *Chihwaseon* (*Ch'wihwasŏn*, 2002). More significantly, however, while those films aestheticising 'traditional' Korean culture have attracted Western audiences, a majority of Korean films marketed in East Asia, including in Korea, tend to foreground a sense of Asian modernity rooted in hybrid culture.

DOMESTIC SUCCESS AND HYBRID CULTURE

Under the government's promotion policies, the Korean film industry experienced gradual growth, a growth that then accelerated towards the end of the 1990s. Although the Asian financial crisis hit the Korean economy hard, causing a decrease in domestic film production, the domestic market share of Korean films leaped to 38 per cent in 1999 from 24 per cent in 1998 (Yu 2000: 6). Undermining scepticism concerning its sustained success, domestic films captured 49.8 per cent of market share in Korea in 2001 and 48.5 per cent in 2002 (Korean Film Observatory 2003: 18).

The domestic success of Korean cinema was accompanied by a series of local box-office hits. Recent years have seen several Korean films setting box-office records, even outdoing the biggest Hollywood blockbusters. For example, the hit film *Shiri* (*Swiri*, 1999) attracted 5.78 million viewers, breaking the local attendance record of 4.7 million tickets for *Titanic* (US, 1997) (*The Korea Herald* 2000). Moreover, *Shiri*'s record has subsequently been broken by two other domestic films: *Joint Security Area* (*Kongdong kyŏngbi guyŏk JSA*) in 2000 (Paquet 2001a) and *Friend* (*Ch'in'gu*) in 2001, which set a new record of 8.14 million viewers (Paquet 2002). While several factors contribute to the popular success of Korean cinema at home, one of note is a generational shift in the local film community, which has provided opportunities for young, talented film-makers. Enjoying greater freedom of expression under the noticeably loosened state censorship and increased financing brought by the involvement of *chaebŏl* and investment companies in film production, the films of this younger generation have brought a much needed vitality to the Korean film scene.

Yet, more importantly, by utilising a style that effortlessly mixes indigenous cultural elements with regional and Western influences, recent Korean films respond to the sensibilities of contemporary Koreans. Like their own domestic audiences, young directors have been deeply influenced by foreign, particularly Western, cultures and media, while they are also responsive to contemporary domestic affairs and politics. As Richard King and Timothy J. Craig note of other Asian popular cultural scenes, successful young Korean directors, in their creative use, appropriation and adaptation of foreign cultural influences, construct 'new hybrid cultural forms that are appealing and accessible to their audiences' (King and Craig 2002: 7). These hybrid cultural forms provide an important means for their self-definition, a self-definition that not only distances itself from a xenophobic and moralising adherence to local cultural 'tradition' but also challenges Western cultural hegemony.

In short, the recent success of Korean films has in large measure been a result of creative interaction between the transnational and the local media, rather than a regressive insistence on 'traditional' cultural heritage or a simple adoption and imitation of foreign culture. Equally important, contemporary Korean cinema also shows that the contact between different cultures results in hybridisation, not homogenisation. The hybrid nature of Korean cinema is a product of the localisation of global media culture. Consequently, New Korean Cinema reflects Jenny Kwok Wah Lau's acute observation of the new Asia in formation, which consists of not one universal modernity but 'multiple modernities' that reject the prescriptions of globalists/universalists and the demands of the localists/indigenists (Lau 2003). Furthermore, as a hybrid cultural form and as resistance to Western economic and cultural hegemony, New Korean Cinema is both an effect of and a response to media globalisation.

NEW KOREAN CINEMA AND MEDIA REGIONALISATION

Since the late 1990s, Korean cinema embodying hybrid culture has been popular abroad, particularly in East Asia. Many local box-office hits have increasingly been entertaining regional viewers in theatres, as well as on DVD and VCD (Video Compact Disks), a medium extremely popular in East Asia, or in the form of copies downloaded from the Internet. Those films that have appealed to audiences across borders include *The Foul King* (*Panch'ik wang*, 1998), *Shiri, Joint Security Area, My Sassy Girl* (*Yŏpki chŏk-in kŭnyŏ*, 2001) and *Phone* (*P'on*, 2002). Notably, *Shiri* also reached the top of the box-office in Hong Kong at the end of 1999 (M. H. Kim 2001) and attracted 1.2 million viewers in Japan (Macintyre 2001), while *Joint Security Area* sold for US$2 million to Japan (Paquet 2001a) and stayed among the top ten hits at the Japanese box-office for eight weeks in 2001 (Paquet 2001b).

The recent success of Korean films in the region is, in fact, part of the craze for Korean popular culture across Asia, often referred to as *Hanryu* ('Korean Wave'). The term *Hanryu* was first coined by Chinese journalists to describe a sudden influx of South Korean pop culture, from dance music to television dramas and films, and its fast-growing popularity among Chinese youth in the late 1990s (Jang 2003: 144). Soon the phenomenon extended to other parts of Asia, including Hong Kong, Taiwan, Vietnam and Singapore. *Hanryu* is demonstrated by Korean television dramas aired on the main television networks, Korean songs played on local radio, Korean stars featured in local media productions and fan magazines, and Internet fan sites devoted to a shared penchant for Korean popular media and stars.

Several factors contribute to the regional success of Korean popular media including films. First, the rapid spread of existing and new media technologies such as satellites, the Internet and DVD has helped broaden the exposure of Korean media. Increased market deregulation has also favoured the wide regional circulation of Korean media, since it, coupled with the opening of China's vast market, has resulted in the tremendous expansion of the regional media market and the subsequent huge growth in demand for content. Equally important is the relatively weak performance of other film industries in the

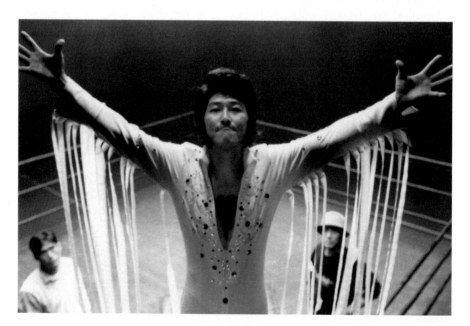

Figure 11 A regional hit in East Asia: *The Foul King* (1998).

Figure 12 A story of contact between Korea and China: *Failan* (2001).

region, particularly the Hong Kong film industry, which had previously been a particularly energetic force.

Cultural proximity is another significant factor. While many Asian nation-states are still wary of Western cultural imperialism, a growing proportion of regional audiences is inclined towards Korean films that reflect cultural values closer to its own. According to one Korean critic, Korean television dramas and films present an image of Korean society as highly modernised, but still reflecting Asian traits such as Confucian traditions with their emphasis on family, group orientation and social hierarchy (Jang 2003: 146). A Chinese professor also attributes the local appeal of Korean popular culture to cultural similarity. He notes that although Korean popular cultural forms are recognised as hybrid, or influenced by Western culture, they are easy to relate to because they are based on Asian culture (ibid.: 147–8).

In addition, to overcome the backward image of the East found in the East and in the West, East Asian audiences are consuming Korean media with cultural affinity to promote an Asian sense of modernity. In this respect, the phenomenon of the regional circulation of Korean cinema is an excellent example of 'geo-cultural markets' (Straubhaar 1997) that are organised around close cultural, linguistic and geographic links within the highly internationalised contemporary world. As Straubhaar (1997) aptly notes, the vitality of regional media shown in the presence of the geo-cultural market demonstrates the co-existence of regionalisation and globalisation in the world media cultural economy.

Furthermore, along with the growing popularity of Korean entertainment media in the region, bilateral cultural exchange between Korea and other East Asian countries has also increased. For example, while Korean stars have been featured in various local media productions, including television dramas, commercials and films in the region, several regional stars from mainland China (e.g. Zhang Ziyi in *Musa*, 2001) and Hong Kong (e.g. Cecilia Cheung in *Failan* [*P'airan*], 2001) have also appeared in Korean media. In addition, there has been an increasing number of co-productions between Korea and other East Asian countries. *Bichunmoo* (*Bich'ŏnmu*, 2000) and *Musa* were co-produced with China, whereas *One Fine Spring Day* (*Bomnalŭn kanda*, 2001) is a Korean/Hong Kong/Japanese co-production, and *Three* (*Ssŭri* 2002) is an omnibus film co-produced by Hong Kong, Korea and Thailand.

CONCLUSION

The remarkable success of Korean films at home and in East Asia has begun to draw attention from Hollywood companies. Significantly, some of the Korean branch offices of Hollywood firms have recently begun distributing domestic films. For example, the local direct distributor of Disney, Buena Vista International Korea/Disney, distributed *Il Mare* (*Siwŏlae*) in 2000 and *Bungee Jumping of Their Own* (*Pŏnjijŏmpŭrŭl hada*) in 2001, while the Korean branch of Twentieth Century Fox distributed *Calla* (*K'ara*, 1999) (see Mun 2001). Some Korean films were even exported for US distribution, among them Yi Myŏng-se's *Nowhere to Hide* (*Injŏngsajŏng polgŏt ŏpda*, 1999), Im Kwon-Taek's *Chunhyang* (*Ch'unhyangdyŏn*, 2000) and Yi Jŏng-hyang's *The Way Home* (*Chipŭrŏ*, 2002). Nevertheless, with Korean cinema still relatively unknown to the American public, American companies have primarily been eager to buy remake rights. The films sold for American remakes thus far include *My Sassy Girl*, bought by DreamWorks SKG, *Hi, Dharma* (*Dalmaya nolja*, 2001) bought by MGM, and *Marrying the Mafia* (*Kamun-ŭi yŏng'gwang*, 2002) bought by Warner Bros. (Korea Culture and Contents Agency 2003).

Increased international attention to Korean cinema has also inspired a rise in Korean film festivals around the world. Notable Korean film festivals held in North America include the annual New York Korean Film Festival, which started in 2001, and the 2002 Toronto International Film Festival's 'Harvest: South Korean Renaissance'. Korean film festivals also appeared in Europe in 2001, first in London (BBC 2001), and then in Paris (Paquet 1999), as well as in Hong Kong in 2001 and 2003.

After a long and unflattering history of foreign domination and poor international standing, many Korean journalists and critics are celebrating the ascendancy of the Korean film industry in the local and regional media scene. Pointing to the increasing production of blockbuster films that have met with little success and sky-rocketing production costs, however, some question the sustainability of the current success of Korean films, and they worry about the potential lowering of quality that such commercialism might generate. Others remain wary of the continuing popularity of foreign films and media products in Korea, as well as their impact on local culture and people.

The local and regional success of Korean cinema has not yet been challenged. While fostering awe and fascination, however, the continuing popularity of Korean cinema has begun to provoke anxiety in the region. Consequently, to maintain the strength of New Korean Cinema, especially as it struggles against becoming a replica of Hollywood, the Korean film industry must also enhance co-promotion strategies with other East Asian nations. One example of such a strategy is the Pusan Promotion Project of the Pusan International Film Festival, a pre-market for Asian films at which potential co-producers and co-financiers may be found. Through these kinds of efforts, New Korean Cinema can continue to prosper at home and within the East Asian market.

REFERENCES

BBC (2001) 'Korean Film Festival Opens in London', 29 April. Online. http://news.bbc.co.uk.

Bobrow, Davis B. and Na, James J. (1999) 'Korea's Affair with Globalization: Deconstructing *Segyehwa*', in Chung-in Moon and Jongryn Mo (eds), *Democratization and Globalization in Korea: Assessments and Prospects*, Yonsei University Press: 179–208.

Chin, Sŏng-ho (1994) 'Yŏngsang chinhŭng pŏp – yŏnghwa hak'kyo sinsŭl-ŭl [Basic Motion Picture Law, film school to be established]', *Chosun Ilbo*, 25 October: 17.

Gills, Barry K. and Gills, Dong-sook (2000) 'South Korea and Globalization: The Rise to Globalism?', in Samuel S. Kim (ed.), *East Asia and Globalization*, Lanham, MD: Rowman and Littlefield: 81–104.

Jang, Soo Hyun (2003) 'Contemporary Chinese Narratives on Korean Culture', *Korean Journal*, 43, 1: 128–63.

Kim, Dong-ho (2000) 'Pusan International Film Festival: Catalyst for Asian Cinema', *Koreana*, 14, no. 2: 24–9.

—— (2003) 'Pusan International Festival Boosts Korean Filmdom', *The Korea Times*, 15 September. Online. Available through http://search.hankooki.com.

Kim, Hong (1994) 'Juragi Kongwŭn 1nyŏn hŭnghaeng suip [One year's Revenue of *Jurassic Park*]', *Chosun Ilbo*, 18 May: 31.

Kim, Hyoun-soo and Kim, Jay (2002) 'Final Report on the 2001 Korean Film Industry: Sustainable Growth?', Korean Film Observatory, report # 4: 2–18.

Kim, Min-bae (1994) 'Yŏngsang chinhŭng pŏp chejŏngk'iro [Basic Motion Picture Promotion Law to be Established]', *Chosun Ilbo*, 5 July: 2.

Kim, Mi-hui (2001) '2000: A Year of Profits and Accolades for Korean Films', *Korea Now*. Online. http://kn.koreaherald.co.kr.

Kim, Samuel S. (2000) 'Korea and Globalization (Segyehwa): A Framework for Analysis', in Samuel S. Kim (ed.), *Korea's Globalization*, Cambridge: Cambridge University Press: 1–28.

Kim, Young-sam (1995) 'Outlining the Blueprint for Globalization', in *Korea's Quest for Reform and Globalization: Selected Speeches of President Kim Young-sam*, Presidential Secretariat, Republic of Korea: 268–73.

King, Richard and Craig, Timothy J. (2002) 'Asia and Global Popular Culture: The View from He Yong's Garbage Dump', in Timothy J. Craig and Richard King (eds),

Global Goes Local: Popular Culture in Asia, Vancouver: University of British Columbia Press: 3–11.

Korea Culture and Contents Agency (2003) 'World's Interest in Korean Film Growing', 24 March. Online. www.kocca.or.kr.

Korean Film Observatory (2003) '2002 Box Office Result for Korean Films, 48.5% of the Overall Domestic Market', report # 8: 18–9.

The Korea Herald (2000) ' "Swiri" Director Buys Kangnam Theater', 21 July. Online. www.koreaherald.co.kr.

Lau, Jenny Kwok Wah Lau (2003) 'Introduction', in Jenny Kwok Wah Lau (ed.), *Multiple Modernities: Cinemas and Popular Media in Transcultural East Asia*, Philadelphia: Temple University Press: 1–10.

Macintyre, Donald (2001) 'Korea's Big Moment', *Time Asia*, 10 September. Online. www.time.com.

Mun, So-hyŏn (2001) 'Hanguk yŏnghwa usŭpke pojimara [Don't Ignore Korean Films]', *MBC News in News*, 8 March. www.imbc.com.

Paquet, Darcy (1999) 'Korean Film Newsletter #3: September 17, 2001'. Online. www.koreanfilm.org.

——(2001a) 'Korean Film Newsletter #9: February 26, 2001'. Online.www. koreanfilm.org.

——(2001b) 'Korean Film Newsletter #11: August 26, 2001'. Online.www. koreanfilm.org.

——(2001c) 'Korean Film Newsletter #12: December 15, 2001'. Online. www. koreanfilm.org.

——(2002) 'Korean Film Newsletter #13: March 21, 2002'. Online. www.koreanfilm.org.

Shim, Doobo (2002) 'South Korean Media Industry in the 1990s and the Economic Crisis', *Prometheus*, 20, 4: 337–50.

Shin, Jeeyoung (forthcoming) 'Contradiction in the Visible: Globalism and Nationalism in Two Contemporary South Korean Films', in Frances Gateward (ed.), *Seoul Searching: Identity and Culture in Korean Cinema*, New York: SUNY Press (forthcoming).

Straubhaar, Joseph D. (1997) 'Distinguishing the Local, Regional and the National Levels of World Television', in Annabelle Sreberny-Mohammadi et al. (eds), *Media in Global Context*, London: Arnold: 284–98.

Yu, Gina (2000) 'Renaissance of Korean Movies', *Koreana*, 14, 2: 4–15.

NOTES

I would like to thank Julian Stringer for his feedback on an earlier draft of this chapter.

1. The Uruguay Round refers to a series of multilateral trade negotiations held between 1986 and 1994. The agreement was reached on 15 December 1993, and was signed by most of its 123 participating governments on 15 April 1994. The Uruguay Round settlement created the World Trade Organization (see www.wto.org).
2. The full content of the laws referred to in this chapter can be found on the website of the Ministry of Government Legislation (at www.moleg.co.kr), unless stated otherwise.
3. The changes in the Film Promotion Law are also summarised in 'The History of Korean Film Laws (Yŏnghwa pŏp pyŏnch'ŏnsa)', available on the website of the Korean Film Archive (www.koreafilm.or.kr).
4. *Source:* KOFIC's introduction to its international promotion department at the KOFIC website: http://www.kofic.or.kr/english/aboutus/aboutus.html.

4. *CHUNHYANG*: MARKETING AN OLD TRADITION IN NEW KOREAN CINEMA

Hyangjin Lee

The story of a beautiful woman who challenges the social prejudice of her lower-class origin and marries above her social position is a universal source material of romantic tales in many cultures. *The Tale of Chunhyang* is the Korean archetype of this notion of feminine beauty. *Chunhyang* appeared in a shamanistic legend in early eighteenth-century Korea. Henceforth, her story appeared in many oral-narrative folk traditions. Through time, her beauty has been variously recreated and refined according to the specific demands and concerns of successive audiences. Furthermore, her story has been remade in almost every medium for popular entertainment in each period, such as *P'ansori* (Korean traditional operatic drama), Chinese poems, popular novels, stage dramas, Western-style operas, films and television dramas. The various aesthetic orientations of each medium can be seen in the relationship between text and audience as revealed through the various transformations (Chŏn 1998). The essence of the folk-tale embodies the popular desire of a Utopian society. Her courageous rebellion triumphs over the prevailing class system. The inevitability of the narrative's internal motif and appropriateness of external elements, however, determine the extent of acceptance or rejection by the audience. Therefore, the dramatic variations between the versions clearly reflect the deciding role of the audience as the subjects of the oral tradition through its historical transmission (Chŏn 2003). The significance of the tale in Korean film history can be seen in its many versions. To date, there have been more than sixteen works based on this narrative, including three North Korean films. In each version, the traditional beauty appears in different guises, identifying the specific demands of the contemporary audience.[1] What makes the tale an enduring tradition is the creative imagination of its audience rather than its authenticity.

Im Kwon-Taek's *Chunhyang* (*Ch'unhyangdyŏn*, 2000) presents a new interpretation of this oral tradition but it is created for a more global audience. Im

Figure 13 Mongryong and Chunhyang with her Kŏmungo: *Chunhyang* (2000).

is one of the most notable figures in the history of Korean national cinema. His directing career, spanning more than four decades, reflects the turbulent history of the national cinema. In the second half of the twentieth century, the Korean film industry experienced continual conflict against political intervention and the desire to protect an industry constantly under threat from Hollywood. Im survived the dark age of Korean film history, under Park Chung Hee's authoritarian military regime, and he transformed himself into a leading figure of the Korean 'New Wave' in the early 1980s. Since the mid-1980s democratisation movement, Im has earned an international reputation as 'the old master' of New Korean Cinema.

As an old-generation film-maker, Im is actively engaged in setting new trends in the New Korean Cinema. Having completed *A Life Downstream* (*Haryu insaeng*, 2004), the director has now made ninety-nine films since his directing début in 1962. The general direction of his film-making, therefore, cannot be singled out by use of the term 'New Korean Cinema'. During the pre-democratisation period, he made a series of anti-Communist war films and national policy films about 'good' citizens upholding the dreams of rapid economic modernisation. His works also include historical dramas, horror films, action thrillers, modern urban films and romantic melodramas. As a result of his prolific output and the quality of his work, his reputation as one of the most popular commercial film-makers in his homeland has never been seriously challenged. In the early 1980s, however, there was a significant change in Im's approach to film-making. This was largely due to his self-criticism of his former films which, he believed, could no longer address the pressing issues of society. Im has the uncanny ability to understand the cinematic needs of society at any given time and the intelligence to produce what audiences desire. Although his film-making has often been threatened by political interference, such interference has never seriously interrupted his film-making. He always seeks to communicate with his audience through stories about people who are marginalised by mainstream society. This approach is the key factor in understanding his present status as a national figure in Korean cinema.

The most noteworthy contribution made by Im to the current renaissance of Korean national cinema lies in his pursuit of creating a national identity. In particular, his persistent cinematic enquiry into the notion of Korean-ness encourages the younger generation of film-makers to redefine cultural tradition through new creativity and experimentation. Examples of such works include Im's own films: *Sopyonje* (*Sŏp'yŏnje*, 1993), *Festival* (*Ch'ukche*, 1996), *Chunhyang*, and *Chihwaseon* (*Ch'wihasŏn*, 2002); Pae Ch'ang-ho's *My Heart* (*Chŏng*, 1999); Kim Ki-dŏk's *Spring, Summer, Fall, Winter . . . and Spring* (*Pom yŏrŭm kaŭl kyŏul kŭrigo pom*, 2003); Kim Hyŏn-sŏk's *YMCA Baseball Team* (*YMCA yagudan*, 2002); and Chu Kyŏng-jong's *Little Monk* (*Dongsŭng*, 2003). The nostalgic sentimentalism which these films convey relieves audiences from their collective historical trauma, such as memories of Japanese colonial rule (1910–45), the Korean War (1950–53) or military dictatorship (1962–87).

Also, regardless of whether it is promoted by commercialism or artistic experimentalism, this type of nostalgic or historical film clearly reflects changed perceptions of Korean identity. Im has deeply influenced major trends in New Korean Cinema by urging his audiences to think about what they have lost through processes of modernisation and political change. This de-politicised approach to history and society lends a different quality to New Korean Cinema from that of the Korean 'New Wave' which appeared between the 1980s and early 1990s. If the New Wave was a part of the South Korean democratisation movements, New Korean Cinema since the mid-1990s can be understood as the outcome of past political struggles. The practitioners of New Korean Cinema now seek to realise cultural democracy in Korea by searching for a new national identity and the autonomy of film-making from political control.

Chunhyang is the most ambitious project in Im's directing career, and arguably his masterpiece (Chŏng 2003: 411).[2] By remaking the old tale, he attempts to entertain international as well as domestic audiences. The difference between *Chunhyang* and his previous films is that the latter were made either for a Korean audience or for international film festivals. The formal, stylistic experiments that visualise the lyrical music *P'ansori* are the quintessence of Im's rendition of this folk-tale. Through this contemporary artistic approach to folklore, *Chunhyang* tries to address the notion that the 'distinctive uniqueness of cultural tradition is crucial for global audiences to be aware of the notion of Koreanness' (Sŏ 2002: 8–9). It reflects the prevailing beliefs of Koreans regarding their national identity. Korean-ness, extracted from cultural tradition, can be a unifying concept in defining the collective identity of the people, regardless of their experiences of historical and social processes of Westernisation and modernisation (Hŏ 2000). *Chunhyang* attempts to realise the fantasy that 'the essence of Korean beauty . . . could be accepted as a universal aesthetic ideal' (Yi 1993: 173). In this sense, Korean beauty, as pursued by Im's *Chunhyang*, seems successfully to have generated a great deal of interest and enthusiasm at film festivals and art-house circuits around the world. Among Korean audiences at commercial theatres, however, the film's reception can only be described as, at best, lukewarm. Consequently, it is destined to be a film created for the international film festival or art-houses.

This chapter will explore the ways in which *Chunhyang* presents folk art and cultural traditions in Korea to a wider, international audience, in order to evaluate the validity of the creation of a national identity. The reinvention of tradition pursued by *Chunhyang* is a distinctive marketing strategy of New Korean Cinema and it works to highlight its cultural uniqueness from other national cinemas. *Chunhyang* locates Korean national cinema in the 'official' history of world film. The artistic achievement of the film can also be considered a measure of the maturity of the Korean film industry (Min 2001: 28). The film illustrates the dynamics of the Korean film industry in response to the simultaneous cross-trends of globalisation and localisation in world film culture. The thesis here is that the rapid expansion of the Korean film industry in recent years, due to the commercial success of modern films, provides the means to accommodate further domestic and international connoisseurs. Furthermore, examination of the director's lifelong cinematic journey searching for so-called Korean-ness (S. Chŏng 1987: 216–39; Im 1993) can help create new directions in Korean cinema.

CREATING A NEW NATIONAL IDENTITY FOR GLOBAL AUDIENCES

The notion of Korean-ness assumes that the collective identity of the nation can be defined by its unique cultural experiences and traditions. It is invented for others' recognition of the presence of 'us', or vice versa, by stressing the distinctiveness of national traits through cultural traditions.[3] This conceptual artificiality does not accurately reflect the heterogeneity of social reality, however. In fact, the hybridisation between tradition and modernity is clearly evident in contemporary Korean cultural life (Yi 1993: 174). Furthermore, the imported idea of oriental or fusion style in an urban life creates a new trend in contemporary cultural consumerism. This perception of 'Korean-ness', therefore, does not necessarily apply to all South Koreans. In particular, the locality constructed by the popular discourse is articulated in a relative sense, depending on the specific demands of consumers.

The creation of a new national identity for global audiences pursued by New Korean Cinema practitioners should be understood in this context. Since the 1980s, Korean film-makers and policy-makers began to look for ways to present the national cinema as a new force of world cinema. During the democratisation movement period of the mid-1980s and early 1990s, the issues of modernisation, colonialism, Cold War conflicts and military dictatorship were among the themes to be found in films. The leaders of this new group were young, progressive film-makers who were university graduates and sympathetic towards student activism, such as Park Kwang-su, Jang Sun-woo and Park Chŏng-won. They opposed the political passivity of the existing film culture and sought to expose political corruption and economic inequality in their recently prosperous, capitalist society. On the other hand, a group of the older generation of film-makers from the existing film production system also voiced criticisms of the country's post-colonial condition after suffering the consequences of national division. Yi Chang-ho, Chŏng Chi-yŏng (Jŏng Chi-yŏng) and Chang Gil-su were some of the leading figures. Park Kwang-su's *Chilsu and Mansu* (*Ch'ilsu-wa Mansu*, 1988) and *Black Republic* (*Kŭdŭldo uri ch'ŏrŏm*, 1992), Park Chong-won's *Kuro Arirang* (1989) and *Our Twisted Hero* (*Uridŭl-ŭi ilkŭrŏjin yŏngung*, 1992), and Jang Sun-woo's *Lovers in Woomuk-Baemi* (*Umukbaemi-ŭi sarang*, 1989) subtly deal with the sufferings of ordinary citizens by the political abuses of Park Chung Hee's military regime and the deepening gap between the rich and the poor. Yi Chang-ho's *A Wayfarer Never Rests on the Road* (*Nakŭnenŭn kilesŏdo swiji annŭnda*, 1987), Chŏng Chi-yŏng's *Southern Guerrilla Forces* (*Nambugun*, 1990), Chang Kil-su's *Silver Stallion* (*Ŭnmanŭn oji annŭnda*,

1991) and Park Kwang-su's *To the Starry Island* (*Kŭ sŏme kago ship'da*, 1993) reject the 'official' interpretation of the Korean War. They dramatise the human sacrifice and hatred between Koreans who were caught up in the conflict through redefining the meaning of the war conducted on behalf of the world powers. In dealing with such issues, cultural tradition is often portrayed as the central motif in resolving the present socio-political conflicts. In addition, pressure from Hollywood to open up the domestic film market has been increasing since 1987, although this has tended to fuel anti-Americanism. Consequently, film-makers have begun to challenge the powerful presence of Americans in Korean film culture. In this sense, it can be said that 'Korean-ness', as conveyed through the national cinema, is constantly being reconstructed.

The three major international film festivals, Cannes, Venice and Berlin, are regarded by many Korean film practitioners and policy-makers as the best venues where a national cinema can be promoted. In particular, Cannes is regarded as an almost sacred arena for Korean cinema on the global stage. The competitive psychology of Koreans had often demanded why Korea had not won the Grand Prix at Cannes or Venice whereas Japan won it in the 1950s, and Taiwan and China in the 1980s (Jeon 2001: 266). Im Kwon-Taek stated that he was at last relieved of the psychological burden from national pressure when he received the Best Director award at Cannes with *Chihwaseon* in 2002. Yi Ch'ang-dong's *Oasis* (*Oasisǔ*) won the Best Director award in Venice in the same year. The film critics listed the three Best Director-awarded films, including Kang Tae-jin's *Horseman* (*Mabu*) which won in Berlin in 1961.

Despite the later success by other films, Im's *Chunhyang* marked a significant event in contemporary Korean film history. Im's small-budget art film, *Sopyonje* (1993), had set the highest box-office record up to that time. As a result, Im was given the title of '*Kungmin Gamdok*', i.e. the people's director. The entry of this people's director in the official competition session with *Chunhyang* at Cannes 2000 emphasised the nation's yearning for international recognition.

Reversed orientalism or orientalist discourse on the oppressive gender relationship informed by Confucian social norms tends to be referred to as the most familiar marketing strategy of Korean cinema at international film festivals (Sŏ 2002: 8–16). It is often criticised as an attempt to endorse the identity of a national cinema. The fragmented, heterogeneous images of the feminised masses signify the post-colonial status of the divided nation. For example, three of Im's films, *Mandala* (*Mandara*), *Gilsottum* (*Kilsottǔm*) and *The Taebaek Mountains* (*T'aebaek sanmaek*), were awarded prizes at the Berlin International Film Festival in 1981, 1985 and 1994 respectively. They deal with the agony of individuals, victimised by the developmental state's political abuses, or by the ideological confrontations among the people, due to national division. On the other hand, his two Venice International Film Festival award-winning films, *The Surrogate Mother* (*Ssibaji*, 1987) and *Come, Come, Come Upward* (*Aje aje bara aje*, 1989), portray the depressing lives of women who struggle against the existing patriarchal social systems and cultural prejudices. Regarding the last two works, the figuration of female characters as victims of oppressive Confucian patriarchy and social change envisages the female body as a metaphor for the post-colonial status of the nation (James and Kim 2002). Furthermore, his gendered discourse on nationhood as feminine, inferior and passive extends to signify Korean woman as exotic, seductive and primitive, reinforcing her image as 'consistently oppressive and repressive' (Doane 1988: 216).

Despite its ideological shortcomings and male-centred stance, Im's cinematic sublimation of 'Korean-ness' still focuses on the contradictions between tradition and modernity among precarious lives existing on the periphery of a capitalist society. This portrayal of society and its resulting social pressures is the overriding theme in Im's films. More importantly, his concepts of nation and national tradition are expressed through the voices of the socially and politically marginalised masses in history.

Korean identity, as pursued by *Chunhyang*, also relies heavily on the aesthetic quality of cultural tradition, and especially on the feminine image of the nation as a woman covered by a veil. On the other hand, the visualisation of *P'ansori* in *Chunhyang* tends to silence the authoritative voices of the subjects. It focuses on the visualisation of *sori*, that is, sound, but largely dismisses *imyŏn*, that is, the inner dimension of the narrative (Park 2003: 19–20). In the film's beautiful images of medieval Korea, therefore, the people are often portrayed merely as props. The narrative's emotional dimensions lend melodramatic effects to the images, but they fail to communicate the historical experiences of the people. Their subjectivity, as expressed by the inner dimensions of the narrative, is alienated from the main concerns of the film. Furthermore, history as portrayed by the film attempts to entertain the audience with an idolised image of old Korea.

This stylish representation of 'Korean-ness' embellished by cultural tradition in *Chunhyang* constitutes a state of rebellion by the director against the exclusivist national film culture in Korea. In this sense, *Chunhyang* predicts *Chihwaseon*, the next artistic journey of Im Kwon-Taek to Cannes. *Chihwaseon* dramatises the anarchistic life of the famous painter, Jang Sŭng-ŏp, who lived in the late Chosŏn Dynasty (1392–1910). Im regards this film as his most self-reflective work.[4]

For a Korean film-maker who experienced the violent social upheavals of the country's recent past, the pursuit of artistic experiments beyond the daily concerns of the local audience and their escapist fantasies is rather an alienating concept. The restoration of democracy and civil governance, however, now allows film-makers more freedom to seek out new international audiences. In a democratic society, film does not have to be subject to political control in the name of the so-called 'suffering masses'. From this perspective, *Chunhyang* seems to explore a new Korean identity which is construed by the contemporary reconstruction of culture tradition. The significance of *Chunhyang*'s place in Korean cinema history lies in this challenging new aspect: the redefining of an audience's expectations in a global context.

FROM SOUND TO IMAGE: *CHUNHYANG* IN CANNES AND IN SEOUL

As a cultural commodity in a capitalist society, a film needs to satisfy the audiences who pay for it. Standardisation and universality are principal marketing strategies used to help maximise the financial accountability of a national cinema. From this commercial perspective, marketing the old traditions of a nation seems to lead to more complex pictures because the unfamiliar scenes of alienated people can produce different meanings for various audiences.

An investigation of the different responses of the audiences in Cannes and Seoul to the ideas of 'Korean-ness' expressed in *Chunhyang* can define Im's primary target audience, who would share his ideas of time in reconstructing tradition. To capture the traditional Korean beauty on screen is the philosophy of Im's lifelong film-making practice (J. Chŏng 2002: 173). His pursuit of artistic experimentation, however, was only possible after working for over forty years as a successful commercial film-maker (Chŏng 1987: 136–61). *Chunhyang* denotes Im's transformation from a commercial film-maker to an art film-maker. Im stated in an interview that many of his early films were nothing but 'low-budget' films (James and Kim 2002: 276), and he stressed that the reason why he intended to make a new *Chunhyang* film at the beginning of the new millennium was to present the beauty of a Korean cultural tradition to a new generation. Moreover, he stated that he wanted to prove that *Chunhyang* is an harmonic encounter between Korean traditional aesthetics and the Western film medium. His innovative ideas are an attempt to synthesise the formal properties of *P'ansori* with the cinematic techniques in *Chunhyang*. These concepts recreate the popular operatic tradition, which originates from local culture, as a modern art form for a global audience. As a direct result of the recognition it received in Cannes, *Chunhyang* became the first Korean film to be released in commercial theatres in the United States. Domestic theatres also extended to show it when they heard the news from Cannes, despite its poor performance at the box-office during its first screenings at home. The result, however, was not very different from before. The film's lacklustre reception in Seoul confirmed the alienating effects of 'international film festival awards', highlighting the difference between the symbolic significance of Cannes in the long term and its short-term effects on the local film industry.

The Tale of Chunhyang or *The Song of Chunhyang* is the oldest existing text of *P'ansori*, which flourished in Korea in the late eighteenth and early nineteenth centuries. One spring day, Chunhyang meets Mongryong, a son of the local magistrate and they fall in love with each other. Mongryong, however, has to leave Namwon, to go to Seoul with his family. After his departure, Chunhyang is ordered to entertain the new magistrate, Pyŏn Hakto. Chunhyang rejects his advances and is consequently imprisoned. She is to be executed at the new magistrate's birthday party but Mongryong passes a state exam to return to the village as a secret royal inspector to rescue her from her death.

The Tale of Chunhyang is the Korean equivalent of Shakespeare's *Romeo and Juliet*. It differs from the latter because the story of Chunhyang involves popular criticism of a patriarchal class system which confines women's sexual identity and their bodies as objects of male desire. Sexuality functions as a 'malleable feature of self, a prime connecting point between body, self-identity and social norms' (Giddens 1993: 5). Whereas family women are supposed to learn the ideals of 'wise mother and good wife', certain types of women are socially created from the lower class to assist the dualistic standards of sexuality in Confucian society. The first type of woman is the 'good breast' (Sceats 1996: 118) who is created for rearing a family; and the latter type is 'the dirty body', who is designed for liaisons with the opposite sex. Both of them, however, are deprived of their rights to construct their sexual identities according to their own ideas and desires. Chunhyang rejects the sexual identity of women as dictated by patriarchal class distinctions. She pursues the status of 'respectable wife' and at the same time seeks to realise her sexual desire. Her choice of a privileged nobleman as a marriage partner challenges the authority of the power-élites who attempt to monopolise the reproduction of knowledge and value systems (Sŏl 1999: 324–8). By granting the premarital relationship and inter-class marriage, the story's happy ending signifies popular wishes for a freer society which does not suffer from hypocritical sexual morality and class distinctions. Im's *Chunhyang* tries to validate rebellious ideas as construed by folklore by placing them against creative and experimental ideas expressed through the hybridisation of the formal properties of both *P'ansori* and film art.

In essence, *Chunhyang* transforms the rhythm, pitch and dynamics of *P'ansori* into rich, picturesque images. *P'ansori* is an operatic drama played by a solo singer (*kwangdae*) accompanied by a drummer (*kosu*). The primary medium of *P'ansori* is sound not image. The prefix *p'an* refers to an open space and *sori* means sound or song/vocal narrative. The singer, usually male, stands centre-stage and delivers a dramatic story by songs (*sori*) and narration (*aniri*). He sometimes uses symbolic gestures (*pallim*) to give dramatic effects to the sound or to arouse sympathy among the audience, but his movements are extremely moderated and stylised. In other words, in contrast to Chinese Peking Opera or Japanese *Kabuki*, *P'ansori* does not include theatrical acting, dramatic gestures or representational dances by various characters in colourful costumes against vivid backdrops. This is the reason why the response (*ch'uimsae*) of the audience is crucial in performing *P'ansori*, offering their creative imagination of the story as dictated by the singer (Ch'oi 1990: 109). In *Chunhyang*, the *P'ansori* audience appears as the actors in the framing story, applauding, laughing, dancing, sighing, raging and crying in response to the sound of the singer. In a sense, the frame-like nature of narrative structure (*mise-en-abîme*) in *Chunhyang* attempts to validate the dramatic effects of the mutual response between audience and singer in transforming traditional performing art into cinematic form.

The creativeness of *Chunhyang* as an art film lies in its experimental presentation of a reversed relationship between sound and image. It uses sound as the primary medium to convey the narrative as *P'ansori*, in opposition to the ways of using sound in conventional narrative film-making. Traditionally, sound supports the development of the narrative by creating atmosphere or by expressing the psychological state of characters (Hill and Gibson 1998: 43–4). The perfectly coincident rhythms between acting and music, the synchronised editing according to the dictates of the songs, and the visualisation of lyrics concerning beautiful landscapes and affectionate love, present new artistic experiences to a global audience. This, in turn, challenges conventional ideas of film as a contemporary form that evolved from the history of the photograph, and attempts to link it instead with the history of the performing arts. In short, *Chunhyang* places the cultural traditions of the nation in a transnational space, blending together two different aesthetic worlds: performing art and cinema. At the same time, it firmly anchors film in the art history of Korea.

The locality and complex linguistic features of *P'ansori* (Chŏn 2003: 12) make Im's artistic experiments with the synchronisation of sound and image more complex and dynamic. *Chunhyang* is a *P'ansori* film, not a film about *P'ansori*, such as *Sopyonje*. *Sopyonje* dramatises the tragic story of *P'ansori* singers in modern Korea. It contains some *P'ansori* repertoires familiar to Korean audiences, such as the songs from *The Tale of Simchong* or from *The Tale of Chunhyang*. The film uses *P'ansori* as a motif in the narrative, however, or to create a specific mood for a scene as required by the internal logic of the story. By comparison, the narrativity of *P'ansori* is a key element in *Chunhyang*. The cinematic version cannot ignore the interpretive disposition of language, the intrinsic nature of *P'ansori*. Audiences unfamiliar with foreign-language films tend to be preoccupied with reading the subtitled translations so as to be able to follow the development of the narrative. In fact, for any ordinary audience members, including Koreans, such an experience – consuming a film which requires a full and simultaneous understanding of visual messages, vocal narratives and subtitles – should be an alienating experience. Therefore, they can easily miss out on the synchronising effects created between the images and the rhythmical, verbal expression of the lyrics. In stricter terms, without the prior knowledge of the rich cultural and social implications lying beneath the overt verbal expressions, the cinematic rendition of a performing art narrated in its original language cannot fully capture the synchronising effects between image and sound. The images have to be mediated by the interpretation of another language. This is a linguistic and cultural limitation in translating the locality of an oral tradition into the universal language of cinema art.

There are two scenes which well support this argument. In the first scene, Pangja, the servant of Mongryong, is sent to call Chunhyang in the forest. In the second, two officials are dispatched by a new magistrate to summon Chunhyang from her home. In these scenes, the characters' rhythmical, comic steps crossing the forest or village are almost perfectly synchronised with the fast rhythmical cycles (*chungjungmori*) of songs sung by Cho Sang-hyŏn, the 'human national treasure' of *P'ansori*.[5] On the other hand, the synchronising effects between sound and image have to be mediated by the detailed verbal expressions given by the songs. Otherwise, the seemingly similar atmosphere in the two scenes cannot

Figure 14 Mongryong points at Chunhyang on the swing with his fan and commands Pangja to bring her to him.

easily be distinguished one from the other: the complex, changing relationship between Chunhyang and surrounding characters; the different psychological states of the characters; or the contrastive dramatic function of the two scenes in the narrative. The 'Song of Love' scene and the 'Song of Ten Beats' scene are more illustrative in discussing these specific linguistic features of *P'ansori*. In these scenes, Cho's voice runs over from the actors' dialogue, and soon takes over the actors. He speaks for the actors, who become part of the visual images. The dynamic nature of the various speeds and rhythmical cycles which comprise his narration and songs, such as *chinyang, chungmori, chungjungmori, chajǔnmori* and *hwimori*, clearly conveys the sense of joy, sorrow or anxiety experienced by the characters, leading the development of conflict into the climax (Kim 1990: 261). The rhyme and vocal narration succinctly lead the climax of emotional identification between the fictional figures and real people, that is, the subjects of the stories. The deep feeling and overwhelming emotional power which are expressed in *imyǒn* cannot easily be translated into the images. On the other hand, Cho's literary interpretation of the scenes is far more complicated than the simple description of reconstructed images. It is full of humour, satire and refined metaphoric expressions, informed by the rich poetic tradition and folklore of Korea.

The 'Korean-ness' proposed by *Chunhyang* is a newly invented concept for contemporaries who aspire to a new aesthetic sense (Sato 2000: 321–4). In this sense, it foregoes populism in order to create a new identity for global film audiences who embody the high sense of artistic experience. Conversely, the rather

Figure 15 Pangja runs to bring Chunhyang to Mongryong upon his master's order.

disappointing response of Korean audiences to *Chunhyang* may be in part because the director's formal, stylish experiments are not widely appreciated by the majority of audience members who prefer light entertainment. Also worth noting is the insufficient nature of the critical commentary on Im's new interpretation of this old tradition: it was almost close to total silence (Jeon 2001: 266). Korean-ness, which was recognised by the judges at Cannes, could not help *Chunhyang* avoid the widespread indifference of Koreans. The artistic representation of the national folk culture still remains within the exclusive circles of film connoisseurs.

The general response to *Chunhyang* in Seoul can support sceptical ideas regarding the contemporary meaning of *P'ansori* as a popular art: it does not communicate the resentment (*han*) and excitement (*shinmyŏng* or *hŭng*) of the masses in this era, which are said to be the most important socio-psychological functions of *P'ansori* (Sŏl 1998: 416). Yet if this is the case, how can we explain the astonishing popularity of *Sopyonje* with Korean audiences? Certainly, as an art film, *Sopyonje* rewrote Korean film history by generating a harmony between film critics and ordinary film-goers which helped orchestrate the successful realisation of the old tradition in a contemporary form (Im 1993). As Cho Hae Joang points out, the success of *Sopyonje* greatly benefited from a popular movement of the time, the so-called 'search for our culture' (Cho 2002: 138). The overwhelming response of the nation created the '*Sopyonje* Syndrome', thus revealing Koreans' nostalgic sentiments and sense of loss.

Im proposed that '*P'ansori* is enjoyable to anybody regardless of time and space' (Im 1993). The different reception among Koreans to *Chunhyang* and

Sopyonje, however, contradicts his belief in the universality of old traditions regardless of time and space. Despite its challenging aspects in hybridising the aesthetic qualities of film and oral tradition, *Chunhyang* does not rely on the role of the audience in visualising the lyric music. Some critics were rather harsh even on his Cannes-winning film, *Chihwaseon*: it is almost a 'stuffed beauty' of old tradition and there is no new interpretation or cinematic sublimation for contemporary audiences (Chŏng 2002: 174). The disappointing box-office returns of *Chunhyang* and *Chihwaseon* seem to support this criticism.

Indeed, the active engagement of an audience comprises the textuality of *P'ansori*. This is a different concept from the viewpoint of the film audience. The photographic nature of images tends to remove the subjectivity and spontaneity of the viewer in reconstructing the text. As the result, the visualisation of the narrative is completed by the text, thus, it satisfies audiences who tend not to identify with the people and history as narrated by the film. On the other hand, Im's artistic experimentation in the oral tradition through *Chunhyang* draws on a new relationship between text and its consumer. It is a new form of representation in search of a new audience. The new audience is expected to explore a different subjectivity and receptivity as a new patron of the old tradition.

THE OLD TRADITION AS THE NEW CHALLENGE

The representation of cultural tradition is a useful paradigm to explore the new identity of a national cinema. Like a tourist poster, the exotic images of the national cultural heritage can satisfy notions of 'otherness'. The artistic recreation of traditional culture without a heavy handed ideological slant is certainly a strong feature of many non-Western films that venture into the world film market. In most cases, the aesthetic, experimental quality pursued by such films does not mute the voices of the people who are the actors of history and creators of tradition. It still comments on the reality of the present society. The rebellion of the individual director is against the prevailing social norms and ideological values dictating the ordinary people's lives.

Im's *Chunhyang* silences the people's voices, however, and removes their concern with history and tradition from cinematic representation. It rejects the contemporary interpretation of tradition from the people's point of view. Ironically, this anarchist-individualistic approach expresses contemporary Korean identity in transition. After the long struggle for democracy, Korean society has become more diverse and complex but less of an entity as one nation. It can not overrule the different concerns between the people and their changing interests any more. *Chunhyang* skilfully expresses this transitional period of Korean society.

Furthermore, the varying responses to *Chunhyang* suggest the uncertainty and ambivalence of the new identity politics expressed in New Korean Cinema. The democratisation of the country profoundly influenced the film industry. It now enjoys more freedom. The government dropped notorious pre-censorship stipulations, allowing film-makers more autonomy in choosing their subject matter and ideological stance. In short, Korea is undergoing rapid social change in parallel with its film industry. Film-makers now have to deal with these changes so as to communicate the transitional, multi-layered dimensions of contemporary Korean identity. Korean society now does not request ideological values as the foremost criteria for the creation of its national cinema.

The creation of a new identity is a conflict-ridden process, and film-makers need to understand the complex and unpredictable consuming patterns of their audiences. The intriguing contrast between the muted response to *Chunhyang* in Seoul and the keen interest shown by Korea to its success at Cannes supports this argument. The nation wants to promote 'Korean-ness' to the world. At the same time, Korea's conflicting ideas in identifying self from others highlights the limited accountability of the notion of 'Korean-ness' informed by the stereotypical interpretation of tradition. Moreover, Korean audiences' recent preference for Korean themes, but in a Hollywood style of entertainment, reflects notions of hybridity, heterogeneity and mimicry. This is important in understanding perceptions of cultural tradition. The new identity politics of Korean film underlines the interplay between unification and fragmentation in marketing 'Korean-ness' to the world, suggesting the maturity of the national film industry both artistically and financially.

The production of historical films in Korea may simply echo the increasing needs of the global film market in recent years. But, more significantly, it questions the contemporary interpretation of cultural tradition beyond commercial interests. The continuing artistic achievements, daring generic experiments and commercial success of New Korean Cinema cannot be assessed separately. In this sense, Im's *Chunhyang* should be considered representative of the healthy state of the current Korean film industry. It set a significant trend in New Korean Cinema and has opened up a new market. The artistic, nostalgic recreation of tradition and history pursued by Im is now challenged by a new generation of film-makers who lead the revival of historical films in current Korean cinema. As suggested by the astonishing commercial success of recent historical films, such as Yi Chae-yong's *Untold Scandal (Sŭk'aendŭl – Chosŏnnamnyŏsangyŏljisa*, 2003) and Yi Jun-ik's *Hansanbŏl* (2003), history and tradition are attracting more interest from audiences and investors. The new film-makers are eager to return to history and tradition so as to satisfy the new, creative imagination of the contemporary audience. Marketing an old tradition in New Korean Cinema should be understood as the product of the profit-making motives of the film industry and of the diverse demands of its audience.

REFERENCES

Befu, Harami (ed.) (1993) *Cultural Nationalism in East Asia*, Berkeley: University of California Press.

Cho, Hae Joang (2002), '*Sopyonje*: Its Cultural and Historical Meaning', in David

E. James and Kyung Hyun Kim (eds), *Im Kwon-Taek: The Making of a Korean National Cinema*, Detroit: Wayne State University Press: 134–56.

Ch'oi, Chŏng-sŏn, (1990) 'P'ansori-ŭi Ch'uimsae' [The Responses of *P'ansori*], in Yi Ki-u, and Ch'oi Tong-hyŏn (eds), *P'ansori-ŭ chipyeong* [The Horizon of *P'ansori*], Seoul: Sina: 90–128.

Chŏn, Pyŏng-hyŏng (1998) 'P'ansori-ŭi Hyŏngsŏng-gwa Pyŏnhwa' [The Formation of *P'ansori* and its Transformation], in the Academy of Korean Language and Literature (ed.), *P'ansori Yŏngu* [A Study of *P'ansori*], Seoul: T'aehaksa: 9–47.

Chŏn, Yŏng-sŏn (2003) *Kojŏn Sosŏl-ŭi Yŏksajŏk Chŏn'gae-wa Nambukhan-ŭi Ch'unhyangjŏn* [The Historical Development of Classic Novels and North and South Korean *The Tale of Chunhyang*], Seoul: Munhakmaŭlsa.

Chŏng, Chae-hyŏng (2002) 'Punailyŏjŏkin Tongyangjŏk Sayu-ŭi Hyŏngsanghwa' [The Realisation of Trans-self, Oriental Thought], in *Yŏnghwa P'ŏngron* [Korean Film Critiques], 14: 170–4.

Chŏng, Sŏng-il (ed.) (1987) *Han'guk Yŏnghwa Yŏn'gu I: Im Kwontaek* [Korean Film Studies I: Im Kwon-Taek], Seoul: Onŭl.

——(ed.) (2003a) *Im Kwontaek-i Im Kwontaek-ŭl Malhada 1* [Im Kwon-Taek on Im Kwon-Taek 1], Seoul: Hyŏnmum Sŏga.

——(ed.) (2003b) *Im Kwontaek-i Im Kwontaek-ŭl Malhada 2* [Im Kwon-Taek on Im Kwon-Taek 2], Seoul: Hyŏnmum Sŏga.

Doane, Mary Ann (1988) 'Woman's Stake: Filming the Female Body', in Constance Penley (ed.), *Feminism and Film Theory*, London: British Film Institute: 216–28.

Giddens, Anthony (1993) *The Transformation of Intimacy: Sexuality, Love and Eroticism in Modern Societies*, Cambridge: Polity Press.

Hill, John and Church Gibson, Pamela (eds) (1998) *The Oxford Guide to Film Studies*, Oxford: Oxford University Press.

Hŏ, Mun-yŏng, (2000) 'Chunhangdyon', *Cine 21*, 2: 1.

Im, Kwon-Taek (ed.) (1993) *Sopyonje, Yŏnghwa Iyŏgi* [*Sopyonje, Movie Book*], Seoul: Haneul.

James, David E. and Kim, Kyung Hyun (eds) (2002) *Im Kwon-Taek: The Making of a Korean National Cinema*, Detroit: Wayne State University Press.

Jeon, Pyeong-Kuk (2001) 'International Critique on Korean Cinema and Its Aesthetic Properties – Focusing on the Award-Winning Works at International Film Festivals', *Yŏnghwa Yŏn'gu* [Film Studies], 17: 265–303.

Kim, Ik-tu (1990) 'Ch'anggŭkhwa-ŭi Munjejŏms' [The Problems of Making Korean Classical Opera], in Yi Ki-u and Ch'oi Tong-hyŏn (eds), *P'ansori-ŭi Chipyŏng* [The Horizon of *P'ansori*], Seoul: Sina: 241–69.

Lee, Hyangjin (2000) *Contemporary Korean Cinema: Identity, Culture and Politics*, Manchester: Manchester University Press.

Min Pyŏng-rok (2001) 'Han'guk Yŏnghwa Sanŏp-ŭi Hyŏnhwang-gwa Taean Yeongu' [The Current Stage of Korean Film Industry and A Study of Alternatives], in *Yŏnghwa P'yŏngron* [Korean Film Critiques], 13: 25–40.

Park, Chan E. (2003) *Voices from the Straw Mat: Toward an Ethnography of Korean Story Singing*, Honolulu: University of Hawai'i Press.

Sato, Tadao (2000) *Kankoku Eiga no Seishin* [Korean Cinema and Im Kwon-Taek], Koyang: Kangukhaksuljungbo.

Sceats, Sarah (1996) 'Eating the Evidence: Women, Power and Food', in Sarah Sceats and Gail Cunningham (eds), *Images and Power: Women in Fiction in the Twentieth Century*, London: Longman: 117–27.

Sŏ, Chŏng-nam (2002) 'Chihwaseon-gwa Oasis, Krigo Major Yŏnghwaje-ro Kanŭn Kil' [*Chihwaseon* and *Oasis*, the Road to the Major Film Festivals], in *Yŏnghwa P'yŏngron* [Korean Film Critiques], 14: 8–16.

Sŏl, Sŏng-gyŏng (1998) 'Ch'unhyangjŏn-ŭi Kyetong' [A Genealogy of *The Tale of Chunhyang*], in the Academy of Korean Language and Literature (ed.), *P'ansori Yŏngu* [A Study of *P'ansori*], Seoul: T'aehaksa: 405–17.

——(1999) 'Shin Chae-hyo *P'ansori* Sasŏl-ŭi T'ŭksŏng' [The Characteristics of *P'ansori* Narration of Shin Chae-hyo], in Yi and Ki-u, Ch'oi Tong-hyŏn (eds), *P'ansori-ŭi Chip'yŏng* [The Horizon of *P'ansori*], Seoul: Sina: 322–45.

Yi, Chae-hyŏn (1993) 'Uri Mŏrit'ong-ŭi Sukpyŏn – "*Sopyonje* Syndrome" and Sŏ T'aeji Syndrome' [Excreta in Our Head: '*Sopyonje* Syndrome' and Sŏ T'aeji Syndrome], in *Sangsang* [Imagination], 1:2: 162–77.

NOTES

1. For more detailed analysis of the North and South Korean film versions of *Chunhyang*, see Lee (2000): 67–101.
2. Im has stated that he will still be remembered as the director of *Chunhyang* even though he later won the Best Director award at Cannes for *Chihwaseon*.
3. Harumi Befu cogently notes that 'national identity is not a fixed, objectified, and eternally defined entity; instead, it is continually in the making to fit the needs of the creators and consumers' (Befu 1993: 5).
4. From a personal interview, conducted 21 October 2003, in Seoul.
5. Im used a *P'ansori* performance recorded by Cho in 1976 for *Chunhyang*.

5. 'CINE-MANIA' OR CINEPHILIA: FILM FESTIVALS AND THE IDENTITY QUESTION

Soyoung Kim

Reprinted from *UTS Review* (now *Cultural Studies Review*) vol. 4, no. 2 (1998): 174–87.

RECOGNITION OR REFUSAL AND SOMETHING ELSE

Organising the Women's Film Festival in Seoul during April of 1996, one among many film festivals launched in South Korea in the mid-nineties, I came to wonder about the ways in which certain Korean film festivals mobilise specific identities. In fact, each festival claims a *raison d'être* which includes not only the coverage of identity-oriented themes, but also the endeavour to construct a discursive space where the relevant issues can emerge and take shape.

Various factors have contributed to the recent proliferation of all kinds of film festivals in South Korea. First, there is cine-mania, the Korean version of cinephilia. Second is the enactment of a local self-government system. Third, there has been a shift in the site of Korean activism from the politico-economic to the cultural sphere. And last, there is the ambitious project of *Saegaehwa*, the Korean official version of globalisation. *Saegaehwa* was initiated with the establishment of civil government in 1991. It reverberates in 1997 as follows:

> As the newest member of the Organization of Economic Cooperation and Development, and one of the world's strongest trading nations, the Republic of Korea will further accelerate *Saegaehwa*, its ambitious economic liberalization effort aimed at greater globalization. *Saegaehwa* will open the Korean market to foreign trade and investment and will further strengthen corporate Korea's role on the international business stage . . .[1]

In a breathless and condensed narrative of *Saegaehwa* and civil society, cultural critics often mention a paradigm shift as having occurred in the 1990s. Their argument is that the social change of the 1980s that was mobilised by the massive labour movement in alliance with student protests is being severely damaged by the retreat from the notion of class. The problem with this rhetoric is that it not only fails to perceive emerging social forces and new political agents but also the transformation of class identities.

Facing the need for a new direction in the social movement which no longer appears totally grounded on a proletarian class perspective, groups composed of feminists, gay/lesbian activists, some members of youth subcultures and civil activists have all initiated film festivals as public platforms to address their rights and concerns. The desire to be represented or recognised in public prevails in the various modes of festivals. It seems the various film festivals have become not only a space of negotiation among different forces but also a cultural practice which links the audience to the specific agendas raised by new identities, subject positions and organisations.

Generally speaking, the film festivals can be classified into three categories. First, there are those derived from a coalition of the state, local governments, corporations and intellectuals equipped with film expertise, as exemplified by the Pusan International Film Festival and Puchon International Fantastic Film Festival. Second, there are corporate-sponsored festivals such as the Q Channel Seoul Documentary Film and Video Festival and the Samsung Nices Short Film Festival. Third, there are festivals organised by new and old activist groups.[2]

In a social formation where state intervention into every aspect of people's lives is still highly visible, even the second kind of festival needs to compromise with the power of the state exerted through censorship and exhibition laws. The third kind of festival is relatively autonomous from the state and the corporate sector. Therefore, it provides an interesting example of how the new social movement of the 1990s is taking tentative steps away from the preceding 1980s social movement that was pivoted on the labour movement.

In this third category, the discourses of the 1980s and '90s are simultaneously operative. The similarities and continuities and the differences and ruptures between the two periods become visible when the different film festivals are examined closely. Also, through the politics of these festivals, the notion of identity politics and the possible formation of alternative public spheres may be tested against the civil society claimed by the present government and the mainstream media. So far, the third category has included the Women's Film Festival in Seoul, the Seoul Queer Film and Video Festival, the Human Rights Watch Film Festival (organised by an ex-political prisoner previously gaoled for violation of the National Security Law), IndeForum (held by young filmmakers), and various other small-scale festivals that take place on college campuses, in videotheques and so forth.

The way the three categories of film festival operate may be viewed as an index to the new contours of cultural specificity in the 1990s. The notion of the public sphere and the alternative public spheres in which each film festival is located (or dislocated) has to be taken into consideration *vis-à-vis* the inauguration of the civil government, the retreat of the labour movement as the privileged force of social change, and the concomitant endeavour to find new agencies for social change. Around the same period, the discourse on nationalism has been remobilised with the discourse of *Saegaehwa* in order to dictate a social programme marked by a bourgeois project of appealing to unity to neutralise class conflict.[3] The international-scale film festivals in particular thrive on the manifold manifestations of the global and the local and the national and the local. The local is a fragmented site contested by central and newly formed local governments. As noted above, the film festival provides a condensed space where different interests and ideologies all come into play at the contested intersection of residual authoritarian and emergent democratic modes. The negotiations and compromises between the state, the corporations, the intellectuals and the audiences betray how the different social forces are contesting with one another in this historical conjuncture.

The concern of this paper is to point out the complex structure of articulation working through the various film festivals. They tend to operate in a strategic way so as to render the festival occasion a cultural, political and economic site of ongoing recognition, negotiation and contest. The banning of festivals like the Seoul Queer Film and Video Festival, the Human Rights Watch Film Festival and the IndeForum Festival explicitly indicates pressure points in the hegemonic order. The whole organising, exhibiting and banning process of film festivals reveals blockages, grey areas, niches and points of compromise, as well as a possible direction towards alternative or oppositional platforms. Among the different matrices of emerging groups, collectives and identities engaged in film festival politics, some are not only recognised but also heavily supported by the authorities whereas others are refused recognition or they themselves resist recognition by the authorities.

DESIRE FOR CINEMA, DESIRE FOR RECOGNITION

My focus on film festivals as a distinctive cultural process immediately begs a question. Why has the cinematic mode suddenly been employed in this way from the mid-1990s on? And if that is the case, what is it about cinema that enables such a manifestation? And how is it related to the formation of subcultures, identity questions and cultural politics in general? The reason I do not use the term 'identity politics' but 'identity question' comes from the observation that the mobilisation of politics based on gender, class and race might not be fully materialised in Korea despite the emergence of new identity groups.

Loving cinema or desire for cinema has become a distinctive feature of youth culture since the early 1990s in Korea. Loving cinema is known as 'cine-mania' in the Korean cultural context, or cinematic scopophilia or cinephilia in the West. Cinephilia is historically related to the pre-televisual and pre-1968 mediatisation of the social, as well as to the post-war economic boom in the West.[4] The spread of cinephilia in 1990s Korea is, of course, a different manifestation owing to cultural and historical differences. It seems, however, that two things observed in relation to cinephilia in general are also relevant to understanding the phenomenal increase in Korea's cinema-loving audience. One is a quasi-mystical aspect of cinephilia, which encourages the viewer to recognise her/his soul projected on to the screen or the soul of actors and directors. In other words, there is a moment of recognition related to the viewer's aesthetic as expressed in the concept of photogenie.

> (Photogenie) as the 'law of cinema', it clearly sets in place a viewer's aesthetic. The defining characteristic of cinema is said to be something that pertains to the relationship between viewer and image, a momentary flash of recognition, or a moment when the look at . . . something suddenly flares up with a particularly affective, emotional intensity. The founding aspect of cinematic quality, instead of its specificity, is located not in the recognition of an artistic sensibility or intentionality beyond the screen, as it were, but in the particular relationship supported or constituted by the spectatorial look, between projected image and viewer.[5]

In cinephilia, because people are looking for something they desire to see but which is not actually there to be seen, the mode of spectatorship allows for a diversity of reading activities. Along with the notion of recognition in relation to the viewer's sense of identity, cinephilia functions to unify different groups with different positions under the rubric of the desire for cinema. The growth of cinephilia in Korea is linked to the growth of film culture through the proliferation of film festivals, art-house cinema theatres, cinematheques, videotheques, film magazines, journals and cinema groups housed in cyberspace and in real space.

As is often noted, the quasi-religious energy of the 1980s Korean student movement – in fact a kind of youth culture – is hardly detectable on 1990s streets and campuses. Unexpectedly, and unlike the 1980s, quasi-religious energy is found in film spectatorship. The fascination for cult movies or a mode of cult spectatorship around American B-movies, European art-house cinema, Hong Kong action movies and Wong Kar-wai, in particular, are phenomenal in Korean youth culture. The term 'cine-mania' was coined in recognition of the large number of such spectators.

In my view, the present mode of spectatorship detected on the Korean cultural scene is a hybrid form of cinephilia and cine-mania. Cine-mania connotes the swallowing-up of incredible numbers of films. It is a frenzied mode of film consumption. Cine-maniacs are estimated at as many as 30,000, mostly in their twenties and thirties.[6] This is the pool or potential audience available to fill festival seats, subscribe to film magazines and so on. In fact, the thematic film festivals, such as the Seoul Women's Film Festival and the Seoul Queer Film and

Video Festival, might be characterised as attempts to redirect the energy of mania into something that is grounded on a political agenda via the cinema.

Considering the presence of this movie mania, no one should be surprised to learn that the best-selling weekly magazine on the street kiosks is *Cine-21*, a mixed-form publication, a fan magazine with a touch of cinematic expertise. The success of *Cine-21* is noteworthy. As an allegedly politicised nation, Korea's best-selling magazines used to be monthly social/political commentary magazines.[7] Issued by the progressive newspaper *Hangyurae*, *Cine-21* has reshaped the magazine market and become the best-selling weekly. Is this the replacement of political concerns with cinematic ones? Isn't it the displacement of the real by representation? In response to this hasty and anxious diagnosis which laments the advent of a depoliticised post-modern age, I would argue that new political agency may be found in the topography of cultural politics.

In synchronicity with this outburst of cinephilia, Korean society has witnessed the emergence of new identities and subject positions that are usually considered the premise for identity politics and struggles for recognition. Nancy Frazer, in her argument on the politics of redistribution and recognition, makes a distinction between two areas of injustice. One is economic and the other is cultural although they are necessarily entwined. The remedy for economic injustice entails political-economic restructuring requiring 'redistributing income, reorganising the division of labour, subjecting investment to democratic decision-making, or transforming other basic economic structures'. The remedy for cultural injustice, she suggests, is cultural or symbolic change that involves 'upwardly revaluing disrespected identities and the cultural products of maligned groups . . . The wholesale transformation of social patterns of representation, interpretation, and communication in ways that would change *everybody's* sense of self.' She refers to this kind of remedy as 'recognition'.[8]

As noted above, the desire for cinema is clustered around the notion of recognition and viewers' diverse interpretive activities. Identity politics or the politics of recognition as Nancy Frazer rephrases it, are likely to be positioned in the cultural sphere, which is not totally removed from the one inhabited by the cinephile. Along these lines, I'd like to suggest that the emergence of cinephilia and different identity groups in 1990s Korea should be articulated via the notion of recognition. And how to re-articulate the politics of recognition to the politics of redistribution might be rephrased as how to re-articulate the emergence of group identities in the 1990s to the class problematic of the '80s. The cinematic apparatus as social fantasy seems to mediate two areas of concern.

Group identity dissociated from class identity came on to the scene with the appearance of the 'Orange Tribe' in the early 1990s. The term was coined for a certain group in their twenties who were spotted in the most affluent and *nouveau riche* part of Apgujungdong in Seoul. Despite their insignificant numbers, the mainstream media devoted an hysterical amount of space to stories about them. They were condemned as a morally and sexually corrupt and overspending group of young people. At the same time there was a collective envy directed towards this handful of people who could afford such a luxurious life-style with their parents' money. The 'Yata Tribe' soon eclipsed the Orange Tribe.[9] The linguistic use of the terms 'Orange Tribe' and 'Yata Tribe' is highly suggestive. About the same time, the consequences of the Uruguay Round were forcing Korea to import foreign agricultural products. Due to its high price, the Californian orange represented something expensive, upper class and American in flavour. The ownership of foreign cars and leisure time connoted by the term 'Yata Tribe' indicate the upper classes. The way the words 'Orange' and 'Yata' are articulated to the explicitly feudal connotations of the term 'tribe', however, reveals an interesting mixture of signifiers for both the post-modern and the pre-modern. Considering the current diffusion of post-modernism in both academic and mass media discourse as a replacement for Marxism in Korea and the con-sequent naming of anything new as post-modern, these names effectively articu-late the pre-modern to the post-modern. Hence, Korea's alleged entry into the post-modern era since the 1988 Olympics is marked by group names invoking the feudal in the guise of the post-modern.

Subjected to the authoritarian gaze of the media and society, these groups were constructed as an imagined community of upper-middle-class consumers. With the expansion of consumerism, another identity, called Missy, has been named for certain targeted consumers. This started as a commercial phrase used by a certain department store in about 1993. Young housewives in their late twenties and thirties began to set up a mode of consumption for married women. Thus, these new identities were constructed only to offer identification for new consumers in the expanding economy.

At about the same time, but with a different twist, the notion of feminist subjectivity emerged. The specific linguistic employment of the term 'feminist' (in Korean, English pronunciation is used) gradually replaced the 'women's movement activist' (*yosong undonga*) as feminism penetrated not only the socio-economic sphere but also the cultural sphere. Whereas '*yosong undonga*' is gen-erally associated with the agents of the social movement in the 1980s, this association is more attenuated in the case of 'feminist'. Feminism of the 1990s brought forth and dealt with the issues of feminine writing and feminist subjec-tivity, mostly in the domains of literature, theatre and film. Toward the mid-1990s, gay/lesbian identities also became visible in public with the outing of gay activists and the organising of a couple of collectives. Feminists and gay/lesbian activists have engaged in questioning of effects of cultural representations on the construction of identities. Again, cinema has provided the space where these questions can be discussed. The circulation of feminist and women's films and films with gay characters has greatly contributed to raising related issues. With its certain distance from society, the cinema has facilitated the incorporation of gay/lesbian issues into a cultural discourse that absolutely refused to recognise these issues before.

It doesn't appear, however, that identity politics based on class, gender and race have entered the cultural scene in South Korea in full force yet. Different groups do exist, but the articulation of identity with politics still sounds strange. Identities are interpellated but politics based on differences are not yet fully recognised in the political sphere. Many factors can be cited to account for this. First, there is Confucian resistance to the notion of multiple identities. Second, the everyday linguistic habit of saying 'we' and 'our' (*uri*) blocks the notion of different identities. For instance, people even tend to call their own partner 'our husband' or 'our wife'. Third, there is a refusal to recognise sexual and gendered identity because of a social norm which regards such matters as 'private' and hence should not be a part of public discourse. In this regard, it is telling that reactionary male critics choose not to use the term '*yosong*' when discussing women's issues, as this has a strong implication of feminine sexuality. Instead they use the more neutral term, '*yosa*', which means only a person who is born as *yosong*.

Last, but most significant, is the dominant force of national identity, safeguarded by the National Security Law, the narrative of the racially homogenous nation, and the ever-present scenario of North Korean invasion. Any challenge to the fiction of the racially homogeneous nation is still a social taboo. Underneath the belief in the collective 'one true self' there lurks uneven regional development, the repression of gender differences and class divisions, and the exploitation of foreign workers. In a way, national identity claims exclusive appropriation of identity politics without referring to its politics, as the idea of one homogenous race with a shared history and shared blood is unquestionably embodied in the understanding of Korean national identity. National identity in this context is never a 'production which is never complete, always in process and always constituted within, not outside, representaion'.[10] Rather, it always remains a trans-historical and essential notion. The hold of national identity disallows the dissemination of different identities into politics.

Certainly, this notion of national identity was used effectively against both the Japanese colonial discourse of the Greater Asian Co-Prosperity Sphere and American neo-colonial discourse. But owing to the appropriation of national identity by the military dictatorship from 1961 to 1990 as the ground on which to legitimise heavily centralised and oppressive regimes, the discourse of national identity has foreclosed upon the development of politics based on the local and gender differences. National identity based on shared ancestry can be used as a strategic essentialism by a nation with a history traumatised by colonial and neo-colonial memories. But it becomes a problem, especially when the multinational corporations of that nation branch out to employ workers from other parts of Asia such as Nepal, the Philippines and India.

In South Korea, any attempt to disrupt nationalistic discourse would be immediately taken as a violation of the National Security Law. In this regard, the emerging groups with an emphasis on gender, sexuality and local politics could be construed as a challenge to the sweeping discourse of national identity in South Korea. Indeed, the present government unwittingly proved this by banning film festivals such as the Seoul Queer Film and Video Festival, the Human Rights Watch Festival and the IndeForum Festival.

The notion of fragmented and multiple identities does not sit well with the claim to a 5,000-year-old nation-state based on a single race. Even the powerful class movement based in the student movement of the 1980s seldom questioned this construction of national identity. Indeed, the class movement often resorted to national identity or the discourse of nationalism to mobilise the people. Irrespective of class position, what has been always at stake is the mode of government but not nationalistic discourse. Furthermore, there is no doubt that the national identity propagated by the hegemonic discourse has primarily represented the middle-class male population. The presence of North Korea as immediate other has also always provided an alibi and ironically contributed to securing the discursive stability of South Korean national identity.

In this aperture, identity (*chongchae*) politics have not grafted on to the social formation of Korea yet. Some might even argue that the topic itself is being imposed upon us as one of the problematics of travelling cultural studies. Despite the fact that identity politics do not provide the most privileged entry point for reading the cultural formation of Korea at this moment, this scarcely means that emergent different identity groups do not exist. Rather, the identity groups deploy a different rhetoric and different strategies to negotiate with the state apparatus and the mainstream media.

Finding themselves in the ever-shifting space between the residual authoritarian government of military dictatorship and hegemonic quasi-democratic government, the non-majority groups tend to employ the discourse of radical differences less than the idea of universal humanism. The appeal to human rights reverberates through the array of feminist and gay/lesbian movements. Although pragmatic, there is a price for this practice. On the one hand, it has helped to reduce the risk of radical separation but, on the other, it has barely touched the critical discourses and practices of nationalism, capitalism and the Confucian patriarchal notion of sexuality.

Unlike those of the United States, identity politics in Korea do not appear to have occupied the space of class identities that previously dominated the economic, social and political landscape.[11] It is unlikely that the class issue can be totally suppressed in Korea considering the massive scale of labour unions across the nation. But it is also true that the general situation is unlike that of the 1980s, when the problematic of class dominated intellectuals and the people (*minjung*). So, it might be asked how other subject positions such as women, gays and lesbians have been able to emerge as political agents during the social transformation of South Korea. In the light of Confucian ageism, a feudal way of maintaining traditional hierarchy and order, the formation of youth culture in the form of cine-mania and rock-mania is also noteworthy in this regard.

FILM FESTIVAL POLITICS AND IDENTITY QUESTIONS

Mapping film festivals allows significant understanding of Korean cultural politics in the 1990s. This is because organising festivals has turned into one of the major cultural practices for feminists, queer groups, young film-makers, college students, youth groups and citizen activists.

Local governments such as Pusan and Puchon, and multinational corporations, such as Daewoo and Samsung, have also joined in. Desire for cinema and desire for globalisation, often encapsulated in the official discourse of *Saegaehwa*, converge in international-scale film festivals. Festivals, such as the Pusan International Film Festival (PIFF) and Puchon International Fantastic Film Festival (PiFan), have emerged as a result of cinephilia and global-philia via an emphasis on local politics. The heavily centralised process of urbanising only Seoul during the authoritarian regime is now being challenged by the inauguration of local governments. The cities of Pusan and Puchon are trying to promote their local identities by mobilising international-scale film festivals.

Evoking its geographic proximity to the rest of Asia, Pusan claims the region as its main focus. The highlighted programme 'A Window on Asian Cinema' is an attempt to locate the city of Pusan as a new focus for Asian cinema in competition with the Hong Kong and Tokyo international film festivals. With rising interest in the Asian region, and North-East Asia in particular, Pusan selectively promotes Asian identity to reach out towards the global. In the process of constructing a major film studio, the city of Puchon has become the host city for a festival of films in the fantastic genre. The culturally impoverished image of Puchon, both as a satellite city to Seoul and as a light industrial area, awaits transformation via its emergent status as a site of cultural production and exhibition at the festival. At least, that is the message the festival organisation sends out.

Film festivals in Korea, however, are not exclusively tied up with or appropriated by the discourse of the global and the local and authorised and patronised by central government, local governments and multinational corporations. As discussed, the post-1988 Olympics era shifted the focus from class identity to diverse groups and subject positions, along with the economic boom. The mainstream media's critique of working-class identity in the 1980s has largely given way to comments upon various sorts of new identities which emerged in the early 1990s. These new identities were concocted mainly by consumer-oriented culture and disseminated through advertisements. As a result, they did not develop into interest groups in a rigorous political sense. This phenomenon succeeded in blurring class demarcations, however, by replacing class identity with highly mediated interpellations of imagined groups composed of affluent teenagers, college students and young housewives in their late twenties and thirties.

Simultaneously, the notion of national identity has re-emerged in 1990s Korea under the slogan of *Shintopuli*, meaning the non-differentiated sameness of the body and the native soil. This essentialised notion, conflating the nation, the body and nature, has arisen as a complicit counter-narrative to the anxiety generated by *Saegaewha*. Again, not unlike the term 'Orange Tribe', the allegedly post-modern discourse of *Saegaehwa* has come into being only by evoking the pre-modern Confucian notion of *Shintopuli*. Between *Saegaehwa* and *Shintopuli*, the notion of the modern remains somewhat abstract, as does the notion of the public sphere, never mind that of the alternative public sphere. In this highly contested force field, where the synchronicity of the non-synchronous collides, new subject positions based on gender and sexuality have emerged.

The women's movement absolutely cannot be characterised as something new to the 1990s, however. From the colonial period (1910–45), women workers and intellectuals joined the social movement with demands for equal wages, the revaluation of housework and the denunciation of Confucian patriarchy. Until recently, however, the women's liberation movement was located in the larger context of the class and national movement, with the possible exception of certain groups launched in the 1980s, such as Another Culture (*Ttohanaui Munhwa*).[12] The identity of activists from the women's liberation movement (*yosong haebang undonga*) of the previous period is considered to occupy a different position from that of the 1990s feminists. The discourse of the latter is often associated with cultural politics.

Although the differences between them are repeatedly noted, and despite its relative withdrawal, the women's liberation movement operates alongside feminist cultural practice. There are tensions and divergences between the groups, collectives and organisations with different positions, but they are not radically alienated from one another. It seems that there is a shared awareness which causes them to avoid public divisions. There are also negative effects, however. Neither the women's movement nor feminist practice has problematised the discourse of nationalism or the notion of sexuality to any great extent.

For instance, the 'comfort women' issue about former Korean sex slaves of the Japanese army has once again been re-appropriated by the nationalistic cause because of the failure to bring out the tension between nationalism and women's issues. The 'comfort women' issue is often reinterpreted to produce an appeal to empower the nation via capitalism and militarism. In the case of the 'comfort women' issue, discursive strategies reliant on universal humanism fail to problematise these issues. Admittedly, in a society that oscillates between the residual mode of an oppressive regime and a quasi-civil mode, the relative distance posited between women's issues and macro-politics has shielded feminist practice from the National Security Law. Intervention has not been fully realised, however. By not problematising these issues, some feminists even find themselves performing in a space which is not only almost risk free but profitable owing to the service they provide for cultural industries geared to women consumers, such as television, publishing, theatre and films.[13] In the regard, the recent boom of professionally successful women's autobiographies has been astonishing.

The Seoul Women's Film Festival is located in this rather vague space where a wide range of women's issues is shared. This has both negative and positive sides. On the one hand, a public platform, such as this festival, can bypass the prescriptive and often dogmatic kind of feminist programme. On the other, it can be easily reincorporated into the hegemonic discourse by allowing itself as a momentary event to be one of the eccentric manifestations of the identity question via cinema.

As illustrated, the growth of cinephilia, the proliferation of theme-based film festivals and the emergence of identity groups in 1990s Korea may be articulated with one another. There is something in cinephiliac culture that can facilitate the process of identity and subject formation and festival politics. In cinephilia, people are looking for something they desire to see. In the same vein, film festivals based on themes and identities encourage and invite viewers who desire to 'share' a relatively vague object of desire they are collectively looking for. This situation may have useful political-cultural dimensions in that it invites an active reading and a sense of a joint project. In this way, it simultaneously engages with group-identity processes and individual creative reading activities, both focused on notions of desire defined in terms of cultural politics in given situations. The mode of festival spectatorship that includes discussion materials and seminars mobilises the process of identity and subjectivity formation. Since a film festival may provide a space for sharing between the viewers, programmers, academics and activists involved, it opens up the possibility of activating the viewers' subjective reading around the overall rubric put on the agenda by the festival. An air of eloquent inarticulateness pervades viewers as there is no dogmatically defined cultural-political project.

In the case of the Seoul Women's Film Festival, this is a preliminary process in the articulation of feminist identity and subjectivity, unevenly desired and searched for by female spectators with multiple positions. If this is part of the politics of recognition, it is not so much about recognition by authority as it is about the recognition of difference among 'women'. Unlike the 1980s women's movement which proposed a direct political agenda via the class movement, today's feminist practice is partly but significantly engaged with, and positioned in, a space of negotiation. As well as ticket sales, the festival was supported by an array of sponsorships including donations from supporters' groups, the city of Seoul, and the Hyundai Corporation. This indicates where women's cultural politics in the form of the film festival are located.

In a way, the feminist movement is positioned at a conjuncture where emerging identities like queer, subcultural youth formations, residual class identity and hegemonic national identity converge in order to contest. How to re-articulate and de-articulate this array of social forces in relation to feminist issues remains an ongoing project. In a society where the notion of the public sphere is not highly valorised or established, the film festival provides an experimental space that might produce an alternative public sphere if not an oppositional one. The banning of the Seoul Queer Film and Video Festival, the Human Rights Watch Film Festival and the IndeForum Festival reveals the rhetoric about the alleged civil society as one which refuses to recognise emerging identities and agencies. From the Orange Tribe to queer, hybrid signifiers of pre-modern and post-modern identities exist. The unacknowledged demands of human rights and freedom of expression, however, demonstrate that the modern notion of the public sphere must not be bypassed. Indeed, the condensed process of localisation and *Saegaehwa* globalisation together with the blend of pre-modern hierarchy and celebratory post-modern consumerism seem to demand 'going on theorizing' by being attentive to the rise of new social movements, as Stuart Hall has emphasised.[14]

Notes

This paper was written during the period when the government of South Korea propagated the discourse of active globalisation. Now, the black magic of globalisation is captivating South Korea with uncompassionate charms of IMF (International Monetary Fund). The mushrooming of film festivals is facing a sudden demise due to expeditious restructuring of the national economy into the global one, as are the identity questions which propelled the search for the alternative public sphere such as film festivals. It remains to be seen if the cultural activists are able to revisit the dynamic but unresolved scenes of the very recent past which anticipated new forms of practices and subjective positions.

I deeply thank Chris Berry who has discussed this topic with me at various stages of writing while he taught at Korean National University of Arts School of Film and Multimedia during the fall semester of 1997. My thanks also go to Hema Ramachandran who shared her thoughts on identity politics when I first conceived the matter. This paper was first delivered at the Second Kwangju Biennale conference in 1997. My thanks go to Chungmoo Choi and Suki Kim who generously allowed me to publish this paper.

1. One-page advertisement from *International Herald Tribune*, Saturday and Sunday, 26–7 July 1997.
2. For instance, the Human Rights Film Festival and Labor Film Festival are organised by activists whose organisations are rooted at 1980s' People (minjung) movement. Whereas the Queer Film and Video Festival is steered by a group of gay and lesbian activists who have emerged in the 1990s, Seoul Women's Film Festival is located between these two categories.
3. As is succinctly put by Jennifer Daryl Slack in 'The Theory and Method of Articulation', in *Stuart Hall: Critical Dialogues in Cultural Studies*, David Morley and Kuan-Hsing Chen, (eds), (London: Routledge, 1996), p. 119.
4. Paul Willemen, *Looks and Frictions* (Bloomington: Indiana University Press, 1994), p. 228.
5. Paul Willemen, *Looks and Frictions*, p. 126.
6. *Cine-21*, film magazine, conducted an unofficial survey when it gauged potential subscribers in 1995. This number also largely overlaps with the average art-house cinemagoers.
7. The monthly magazines published by the major newspapers usually deal with the political and social issues with a focus on political leaders and scandals. Examples include *Monthly Chosun* (*Wolkan Chosun*) and *Monthly Dongah* (*Wolkan Dong-a*). *Hangyurae Daily Newspaper* (*Hangyurae shinmun*) set up by the people's collective fund in the late 1980s, issued the progressive weekly magazine, *Hangyurae 21*, which became the leading magazine of its kind, and displacing the dominance of monthly magazine with the weekly.
8. Nancy Frazer, *Justice Interruptus* (Routledge: New York, 1977), p. 15.
9. The naming of the 'Yata Tribe' came from their style of starting a date. Cruising the night streets in a fancy car, a male would signal his interest to his object of desire by shouting '*Yata!*' (simply meaning 'get in the car'). There are many competing claims concerning the origin of the term 'Orange Tribe'. One story goes that this so-called

Orange Tribe initiates a date by sending a cup of orange juice to the desired person. Members of the Yata Tribe and Orange Tribe have similar class backgrounds. They are beneficiaries of the so-called bubble economy of the 1990s.

10. Stuart Hall, 'Cultural Identity and Diaspora', in *Colonial Discourse and Post-Colonial Theory: A Reader*, ed. and introduced by Patrick Williams and Laura Chrisman (New York: Columbia University Press, 1993), p. 392.

11. Stanley Aronowitz, *The Politics of Identity* (New York: Routledge, 1992), pp. 10–75.

12. This group is largely composed of feminist anthropologists, sociologists and writers. They have not only published the collective works on women's issues but promoted the new society movement in the name of another culture.

13. In relation to women's theatre, literature and translated feminist theory, it has also been through cinema that the representation of women and relevant issues to women has been brought up. Films such as *Orlando, Antonia's Line, Thelma and Louise* and local productions like *The Murmuring*, on the 'comfort women' issue and *The Blue in You* on the trouble caused by the combination of marriage and career have contributed to raising and disseminating the issues.

14. Stuart Hall, 'On Postmodernism and Articulation', in David Morley and Kuan-Hsing Chen (eds), *Stuart Hall* (London: Routledge, 1996), p. 150.

PART II

GENERIC TRANSFORMATIONS

6. PUTTING KOREAN CINEMA IN ITS PLACE: GENRE CLASSIFICATIONS AND THE CONTEXTS OF RECEPTION

Julian Stringer

Mark Jancovich has demonstrated that struggles over genre classification reveal much about how social identities are constructed through the use of cultural distinctions. As he explains, 'genre definitions are produced more by the ways in which films are understood by those who produce, mediate and consume them, than they are by the internal properties of the films themselves' (Jancovich 2001: 33–4). More than this, genres cannot

> simply be defined by the expectations of 'the audience', because the audience is not a coherent body with a consistent set of expectations. Different sections of the audience can have violently opposed expectations. Not only can the generic status of an individual film change over time, it can also be the object of intense struggles at a particular moment. A film which, for some, may seem obviously to belong to one genre may, for others, clearly belong to another genre altogether. (Jancovich 2001: 35)

These observations – which suggest that genre classification is a process to be observed, rather than a fixed destination to be arrived at – are of particular relevance in the case of the simultaneous reception at multiple exhibition sites of New Korean Cinema. South Korea's emerging national film industry is revealing itself to be open to struggles over its meaning and status at home and abroad. Questions of genre have a crucial role to play in this regard. When confronted with a new type of cinema, certain fundamental questions are habitually important. How should a particular movie be approached? What other cultural forms might it be understood against, or in relation to? What position should it occupy within pre-existing and generally accepted notions of what cinema is or could be?

In the face of an object occupying a place outside the usual realms of experience, spectators in diverse locations may reach, with a mixture of anxiety and excitement, for familiar terms of reference through which to comprehend the *kind* of film they are being exposed to. In other words, all spectators in all cultural and historical contexts draw upon paradigms of knowledge with which they are already cognisant. At the same time, it is natural for viewers also to want to draw conclusions regarding what the films they consume may have to tell them about the society that produced them.

Given the hitherto largely 'unknown' character of Korean cinema internationally, many commentators are recognising the keen relevance of such issues. For instance, *Variety* commented in 2001 that 'Korean cinema still lacks a popular hook in audience's minds. Chinese cinema is martial arts extravaganzas and arty peasant dramas, Wong Kar-wai and Zhang Yimou. But Korean? Even upscale Western auds would be hard-pressed to name a single director, let alone a popular genre that identifies Korean cinema' (Elley 2001b: 20). Similarly, the *Village Voice* asserted that '[t]wo years into the country's export thaw, we're seeing more releases out of South Korea . . . and the proliferation makes it virtually impossible to peg the cultural character' (Atkinson 2002: 112).

For outsiders, becoming acquainted with, and making sense of, Korean cinema may be an act of pleasure and of empowerment – a consciousness-raising exercise that allows the urbane spectator to borrow some cultural capital. Yet it is important to bear in mind that neither foreign nor domestic audiences sit back passively and receive the 'true' meaning of a Korean film. The meaning of a Korean movie is not waiting to be discovered – it is not the result of internal textual properties which just need to be unlocked by clever and attentive audiences. Rather, the meaning of Korean cinema in international and in domestic contexts is the result of ongoing and endless processes of negotiation and renegotiation over its identity and status.

This chapter considers two dimensions of the production, mediation and consumption of Korean cinema around genre classifications. First, it makes the simple, but important, point that struggles over the meaning and status of Korean genres begin in Korea itself. Second, it also demonstrates that other struggles over meaning then occur once Korean films are exhibited and consumed elsewhere. Consideration of the turf wars that take place over genre classification in Korea should lay to rest once and for all the lazy assumption that Korean films have an essential meaning magically understood by all native spectators. Just like audiences in other commercial market-places, Korean spectators construct distinctions between various types of cinema in order to help assert and validate their own particular identities. Intense struggles therefore take place in the domestic context over which genres should be named and claimed for this or that preferred version of Korean cinema, and for this or that interpretation of the 'cultural character'.

Some of these claims proceed by characterising Korean cinema in a culturally essentialist manner. For example, one overarching perception is that a specific genre does – or should – hold pride of place above all others in South Korea, namely melodrama. The emergence in the 1990s, however, of a commercially driven and successful motion-picture industry producing an abundance of other kinds of films is at times believed to render problematic previous, widely held views regarding the melodramatic characteristics of the national cinema. For example, one decade after the historic domestic box-office success of *Sopyonje* (*Sŏp'yŏnje*, 1993) – the mother of all Korean melodramas – the *Korea Herald* asked rhetorically whether the 'typically' Korean form of cinematic melodrama is now

> an endangered genre . . . Death, lost loves and tears were once the most common ingredients in Korean movies . . . Appealing unabashedly to women in 20s and 30s who have always made up the largest group of cinemagoers, the soppy tales guaranteed large crowds and warm receptions . . . Now, however, comedies dominate the big screen. (Kim M. H. 2003)[1]

In attempting to explain the contemporary success of such representative comic hits as *My Wife is a Gangster* (*Chop'ok manura*, 2001) and *My Sassy Girl* (*Yŏpki chŏk-in kŭnyŏ*, 2001), the report then presents an economically determinist perspective on the nation's culture: 'History shows that depressing tales usually do well during hard times, such as economic crisis, because they offer viewers a chance to have a good cry and walk out the theaters feeling better . . . the Korean economy has been good the past few years, thus explaining the success of comedies as opposed to the teary stories' (ibid.).

The distinction melodrama versus comedy is utilised here so as to allow the author to impart concerns over the direction South Korea's commercial film industry is moving in. Symbolic associations attached to the latter genre (i.e. frivolity, a care-free attitude, economic success) are represented as the very antithesis of everything symbolically represented by the former (i.e. female resilience, catharsis, deeply felt emotion, pain). Such distinctions provide evidence of the hegemonic struggles which habitually take place over what Korean cinema's identity and meaning could and should be. Across numerous sources published in newspapers, such as the *Korea Herald* and *Korea Times*, a focus of comparison for Korea's comedies and other commercial genres is Hollywood. Hollywood constitutes one of South Korea's great cinematic Others (alongside North Korea, Japan and more recently Hong Kong). For some commentators, Hollywood, as the global capitalist film industry *par excellence* – the holiest of holies – represents everything that the new commercial Korean cinema either promises or threatens to become.

Certainly, this distinction between Korea and Hollywood is maintained through use of highly symbolic language. For example, Kim Jin claims of Im Kwon-Taek's *Chihwaseon* (*Ch'wihwasŏn*, 2002) that 'Im is like a lone lantern shining in the sea of neon lights that is Korean cinema today' (Kim J. 2002a).[2] Here, the signifier 'neon' is used to differentiate between a 'good', authentic artisan Korean cultural tradition and a troublesome, foreign, mass film culture. For such critics, South Korea's commercial cinema virtually prostrates itself when it strives to be little different from Hollywood: 'Mimicry may be a form of flattery, but it eventually becomes a sign of creative spinelessness' (Kim J. 2002b).[3]

Figure 16 Not just a melodrama, but a passionate one: *Ardor* (2002).

All of this is occurring because the 'recent rise of Korean cinema has seen its expansion into diverse genres previously reserved for foreign imports'. (Ibid.)

Yet this last process is far from a simple or a straightforward one. As David Scott Diffrient points out, ambiguities surrounding genre classification are being advanced in Korea itself. At the level of production, generic indeterminacy is a factor built in to the very assembly and promotion of many of the titles now widely classified under the rubric New Korean Cinema.[4] In Diffrient's words, recent years have witnessed the ascendancy of 'a now-internationally acclaimed and generically promiscuous South Korean cinema' which encompasses 'the industry's millenial drive toward genre diversification' (Diffrient 2003: 61). In this sense, genre classification constitutes an attempt to manage potentially violently opposed attitudes to certain kinds of films by cannily appealing to multiple audiences at the same time. As Diffrient explains:

> . . . genres function primarily in South Korea as promotional categories, and thus have as much to do with marketing strategies as they do with critical concepts. The heightened recognition of genre as an unspoken contract between audiences and film companies says a lot about the Ch'ungmuro industry's attempts to forge a reception apparatus through self-definitions. Product differentiation has spawned some unusual neologisms in recent years: . . . *Tell Me Something* (2000) . . . was marketed . . . as 'hard gore' – a 'new' genre that telescoped pornography and the splatter film; *Ardor* (2002) . . . was promoted by its producers not simply as a 'melodrama' but as a '*passionate* melodrama' . . . [gay-themed] *Bungee Jumping on their Own* (2001) was labelled as both a 'a *soulmate* film' and a '*fusion* love story'. (64)

Use of such labels constitute invitations to consume films through indeterminate identities. While these categories may tell us something about the hybrid ways in which films are being positioned in South Korea today, however, they do not by themselves tell us anything about how they are actually being received in diverse markets.[5] To begin to do this, we need to turn our attention to some of the other culturally and historically specific ways in which struggles over genre come into view once Korean films are exhibited and consumed elsewhere.

It is worth drawing attention at the very outset to the sheer diversity of places where audiences around the world can now consume South Korean movies.[6] And at all these sites of film consumption, processes of generic labelling remain important. Public exhibition venues and modes of domestic consumption alike place frames of reference around Korean cinema. While these often comprise specific generic labels, audiences may or may not accept the invitation to understand them on exactly these terms. Looking briefly at how genre classification is negotiated at and beyond international film festivals, for example, demonstrates these procedures. Here, generic identities are first proposed and then either accepted or rejected on a global level.

Focusing on the Pusan International Film Festival, one finds that a notable discrepancy often exists between how the festival presents a film in generic terms and how it is then 'de-genred' and indigenised in overseas markets. For example, *The Way Home* (*Chipŭro* . . ., 2002) was decreed by Pusan to have 'humble content matter' and was considered 'unbankable by the mainstream industry' ('*The Way Home*'). Conversely, it was considered to have a 'universal theme set against the uniquely Korean backdrop' by *Variety* (Kim M. H. 2002). Similarly, Pusan proclaimed with confidence that *Failan* (*P'airan*, 2001) 'succeeds in elevating [*sic*] the level of the "gangster" genre by realistically depicting the lives of the lower-class hoodlums. The film also succeeds in avoiding [*sic*] the cliché solutions abundant in the genre of melodrama' (Joo 2001: 86). For *Variety*, though, this 'flawed but intriguing sophomore outing' is presented as a so-called 'festival film' – 'pic developed a strong critical following locally and could notch up a modest festival career, with some specialised TV sales possible, especially with 10 minutes shaved from its running time' (Elley 2001a).[7] The opening night film of the 2002 event, Kim Ki-dŏk's *The Coast Guard* (*Haeansŏn*, 2002), is described in the Pusan catalogue as 'an explicit and

Figure 17 The opening night film at the 2002 Pusan International Film Festival: *The Coast Guard* (2002).

autobiographical examination of the director's own dark memories and obsessions . . . it is also a shocking report on the oppressiveness that permeates Korean society' (*The Coast Guard*). Yet this assessment becomes transformed into 'a typical big-budget potboiler disguised as social commentary' in the eyes of *The Japan Times* which then goes on to mourn how '[o]nce hailed as a gritty innovator, Kim has turned into Joel Schumacher' (Brasor 2002).

In this last example, a *relational* dimension is once again of importance in encoding and decoding the signs and meanings of Korean cinema. At each and every turn, genre classification helps secure comfortable positions of knowledge from which hitherto unfamiliar films can be talked about. By such means are Korean films assimilated.

North American critics are proving particularly adept at introjecting Korean cinema through cultural distinctions which help establish their 'mastery' over the object at hand. Home-spun references prove especially comforting in this regard. *The New York Times* writes that Im Kwon-Taek's depiction of the artistic temperament in *Chihwaseon* will 'seem familiar to anyone who has seen [the Hollywood bio-pics] "The Agony and the Ecstasy", "Lust for Life", or "Pollock" ' (Scott 2002). Meanwhile, for Michael Atkinson of the *Village Voice*, 'Hollywood's footprint is inedible in the new [Korean] retro', and consequently he comprehends a throng of diverse films through the prism of US movies: *Tell Me Something* (*T'elmissŏmding*, 1999) is therefore a '*Seven*-inflected serial-killer procedural' while *Joint Security Area* (*Kongdong gyŏngbiguyŏk JSA*, 2000) is 'a harrowing political thriller' that 'uses melodramatic Hollywood tropes' and destroys 'the dream of [Howard] Hawksian brotherhood'. Yet for Atkinson, the 'true newsmaker' might be *The Isle* (*Sŏm*, 2000), 'a gorgeously restrained, apocalyptically horrifying *pas de deux* that's notorious for precipitating fainting spells and vomit seizures at press screenings' (Atkinson 2001: 116). *The Boston Globe* helps its readers get their heads around *The Isle*'s distinct geographic setting by writing of its floating cabins resort: 'Think Minnesota in summer' (Smith 2003).

By the time Korean cinema registers on the cultural antennae of American pop critics such as Atkinson, it has experienced a reversal of generic fortune. Instead of providing evidence of a culturally essentialist or economically determinist phenomenon, it has become enlisted in a quest to secure subcultural capital (Jancovich 2002). Clearly working through his own personal illusion of discovery, Atkinson draws upon a highly eclectic range of metaphors so as to present a unique generic understanding of what this new Korean cinema is like: 'Boiling-oil hyperbole and recycled-plastic popness is unapologetically pervasive, but routinely offset by faux-American noir mimeographs, neo-art film minimalism, abattoir farce, punk fashion, and an overall penchant – even in the cheesiest movies – for Hou-like [Hou Hsiao-hsien] distance' (Atkinson 2002: 112).

There are a number of points to make here. First, it is evident that even highly influential cultural institutions such as the Pusan International Film Festival can not dictate once and for all how Korean films will be generically comprehended. Second, American critics – and no doubt critics elsewhere – construct their own generic world views so as to help them make sense of the Korean films they consume.[8] Finally, quoting the examples above begins to suggest how paying attention to different cross-cultural perceptions around Korean cinema may help reveal its variable and complex nature. In one context, the positive mark of a Korean movie is that it is like a lantern shining gracefully and modestly in a sea of vulgar neon. In another context, it is to be valued for precisely the opposite reason – because it has become the sum of all fears: 'To Watch Korean movies is to watch a national culture bar-brawl with itself,' Atkinson writes with evident relish, 'and fight dirty every step of the way. There may not be a more intensely conflicted nation making significant movies now' (Atkinson 2001: 116).

Further research on the illusions of discovery fostered around Korean cinema would no doubt unearth the presence of other cult reading formations. (For example, those to be found on fan discussion forums and in the pages of magazines such as the US-based *Asian Cult Cinema*.) After all, the eager reception of Hong Kong cinema around the world has previously demonstrated that, when Asian popular cinemas become known, their products become enlisted in a war of distinction between fans and other specialised consumers. One of the most fascinating aspects of the contemporary vogue for New Korean Cinema may therefore be that it provides opportunities to observe these processes in operation.

Jancovich suggests that different kinds of audiences – and different members of the same audience – engage in struggles over genre classification so as to assert their own social identities. For these reasons, among others, the meaning of a film genre is never fixed but rather contingent upon circumstances of reception. I would like to conclude my brief discussion of genre and South Korean cinema by making one final point. It might be argued that one purpose of historical scholarship within Film Studies should be to demonstrate that illusions of discovery concerning national cinemas happen at different times and in diverse ways, on the basis of the variously situated and highly contingent positions from which particular spectators advance and gain knowledge and new cultural competencies. In this sense, understanding Korean cinema through generic classifications truly does mean embarking on a journey on a long and winding road, not arriving at a destination.

REFERENCES

Arfah, Sharifah (2002) 'South Korean Films Make Their Mark', *New Straits Times*, 15 October: Entertainment, 3.
Atkinson, Michael (2001) 'Blood Feuds', *Village Voice*, 21 August: 116.
——(2002) 'Leaps of Bliss', *Village Voice*, 20 August: 112.
Berry, Chris (2003) ' "What's Big About the Big Film?": "De-Westernizing" the Blockbuster in Korea and China', in Julian Stringer (ed.), *Movie Blockbusters*, Routledge: London: 217–29.
Brasor, Philip (2002) 'Seeing the Big Picture at the Pusan Film Fest', *The Japan Times*, 27 November.
Choe, Yong-shik (2001) 'Korean Films Turn Up In Asian Black Market', *Korea Herald*, 30 October.

'The Coast Guard' (2002) *Seventh Pusan International Film Festival*, catalogue: n.p.

Diffrient, David Scott (2003) 'South Korean Film Genres and Art-House Anti-Poetics', *Cineaction*, 60: 60–71.

Elley, Derek (2001a) '*Failan*', *Variety*, 6 July. Online. www.variety.com

——(2001b) 'Local Hitmakers Eye Global Breakouts: Marketing on "Korea Fever"', *Variety*, 4 December: 20.

Garlick, Jeremy (2002) 'Korean Films? Never Fear, the DVD Room is Here', *The Korea Herald*, 13 December.

Jancovich, Mark (2001) 'Genre and the Audience: Genre Classifications and Cultural Distinctions in the Mediation of *The Silence of the Lambs*', in Melvyn Stokes and Richard Maltby (eds), *Hollywood Spectatorship: Changing Perceptions of Cinema Audiences*, London: British Film Institute: 33–45.

——(2002) 'Cult Fictions: Cult Movies, Subcultural Capital, and the Production of Cultural Distinctions', *Cultural Studies*, 16, 2: 306–22.

Joo, You-Shin (2001) '*Failan*', *Sixth Pusan International Film Festival*, catalogue: 86.

Kim, Jin (2002a) '*Chihwaseon* Director Im Kwon-Taek Portrays Fading Beauty of Bygone Times', *The Korea Herald*, 10 May.

——(2002b) '*Yesterday*'s Troubles Don't Seem So Far Away', *The Korea Herald*, 14 June.

——(2002c) 'Commercial Interest Driving Hollywood Remakes of Korean Hits', *The Korea Herald*, 18 July.

——(2003a) '*Arirang* Fades on Heartbreak Hill', *The Korea Herald*, 21 May.

(2003b) 'South Korea Enters the Sequel Age: Thriving Film Sector Hopes to Turn Hits Into Franchises', *The Hollywood Reporter*, June 24.

Kim, Mi-hui (2002) 'Korean Femme-Directed Pic Impresses Filmgoers: *Way Home* Beats Out *E.T.*, *Blade II*', *Variety*, 21 April. Online. www.variety.com

——(2003) 'Is Korean Melodrama an Endangered Genre?', *The Korea Herald*, 7 April.

Korean Overseas Information Service (2004) *Korea 2004*, photo diary, Seoul: Government Information Agency.

Korea Times (2001) 'Triumph of Korean Movies Hoped to Continue in New Year', 31 December.

——(2002a) 'Korean Movies to Hit USFK Theaters Next Week', May 24.

——(2002b) 'Fun Movie?', April 13.

Riverfront Times (2001) 'Film/Listings', 14 November.

Scott, A. O. (2002) 'New York Film Festival Reviews: Living the Artistic Life in 19th-Century Korea', *The New York Times*, 28 September: B, 14.

Smith, Damon (2003) 'Evocative, Disturbing Films Show the Richness of Korean Cinema', *The Boston Globe*, Living C6.

Steiner, Christopher, B. (1995) 'The Art of the Trade: On the Creation of Value and Authenticity in the African Art Market', in George E. Marcus and Fred R. Myers (eds), *The Traffic in Culture: Refiguring Art and Anthropology*, Berkeley: University of California Press: 151–65.

Stringer, Julian (2003) *Regarding Film Festivals*, Ann Arbor: UMI Dissertation Services.

'The Way Home' (2002) *Seventh Pusan International Film Festival*, catalogue: 97.

NOTES

This chapter owes a debt to the intellectual influence of Mark Jancovich. I would also like to thank Gianluca Sergi for some thought-provoking comments, and SooJeong Ahn for lending me research materials.

1. Such sentiments are underlined by the *Korea Times*, which states that one 'concern is the proliferation of commercial films that are created with the sole purpose of giving the audience a few laughs' (*Korea Times* 31 December 2001) – as if this were somehow a bad and shameful thing.

2. The Korean Overseas Information Service evidently agrees. Its glossily packaged *Korea 2004* diary – sent out by Korean Embassies to select community leaders in the United Kingdom and other nations – includes one page on the proud fact that 'Korean movies are enjoying a boom' (Korean Overseas Information Service 2004: n.p.). The sole titles mentioned to illustrate this fact, however, are Im Kwon-Taek's historical dramas *Chihwaseon* and *Chunhyang* (*Ch'unhyangdyŏn*, 2000). In the view of this important government-sanctioned publication, these two titles – and these two titles alone – represent what Korean cinema is and ought to be in the eyes of the world.

    Others may wish to point to the existence of a less highbrow, more populist strain in contemporary South Korean film culture. One of the classic tropes through which social identities are maintained via genre classifications is through the construction of binary distinctions between 'average' and other viewers. For example, reporting on the release of *2003 Arirang* (2003), a contemporary remake of the silent Korean classic *Arirang* (1926), the *Korea Herald* laments that the newer film 'compromises the genuine pain of the Japanese colonial period'. Moreover, it directly contradicts the reverential views espoused by *Korea 2004* when it claims that 'the average spectator who didn't care much for the constant pansori singing in director Im Kwon-Taek's *Chunhyang* is not likely to find the incessant growling of an apparently drunk *ajeossi* in this film particularly mellifluous' (Kim J. 2003a).

3. For an overview of debates concerning contemporary South Korean cinema's perceived mimicry of Hollywood models, see Berry 2003.

    The forging of a commercially driven industry is sometimes claimed to have unforeseen effects on the Korean melodrama, foreclosing that genre's ability continually to produce 'soppy tales' for the emotional edification of young women. In a piece exploring the sequel and franchise possibilities of recent Korean box-office hits, *The Hollywood Reporter* notes a specific problem 'tied closely to one of the hallmarks of Korean cinema – the propensity for characters to die. Korean films are often imbued with a deep sense of tragedy, and the death of major characters are [*sic*] quite common' (Kim J. 2003b) – the point here being that the death of major characters makes it relatively difficult to produce sequels.

    Further underlining debates on the allegedly imitative nature of some contemporary Korean genres are claims about universal values rather than culturally specific values. On the subject of Hollywood remakes – a particularly valuable source of information concerning attitudes towards the international circulation, translation and indigenous reception of East Asian movies – two 'Korean-American industry insiders' share their belief that Hollywood-style versions of Korean hits should 'have universal storylines that are understandable in any culture'. Producer Roy Lee thus claims that '*My Wife is a Gangster* is *True Lies* [US, 1994] with a mafia background' and that '*My Sassy Girl* is a universal romantic comedy' (quoted in Kim J. 2002c). (This latter assertion concerning comedy and romance is contradicted elsewhere – see note 5 below.) Author Kim Jin concludes that 'the cluster of big-screen hits currently being adapted for American audiences, is primarily driven by commercial interest rather than an interest in Korea' (ibid.).

4. Genre diversification can be taken to be one mark of a commercially (and artistically) healthy film industry. Another is the existence of generic self-reflexivity. *The Korea Times* (2002b) reports that '[c]alling itself the first parody movie in Korea, *Chae-mit-nun Yong-hwa* (*Fun Movie*) by director Chang Kyu-sung makes fun of all things Korean ... parodying famous scenes from contemporary Korean movies.'

5. The question of why certain South Korean genres, and not others, are perceived to be suitable for particular overseas territories is an important subject requiring further research. Arguments concerning the export and overseas reception of New Korean Cinema need to be verified rather than simply assumed.

    The trade press proves to be of some help in this regard. In *Variety*, Derek Elley reports that 'Japan remains Korea's most fertile export market; Hong Kong, which has been bombarded with an unprecedented 17 Korean movies this year, remains hit and miss; Singapore and Malaysia are better for TV drama; and Taiwan has become a Korean movie graveyard, with even *Friend* bombing there.' Elley quotes Jenifer Muhn, international sales chief at Cinema Service, as claiming that France remains among the most 'receptive' of European markets. According to Muhn, 'Western buyers want arthouse titles and action movies ... The hardest sells are comedies and romances' (Elley 2001b:20).

Preliminary investigation of just one of the specific territories mentioned above – Malaysia – reveals unexpected ambiguities and complexities. A 2002 article from the *New Straits Times* reports that *Shiri* (*Swiri*, 1999) – 'a thriller' – and *2009 Lost Memories* (*2009 Losŭt ŭ memorijŭ*, 2002) – 'a mega action cum sci-fi thriller' – have already been released there, with 'many more South Korean movies to come'. Yet despite the ostensibly masculinist action movie/thriller connotations of the above titles – the very antithesis of the tear-inducing Korean television drama – the latter was promoted in terms of the romantic associations ripe for exploitation around 'heart-throb' lead actor Jang Dong Gun. Chinese newspapers, radio station MY FM and TV3 all participated in a nationwide campaign entitled 'To Jang Dong With Love'. According to the report, all that is required is to 'send in love letters and dedications through the different mediums' (Arfah 2002: 3).

6. As previous chapters in this volume have shown, New Korean Cinema is most obviously associated with two specific forms of contemporary film consumption. First, high-profile international film festivals. Second – and sometimes subsequent to festival screenings – comparatively wide distribution in 35-mm theatrical markets, followed thereafter by home consumption on commercial video, VCD (much more prevalent in Asia than other regions) and DVD.

It is also worth noting, however, the existence of numerous other sites of reception which act as exhibition windows for Korean cinema. In Korea itself, the so-called 'DVD room' – a cross between Internet café and public cinema – has been installed in some cities (Garlick 2002). Domestic box-office hits have also been screened in US military movie theatres to American soldiers and their families in 'a bid to promote understanding of Korean culture'. (*Korea Times* 2002a) Illegal videos and DVDs remain widely available on the Asian black market (Choe 2001). In addition, as fan discussion on Internet forums, such as Darcy Paquet's excellent site koreanfilm.org, testify, new technologies and modes of domestic consumption, e.g. specially imported videos, alternatively sourced DVDs, and Internet (including broadband) downloads, are crucial in facilitating some overseas audiences' sense that they have a stake and emotional investment in Korean cinema. The question of how specific titles have been generically marketed and consumed in these diverse subterranean locations, though, remains an open one.

For the moment, what might be argued is that at multiple sites of reception what Christopher B. Steiner (1995: 154) terms an 'illusion of discovery' circulates around Korean cinema. As Steiner explains, in commercial practices, the success of the distributor necessarily depends upon the separation of buyers from sellers – the distributor works in a space between the primary suppliers of culture and their consumers. Because of this, consumers of commercially distributed culture do not have the opportunity to uncover an object by chance or recognise its potential value before it enters the market-place. This situation therefore encourages the fetishisation of commercial 'discoveries'. Moreover, genre classification plays a key role in anchoring and facilitating these discoveries.

7. For an extended discussion of the 'festival film' as a generic category, see Stringer (2003: 135–238).

8. To provide one more example, the *Riverfront Times*, Missouri, describes *Attack the Gas Station* (*Juyuso sŭpgyŏksagŏn*, 1999) as a 'gone-wrong heist movie in the anarcho-slapstick mode' (*Riverfront Times*, 2001).

7. HORROR AS CRITIQUE IN *TELL ME SOMETHING* AND *SYMPATHY FOR MR. VENGEANCE*

Kyu Hyun Kim

What makes a horror film a horror film? That it evokes an overwhelming sense of terror and abjection in the viewer? That it compels us to watch the unwatchable and name the unnameable? If these definitions hold true, then director Chang Yun-hyŏn's *Tell Me Something* (*T'elmissŏmding*, 1999) and Pak Ch'anuk's *Sympathy for Mr. Vengeance* (*Poksu-nŭn na-ŭi kŏt*, 2002: hereafter *Sympathy*) are horror films through and through. Indeed, they perform the objectives of 'scaring' and 'terrorising' the audience with an almost excessive level of efficiency.

Even so, the marketing campaigns for both films scrupulously avoided the 'horror' label. In South Korea, *Tell Me Something* was confusingly marketed as a 'hardcore thriller'. For the most part, however, the movie was mainly perceived by the audience and film reviewers as a star vehicle for Han Sŏk-kyu and Shim Ŭn-ha, and therefore not really worthy of serious critical analysis. On the other hand, *Sympathy*, stuck with an equally strange tagline, 'authentic hardboiled movie', was received favourably by many film critics, and was selected as the best Korean film of 2002 by *Film 2.0* magazine, among other journals. It turned out, however, to be a box-office disappointment despite the casting of major stars Song Kang-ho, Bae Du-na and Shin Ha-kyun.

Even though horror films no longer constitute a marginalised genre,[1] they are still sometimes considered distastefully misogynist, gratuitously violent or inherently conservative, in the sense that they seem to categorise the outsiders and the underprivileged (homosexuals, ethnic minorities, political critics, women) as 'other' or monstrous, and to punish with acts of graphic violence (in the case of the non-supernatural 'slasher' genre) those who are sexually active or unconventionally minded. Nevertheless, as horror films have gained greater acceptance around the world as mainstream blockbusters – the multiple Oscar-winning *The Silence of the Lambs* (US, 1991) being the most salient example – and objects of serious academic examination, the boundaries of the horror genre have become more contested.

The horror genre has a long history in Korean cinema but it has only recently begun to receive the type of scholarly attention it deserves.[2] The potential of Korean horror films to challenge and critique the cultural conventions and ideological strictures imposed by 'mainstream' Korean society – especially on women, sexual minorities, economically underprivileged youth and other oppressed groups – are just beginning to draw attention.[3]

In this chapter, I would like to focus on the sources and meaning of the terror and abjection created by *Tell Me Something* and *Sympathy*, rather than on their modes of interaction with various genre conventions. By doing so, I would like to claim that the terror and abjection produced by these films originate from their acute and insightful critiques, not simply of the moral conventions and political ideologies underlying contemporary Korean society, but also of the more generalised problems germane to modern society and subjectivity. Let us begin, then, with an analysis of *Tell Me Something*.

Tell Me Something opens with the discovery of a mutilated male body. Detective Cho (Han Sŏk-kyu), assigned to the case, has recently lost his mother to a chronic illness and has had his reputation tarnished by taking money from a local gangster to pay for her medical bills. It turns out that a serial murderer is on the loose. The culprit uses chloroform to sedate a select number of well-to-do young men and then dismembers their bodies. Each victim is missing parts of his body. The killer leaves various body parts – a pair of arms, a torso, a pair of legs – from previous victims while removing the fresh body parts from new victims. Detective Cho discovers that all victims seem to have been involved, romantically or otherwise, with Su-yŏn (Shim Ŭn-ha), a forensic archaeologist working for a museum.

In a double climax reminiscent of Dario Argento's notorious *giallo* masterpiece *The Bird with Crystal Plumage* (Italy, 1969), Su-yŏn's medical resident friend Sŭng-min (Yŏm Chŏng-a) is first identified as the murderer. Sŭng-min, cornered by police, attempts to commit a double suicide with Su-yŏn but is instead shot and killed by her. In the final surprise ending, Su-yŏn is revealed as the real mastermind behind the serial murders.

In her influential essay on the portrayal of women in mainstream Hollywood films, Laura Mulvey asserts that the female body tends to be objectified by the male viewer, resulting in what she calls 'fetishistic scopophilia', the pleasure derived from looking at the female body, idealised as a beautiful and perfect object, and sadistic voyeurism, which stems from the fear of castration and thus renders woman's presence in a motion picture as a 'problem' to be investigated and resolved (Mulvey [1975] 1999). Further developing psychoanalytic interpretations of the horror genre, Barbara Creed argues that horror films seek to purge the abject – for example, bodily fluids, corruption, dead bodies and various forms of the monstrous – from the viewer's consciousness and to 'redraw the boundaries between the human and nonhuman . . . separating out the symbolic order from all that threatens its stability' (Creed [1986] 1996: 46). In Creed's view, the abject is signified by the vagina and the womb – in other words, the mother – which male subjects must renounce in order to maintain their masculinity. Therefore, the 'feminine' is construed as the monstrous, and overcoming the monster restores the stability of male identity and by inference the patriarchal ideology that protects the articulation of male desires while suppressing female desires.

Initially, *Tell Me Something* seems to fit in well with the type of mainstream films that, according to Mulvey and Creed, serve to strengthen the patriarchal ideology. Certainly, at the end of the film, Su-yŏn is unmasked as a monster, a serial killer. Does not this confirm that femininity as presented through her is 'monstrous'? In fact, the situation is not so simple. Director Chang skilfully manipulates the expectations of the audience towards a generic melodramatic plot in which Su-yŏn would fall in love with Detective Cho, only to shock us with the revelation that the serial murders are motivated by a gender-related reason. As in Francis Ford Coppola's *The Conversation*, (US, 1974) this revelation completely changes the meaning of the visual information to which the viewers had access prior to that moment.

Su-yŏn's psychological motivation for murder is hinted at in two flashback sequences. In the first flashback, we are introduced to Su-yŏn's father, Ch'ae. He is a brilliant and renowned painter whose surviving works are considered priceless by art dealers. We learn, in a montage almost completely devoid of exposition by dialogue, that Ch'ae raped Su-yŏn when she was barely a teenager, and continued to have sexual relationships with her until adulthood. In an earlier scene, when Cho is examining Su-yŏn's apartment, he casually picks up a picture-postcard depicting a woman slowly drowning in a river, surrounded by flowers. The picture is John Everett Millais's *Ophelia* (1851–2). Later, during the first sequence of Su-yŏn's recollection, we glimpse another depiction of Ophelia, modelled after Millais's painting but featuring the adult Su-yŏn's face. These shots provide clues for the viewer to identify her mental state as 'unstable' by associating it with Ophelia's madness. They also provide clues for an interpretation that the killer's motivation is gender-related, however. During the second flashback sequence, Su-yŏn and Detective Cho visit Ch'ae's now abandoned house, and we see a series of images in which Ch'ae is seen painting the young nude Su-yŏn, and caressing her legs fetishistically. Here, Ch'ae's scopophilia is directly connected to his sexual domination of his daughter, as well as his artistic potency. Pleasure in seeing equals pleasure in sexual violence equals artistic achievement and authority.

Other murder victims are also marked by their acts of scopophilia and voyeurism: their acts of looking literally spell death for them. Cho's partner Detective O is stabbed to death at the precise moment that he looks at a

Polaroid snapshot of Su-yŏn and her friends (some of whom have since become her victims). More significantly, another murder victim, Ki-yŏn, is shown not only harassing Su-yŏn, but also spying on her with cameras clandestinely installed in her apartment. The walls of his video-surveillance room are covered with fetishistic representations of Su-yŏn. As portrayed in the movie, this set-up acquires an additional layer of meaning because of the Korean viewer's knowledge that Su-yŏn is played by Shim Ŭn-ha, a major star. Korean (male) viewers are thus drawn into complicity with Ki-yŏn's objectification of Su-yŏn, paralleling their own objectification of the actress Shim.

We have seen that Su-yŏn is, in fact, a variant of Ophelia, reconstituted as an angel/demon of vengeance. Unlike the Shakespearean version, however, Su-yŏn does not destroy herself. Her madness is that of a visionary artist freed from (patriarchal) moral constraints rather than that of an hysterical victim of the male ego. Su-yŏn's serial murders are revealed as tools for her (anti-Electra) artistic project with which she usurps the privileged position of the 'artist' from her father.[4] The male viewer is further disoriented by the fact that her character does not display any gender confusion (this function is relegated to the secondary murderer Sŭng-min who, in a flashback, is seen dressed as a boy) or climactic, hysterical outbursts cinematically codifying her as psychotic. The serial-killer films, starting with the classic model *Psycho* (US, 1960), usually end with 'confessions' by the perpetrators or 'rational explanations' of their psychosis. *Tell Me Something* completely dispenses with this genre convention of reinstating the rational order in the filmic narrative by classifying the murderer as psychotic. Let us examine the remarkable final sequence of the film, to clarify the precise meaning of Su-yŏn's 'artistic' project.

The discovery of Su-yŏn's hidden identity is launched into motion, most tellingly, when Detective Cho, convinced that Sŭng-min's death has solved the serial-murder case, casually goes through a secret surveillance video-tape of Su-yŏn compiled by Ki-yŏn. Until then, Cho has been an identification figure for Su-yŏn. Suffering from the loss of his mother, ethically tarnished and implicitly emasculated, he is positioned in a symmetrical relationship with her since she has defeminised herself, albeit covertly, to seek revenge against her father and other men. By viewing the video-tape, Cho joins the rank of voyeuristic males objectifying Su-yŏn: he 'falls from grace'.

While looking at the video-tape, Cho finds a clue that points to Su-yŏn as the real murderer. During the end sequence, again almost entirely devoid of dialogue, Su-yŏn prepares to board a plane bound for Paris. Following his clue, Cho crashes into her private retreat, a small studio in the countryside. There he locates Ch'ae's portrait of Su-yŏn as Ophelia, and next to it a large, aquarium-like water-tank. Cho turns on the illumination of the tank. Inside is Su-yŏn's artwork-in-progress: a headless body of a man, stitched together from missing body parts of her victims. The camera, from Cho's point of view, pans from the preserved body to the portrait of Ophelia and back, firmly linking these two images for the benefit of the viewer who may have missed the earlier allusions.

Horrified, Cho smashes the tank, destroying Su-yŏn's 'sculpture'. In the air-craft, Su-yŏn is accosted by a young, well-dressed man reminiscent of Ki-yŏn. She turns her calm face towards her seat window. The final shot of the film is a slow zoom-out of Cho stumbling out of Su-yŏn's studio, crawling on all fours, emitting inarticulate noises: a picture of a man symbolically castrated. The film ends, not with the reinstitution of the patriarchal order (through the appre-hension/destruction of the 'monstrous' Su-yŏn) but with a truly terrifying con-clusion for the majority of male viewers – that a female 'artist' devoted to the counter-objectification and emasculation of men like themselves is set free: Ophelia's artistic project, that is also her vengeance, continues.

To reiterate, *Tell Me Something* draws its horrific power partly from subvert-ing and disrupting male-oriented scopophilia and the objectification of the female subject, a well-acknowledged pattern in many internationally successful 'art' films made in South Korea, such as Im Kwon-Taek's *Sopyonje* (*Sŏp'yŏnje*, 1992). Considering that *Sopyonje* features a *P'ansori* artist blinding a female singer so that she can be shaped into a better artist, it might not be too far off the mark to characterise *Tell Me Something* as an anti-*Sopyonje,* a stealthy criticism of the way in which Korean female subjects are objectified under the gaze of 'superior' male artists, be they *P'ansori* drummers, novelists or film directors, with the willing complicity and pleasurable participation of the majority of male viewers.

What about *Sympathy for Mr. Vengeance*? There is little question in my mind that *Sympathy* is one of the most frightening and disturbing films ever made in

Figure 18 One of the most frightening and disturbing of all Korean films: *Sympathy for Mr. Vengeance* (2002).

Korea. This can be easily verified by attending any public screening of the film with an audience. Such an experience spurred one Korean film-maker and academic to denounce publicly the 'irresponsibility' of the film-makers for their failure to warn audiences of the excessively violent nature of the film. She describes her experience of watching the film with a paying audience at a local theatre as follows:

> In the beginning, the members of the audience . . . whispered among themselves, trying to follow the plot. However, as the movie passed the middle section, all whispers died out and the audience became silent. The silence did not stem from their comprehension of the twists and turns of the narrative. Neither was it a product of the audience having lost themselves in the pleasures of following the narrative . . . [It resulted from] the sense of helplessness and confusion among the audience, being saturation-bombed with the images of violence, depicted in painstaking detail on the huge silver screen. When the film was finished, the audience left the theatre silently, deathly pale, as if they were the patients who had just undergone particularly excruciating medical treatments. (Kim Yŏng-hye 2002: 316)

When I attended the screening of *Sympathy* at the 2002 Seattle International Film Festival, the audience response was not very different from that described in the above account.[5]

Ryu (Shin Ha-kyun) is a hearing-impaired factory worker, living with his older sister (Im Chi-ŭn) who is critically ill from kidney failure. Unable to raise the money for a kidney transplant, Ryu contacts an illegal organ-harvesting gang and gives them his own kidney (useless for his sister because of blood-type incompatibility) in exchange for one that can be transplanted into his sister's body. The gang, however, merely harvests his organ and leaves him cheated. When the hospital finds a donor and gives him one week to raise the operation fee, Ryu consults his girlfriend Yŏng-mi (Bae Du-na), a self-proclaimed member of a supposedly radical political group, named the Revolutionary Anarchist Association. She persuades him to kidnap a young daughter of Tong-jin (Song Kang-ho), the president of an electrical-equipment company.

Everything that can go wrong in such a scheme does go wrong. Ryu's sister, accidentally finding out that he resorted to kidnapping a child in order to cure her, is overwhelmed by guilt and commits suicide. Grief-stricken, Ryu buries her body at a site of their childhood memory, a rocky mound next to a small river, following her last wish. Tragically, Ryu allows the kidnapped child to be drowned accidentally in the river, unable to hear her shouts for help. Tong-jin, initially devastated by grief, is consumed by a desire for revenge. He investigates the identities of the kidnappers and, using his skills as an electrical engineer, tortures and kills Yŏng-mi. Meanwhile, Ryu wreaks an equally terrible vengeance upon the organ-harvesting gang, and goes after Tong-jin to avenge Yŏng-mi's death. Eventually, Tong-jin captures Ryu and drowns him at the spot where his daughter died. The film, however, ends with a final uncanny twist: Tong-jin is suddenly confronted and assassinated by four members of the Revolutionary Anarchist Association which the audience until then has been led to believe was a fictitious organisation, existing only in Yŏng-mi's imagination.

Like a David Lynch or a Michelangelo Antonioni film, *Sympathy for Mr. Vengeance* immediately declares itself through its style. The style could be called modernist, in the sense that the 'reality' the characters inhabit is ever so slightly distorted, just enough to undercut the viewer's expectations of comforting genre conventions and mundane representations of everyday reality, but without explicitly breaking down the diegetic effect. The cinematography and production designs emphasise a corrupt green colour, reminiscent of algae or wall paints (Ryu's hair is dyed a pale, slightly sickly green as well). Emotionally distancing long-shots are combined with intimate close-ups (supplemented by shockingly sudden zoom-ins) to create a disorienting effect. The sets, while retaining a semblance of realism, are sometimes overly brightly coloured, excessively cluttered or decorated with bizarre artefacts. Eerie silence peppered with faint rumblings (signifying Ryu's subjective realm) alternates with cacophonic clashes of industrial and natural noises. In the steel factory where Ryu works, the sounds of machines pounding, molten steel cooling and rivets and files rolling around on the floor are loud, pervasive and indescribably menacing. The looks and sounds of the film, therefore, render the viewer disoriented, anxious and uncertain.

The three main characters, Ryu, Tong-jin and Yŏng-mi are all given a measure of verisimilitude but their acts progressively escalate into extreme, 'abnormal' behaviour. The viewer is encouraged in early sections to identify with both Ryu and Tong-jin, whose sense of loss following the deaths of their loved ones is palpably communicated through the excellent acting of Shin Ha-kyun and Song Kang-ho. Consequently, the dehumanisation of these two characters as they are driven to heinous acts of vengeance becomes profoundly disturbing for the audience. In one particularly memorable sequence, the unspeakable sorrow of Tong-jin at the scene of his daughter's autopsy is conveyed entirely through a medium close-up of his face while the graphic sounds of a hacksaw and scalpels tearing open the young body fill the soundtrack. Later, however, when Tong-jin participates as an observer at the autopsy of Ryu's sister, he becomes unmoved and bored: he even yawns at one point.

Yŏng-mi's character has been one of the most controversial points in interpreting *Sympathy*. Her political ideology appears to be a hotchpotch of fashionable slogans ('Dissolve the big business conglomerates! Expel the US imperialist army! Smash the exploitative neoliberalist regimes!'), as well as barely articulated resentment against the industrial bourgeoisie. Chŏng Sŏng-il, one of the foremost *auteurist* critics in Korea, severely criticised the film's conception of Yŏng-mi and, by inference, the film's political stance, arguing that *Sympathy* ultimately subscribes to the view that 'class struggle is impossible despite the existence of the class contradictions' that give rise to the misery and death of Ryu, Yŏng-mi and Tong-jin. Chŏng interprets the terrible fates in the film as a form of teleological determinism, precluding any possibility for the recognition on the part of the characters of their inability to transcend their socio-economic positions in the exploitative capitalist system. Chŏng goes so far as to condemn the film's political stance as 'skulking Stalinism', delivering judgements on the characters based on their already predetermined class identities (Chŏng 2002).

Aside from Chŏng's refusal to consider the fact that theoretically befuddled 'leftist' characters such as Yŏng-mi do exist in real life, his criticism shows a curious insistence on the standards of social realism in evaluating a film best understood as a dark parable. By Chŏng's standard, Travis Bickle's almost comically inept attempt to assassinate a presidential candidate in *Taxi Driver* (US, 1976) would be sufficient to write off the movie as politically muddled, or even conservative. Instead of effecting closure in the narrative and presenting the vision of a morally cohesive universe to the viewer (by showing that the torture and murder of Yŏng-mi should not go unpunished), the assassination of Tong-jin by the members of the Revolutionary Anarchist Association heightens the sense of absurdity. In *Sympathy*, political terrorism is as illogical and ridiculous as obsessive acts of personal revenge and, for that reason, far more terrifying than one in a mainstream action film or thriller – just as it is in our 'real' world.

At the 2003 Toronto Film Festival, director Pak Ch'an-uk was reportedly confronted after the screening of *Sympathy* by a viewer who demanded to know why there was no 'salvation' in this film. Regardless of how Pak might have chosen to answer this question, it is postulated here that the overarching theme of *Sympathy* is, indeed, salvation. Many serious cinematic works about salvation ask why we *cannot* be saved. One factor that propels the characters toward doom is their unwillingness to move out of their subjective spheres of experience and connect with one another through acts of communication.

The theme of the absence of communication is brilliantly illustrated in one early scene, set in Ryu's apartment. We first see four punks frantically masturbating as they listen to what sounds like a woman moaning in sexual ecstasy next door. The camera dollies out of their room, passes through the wall that divides two units, and enters Ryu's room. The sounds of 'sexual ecstasy' turn out to be expressions of agony from Ryu's sister. We see her, slightly out of focus on the right side of the frame, rolling around and whimpering in extreme pain: on the left side is a medium close-up of hearing-impaired Ryu slurping *ramen* (*ramyŏn*) noodles, completely oblivious to his sister's pain. This sequence drives home the point that there is no guarantee that even our most loved ones, for whose health we would gladly give up our internal organs, are truly capable of sharing our subjective cognitions of the life-world (*Lebenswelt*).

Sympathy might strike many a viewer as an unadulterated proclamation of nihilism, since it rejects reconciliation among its vengeance-driven characters through communicative action and mutual identification, and a Utopic political action which, as depicted in the film, simply adds to the misery and suffering of the characters, as exemplified by Yŏng-mi's befuddled solution to Ryu's dilemma. Is the film in fact nihilistic, however? Perhaps we should be wary of confusing a presentation of the abjection we feel facing the yawning abyss with an endorsement of the capitulation to that abyss.

In fact, there are two sequences in the film illustrating the lost opportunities for reconciliation between Tong-jin and Ryu. In the first instance, the distraught Tong-jin encounters the ghost of his daughter, wet and dripping water on the floor. They embrace each other tightly, and she brightly tells Tong-jin, 'Daddy, I should have gotten swimming lessons a little earlier, right?'[6] Most interestingly, the next morning, the police officer visiting Tong-jin notices a puddle of water on the floor, hinting to the viewer that her ghost was 'really' there. This is the only rupture in the boundary between supernatural and non-supernatural in the whole film. This rupture allows us to interpret this moment as the only occasion throughout the film where the authorial/divine voice intervenes into the narrative, and editorialises on Tong-jin's desire for revenge. 'Your daughter is not really eternally lost (since her ghost is proven to be "real"), she has not been killed out of malice, it was an accident, do not waste your life on revenge.' This message is not understood by Tong-jin, deeply focused on his sense of loss. Ironically, he seems to gain a clear sense of purpose by convincing himself that he has nothing to live for.

The second sequence is the final confrontation between Tong-jin and Ryu. Both submerged up to the shoulders in the stream and pitifully shivering from cold and emotional struggle, Tong-jin tells Ryu, 'I know you are a good guy . . . so you understand why I must kill you, don't you?' In response, Ryu reaches out with both arms to Tong-jin, as if to embrace him. Tong-jin, however, ignores this gesture, dives down into the water and slashes Ryu's Achilles' heels with a knife. Ryu drowns in extreme agony, bleeding profusely from gaping wounds in his feet. In this final scene, Tong-jin recognises that Ryu and he are identical figures in terms of their objectives and moral positions, and that their acts of vengeance are fundamentally absurd, serving no purpose. By now, however, Tong-jin is unable to abandon his self-proscribed role: he goes through with the murder, as an executioner performing his 'duties', endowing his action with ritualistic qualities dissociated from his subjective moral decisions.

This scene makes a good comparison with a similar confrontation between the main characters, the industrialist Gondō and the drug-dealing kidnapper-murderer Takeuchi in Kurosawa Akira's *High and Low/Tengoku to Jigoku* (Japan, 1963). In the latter, Takeuchi is prepared to accept not only his death by execution, but also the absolute irreconcilability between denizens of the wealthy 'heaven' and the poor 'hell' (the original Japanese title of the film). The film ends ambiguously, the viewer left to guess whether Gondō's conciliatory efforts toward Takeuchi, who has brought him financial ruin and emotional hardship, have had any impact on the kidnapper. For the latter, the prospect of being forgiven by the object of his resentment and anger is apparently more terrifying than his own death. Unlike Kurosawa, however, Pak Ch'an-uk denies his characters the possibility of redemption through reconciliation: unlike Gondō, whom we are suggested to believe has come to accept and even forgive the kidnapper Takeuchi, Tong-jin cannot bring himself to identify with Ryu.

The terror and abjection produced by *Sympathy* are neither accidental nor spurious. As is the case with any truly great horror film, terror and abjection *are* the message. *Sympathy* is, in the final analysis, less concerned with the evils of capitalist exploitation than with our refusal (or inability) to transcend our subjective perspectives and enter into communication with one another. Just as Roman Polanski's *Rosemary's Baby* (US, 1968) is less about the hocus-pocus plot involving the birth of a Satanic infant than about Rosemary's terror at her inability to move out of her life course (we remember the supremely disturbing final image of Rosemary's beatific but hollow smile, conceding the utter loss of free will), *Sympathy* asserts that the demons that drive us to madness and cruelty cannot be expunged by either rituals of exorcism or the political and social acts designed to restore moral equilibrium: for the demons reside in our very subjective beings.

My analysis of *Tell Me Something* and *Sympathy for Mr. Vengeance* shows not only that these two films constitute 'exemplary' horror films, despite the lack of obvious generic codes that identify them as such, but also that they present more trenchant critiques of the patriarchal ideology (in the case of *Tell Me Something*) and breakdown of the communication grounded in the conditions of modern subjectivity (in the case of *Sympathy*). Dismissed as a commercial, star vehicle on the one hand, and debated as a flawed 'leftist' critique of capitalist South Korean society on the other, these two masterworks disclose their true prowess as horror films as critique when we pay attention to their 'messages', in the form of terror and abjection they inspire in us, their viewers.

REFERENCES

Black, Art (2003) 'Coming of Age: The South Korean Horror Film', in Steven Jay Schneider (ed.), *Fear Without Frontiers*, Grange Suite, England: FAB Press: 185–203.

Bradshaw, Peter (2003) '*Sympathy for Mr. Vengeance*: Review', *The Guardian*. 30 May.

Chŏng Sŏng-il (2002) '*Poksu-nŭn na-ŭi kŏt* bip'annon: Kŭdŭrŭn iyu-ŏpshi jungnŭnda, k'omidida (2) [A Critique of *Sympathy for Mr. Vengeance*: They Die Pointlessly, It's a Comedy]', *Cine 21*, 349 (25 April).

Creed, Barbara ([1986] 1996) 'Horror and the Monstrous-Feminine: An Imaginary Abjection', in Barry Keith Grant (ed.), *The Dread of Difference: Gender and the Horror Film*, Austin: University of Texas Press: 35–64. Originally published in *Screen*, 47, 1, 1986.

Jancovich, Mark (2002) (ed.), *Horror: The Film Reader*, London: Routledge.

Kim So-yŏng (Kim Soyoung) (2000) *Kŭndaesŏng-ŭi yuryŏngdŭl: p'ant'asŭt'ik hanguk yŏnghwa* [The Phantoms of Modernity: Fantastic Korean Cinema], Seoul: Ssias-ŭl Ppurinŭn Saram.

Kim Yŏng-hye (2002) 'Yŏnghwa-esŏŭi "p'ongnyŏk" e taehayŏ, hogŭn "p'ongnyŏkjŏk"-in yŏnghwa e taehayŏ [On the 'Violence' in Cinema, or on the 'Violent Cinema']', *Hwanghae munhwa* (summer): 315–20.

Mulvey, Laura ([1975] 1999) 'Visual Pleasure and Narrative Cinema', in Sue Thornham (ed.) *Feminist Film Theory: A Reader*, Edinburgh: Edinburgh University Press: 60–9. Originally published in *Screen*, 16, 3, 1975.

Simpson, Philip L. (2000) *Psycho Paths: Tracking the Serial Killer Through Contemporary American Film and Fiction*, Carbondale and Edwardsville, Illinois: Southern Illinois University Press.

NOTES

1. According to Mark Jancovich, '[in] recent years, it could be argued, the horror film has taken over from the western as the genre that is most written about by genre critics'. (Jancovich 2002: 1)

2. There is no consensus among film scholars as to what title constitutes the first horror film made in Korea. Even though some point to *The Public Cemetery Under the Moon* (*Wŏrha-ŭi kongdong myoji*, 1967), I find this claim hard to believe. Surely there are many more notable precedents, such as Kim Ki-yŏng's *The Housemaid* (*Hanyŏ*, 1960) or Yi Man-hŭi's *Evil Staircase* (*Ma-ŭi kyedan*, 1964), both of which are fine instances of psychological horror in the mould of *Les Diaboliques* (France, 1955). The contemporary Korean horror cinema as a steadily produced genre seems to originate with the surprising financial success of *Whispering Corridors* (*Yŏgo koedam*, 1997). Other notable recent horror films include *Memento Mori* (*Yŏgo koedam tubŏnjjae iyagi*, 1999), the sequel to *Whispering Corridors*; the utterly conventional but effective *Nightmare* (*Kawi*, 2000) and *Phone* (*P'on*, 2002), both directed by An Pyŏng-gi; *Ring Virus* (*Ring*, 1998), based on the famous Japanese novel and film adaptation; Yun Chong-ch'an's powerful, allegorical 'haunted apartment' horror *Sorum* (*Sorŭm*, 2001); the arch-derivative *Say Yes* (*Sei yesŭ*, 2001); and the wickedly humorous horror-satire *Quiet Family* (*Choyonghan kajok*, 1999), directed by Kim Chi-ŭn. For a fascinating read, mostly from a psychoanalytic viewpoint, of some of these films, see Kim So-yŏng (2000).

3. For instance, Art Black claims that *Memento Mori* presents a powerful critique of 'the strict, cruel, sexist and debasing Korean scholastic system and, by implication, the misogynistic nature of Korean society as a whole' (Black 2003: 185).

4. As B. Ruby Rich points out, '[the] romantic linkage of art and divinity to criminality . . . serves as prerequisite for contemporary narrative obsession with serial murder, which substitutes repetition for creativity, pattern for design, and the spilled blood of corpses for paints' (quoted in Simpson 2000: 18).

5. The Seattle festival audience probably displayed greater tolerance to the film, having been inured to various types of 'extreme cinema', than the Korean audience in a local theatre. Peter Bradshaw of the British *Guardian* newspaper reports that the attendees at the 2003 Berlin Film Festival were also 'baffled and repulsed' by the film (Bradshaw 2003).

6. The English-language subtitle in the foreign-release print and the DVD version subtly mistranslates her dialogue as 'Why didn't you teach me how to swim?' The implication is that she is a phantom arising out of Tong-jin's guilty consciousness.

8. TWO OF A KIND: GENDER AND FRIENDSHIP IN *FRIEND* AND *TAKE CARE OF MY CAT*

Chi-Yun Shin

This chapter considers two buddy films released in 2001 that exemplify contrasting tendencies within contemporary South Korean cinema: *Friend* (*Ch'in'gu*) and *Take Care of My Cat* (*Goyangirŭl but'akhae*). Both are 'friendship-themed' films, the narratives of which are primarily concerned with the fluctuating relationships among a circle of close-knit school-friends as they make the transition to adult life, although *Friend* is directed by a man (Kwak Kyŏng-t'aek) and is about four male friends and their macho world, while *Take Care of My Cat* is directed by a woman (Chŏng Jae-ŭn [Jeong Jae-eun]) and is about five female friends. Interestingly, however, only *Friend* was actively promoted as a buddy film. With its straightforward but rather unimaginative title, *Friend* is presented as a film that urges viewers to think about true friendship. Also emphasised in its publicity material is the fact that the film is based on a 'real' story of the film's writer/director, Kwak, and his three childhood friends. Kwak, who dedicated the film to 'my friends and family', expressed a wish that the audience would consider contacting their old friends again after watching his film.[1] As such, the male friendship theme in *Friend* is prominently used and foregrounded, whereas the issue of female friendship in *Take Care of My Cat* is rather subdued, only receiving the occasional passing remark in its promotional material.

Generally speaking, buddy films have long been associated with boys rather than girls. The specific socio-cultural system in Korean society presumes 'true' friendship exists only between men (despite the fact that the traditional patriarchal system has confined women to the domestic arena, thus preventing them from forming strong social ties with anyone outside the family). But, in addition to the gender difference, these two films also represent two supposedly opposing cinematic trends: popular mainstream genre film versus individual art-house film. For many commentators, the box-office performances of the two films testify to the increasing gap between genre films and art-house films. In the case of *Friend*, living up to its pre-release hype, the film opened in fifty-nine screens nationwide and became the highest grossing film in South Korea, with a new record of approximately 8.2 million viewers.[2] In contrast, *Take Care of My Cat* was virtually ignored, with a mere 35,000 admissions (Elley 2001: 28). Despite support from local critics, the film was pulled from most of the nineteen theatres after a week or so of its initial release, even though it has since developed a loyal fan base, mostly by word of mouth.[3]

Friend is certainly a commercial genre film and, more than anything, as two of the four childhood friends eventually become enemies in the organised-crime world, it belongs to the *jop'ok* action cycle that had firmly established itself by the end of 2001 as one of the most commercially viable formulas in the South Korean film industry.[4] This 'new' term *jop'ok* is an abbreviation of '*jo-jik-p'ok-ryŏg-bae*', which is a legal and rather official term (used in the media, for instance) that means organised, criminal gang members. The term *jop'ok* is not a newly coined expression but it is new in the sense that it came to be used as a more colloquial term for gang members. Also, compared to the already existing Korean colloquial terms for individual hoodlums or hooligans, such as *kkangp'ae* or *gŏndal*, *jop'ok* has an added sense of someone belonging to an organised criminal group. In this respect, *jop'ok* can be seen as the Korean equivalent to Japanese *yakuza*, Hong Kong *triad* or Italian (American) *mafia*. It is also interesting to note that everyday usage of *jop'ok* coincides with the rising popularity of the new cycle of gangster action films, especially those released since the mid-1990s.

Gangsters had featured in South Korean films prior to the mid-1990s but the more recent cycle of *jop'ok* films explicitly foreground 'the homo-social hierarchy that [*jop'oks*] belong to' which 'functions as a closed micro-world, within which they ultimately redefine and exercise manhood' (Seo 2002). In particular, the cycle typically features male bonding in the face of adversity as the ultimate virtue of masculinity, often offering a concoction of action, violence, melodrama and humour. As the biggest box-office success at the time of its release, *Friend* also marked the height of the *jop'ok* film's popularity among South Korean audiences. In fact, there seems little doubt that *Friend* has ushered in a cycle of *jop'ok* films which explore and glorify the South Korean underworld. *Jop'oks* dominated the South Korean film scene in 2001, with at least a dozen Korean films featuring gangsters. Apart from *Friend*, other films that topped the box-office in 2001, such as *Kick the Moon* (*Shilaŭ dalbam*), *Failan* (*P'airan*), *My Wife is a Gangster* (*Jop'ok manura*) and *Hi, Dharma* (*Dalma-ya, nolja*) were *jop'ok* films, and the top grossing film in 2002 was also a *jop'ok* film, *Marrying the Mafia* (*Kamun-ŭi yŏng'gwang*).

Publicity for *Take Care of My Cat* proclaimed it to be a 'stylish but realistic portrait of today's twenty year olds', for whom 'there is so much to be curious about besides sex'.[5] Although the inclusion of the word 'sex' in its catchphrase is slightly misleading, as the film does not feature any sexual encounters (in fact, the film purposely evades sex), what is pronounced here is the youthfulness of the film's main characters who are 'cat-like twenty year olds' whose secret code is: 'take care of my cat'. In fact, the film is often described as 'a coming of age drama' in the sense that the film deals with the period in girls' lives between childhood and adulthood. As suggested earlier, the film's narrative is certainly that of a buddy film as well, but *Take Care of My Cat* is mostly considered as an 'individual' art-house film or a drama with a high level of 'artistic value' in South Korea as well as overseas where it was circulated in various film festivals and on the art-house circuit.[6] Indeed, the film has many of the characteristics of an art film or American independent feature in its introspective quality and concern with the mundane, which explains in part why it is not easily identifiable in terms of genre. Despite its generic ambivalence, however, the film operates within mainstream generic paradigms and narrative norms, creatively blending and utilising established genre conventions.

In seeking to strike a balance between detailed textual analysis and a general overview, this chapter compares the different ways in which the two films deal with the theme of friendship in terms of gender and in relation to their historical moment, in which questions about commerce and art, politics and ideology, and text and reception are growing increasingly more complex. More specifically, it focuses on outlining the cultural and historical specificity of the *jop'ok* cycle and its mass appeal during the so-called post-IMF (International Monetary Fund) period, in which hypermasculine ethics seek to resolve national anxieties by recuperating male agency at a time of economic uncertainty. The chapter also considers how *Take Care of My Cat* operates as an example of what E. Ann Kaplan has described as the 'women's film' (as opposed, we might say, to the 'men's *jop'ok* film'), which 'raises the question of what it means to be female' – hence resistant to dominant ideology (Kaplan 1993: 13). The film can be seen to challenge some of the gender assumptions that underpin male-dominated buddy films by revising and updating some of their conventions with a feminist consciousness.

FRIEND

The story of *Friend* spans almost twenty years, from the 1970s to the 1990s, during which time four best friends from various backgrounds grow up to lead very different lives. Tough boy Jun-sŏk (played by Yu Oh-sŏng) is the best fighter at school and the son of a mob boss; Dong-su (Chang Dong-gŭn) is the son of an undertaker and desperately wants to rise up from his background; model student Sang-t'aek (Sŏ T'ae-hwa) is from a stable, middle-class family; and Jung-ho (Chŏng Un-t'aek) is the group's clown, whose mother sells smuggled goods on the black market. As mentioned earlier, the film is a highly personal film for the director, and the role of Sang-t'aek, the wealthier member of the group who goes abroad to study, is based on the director himself. The character also provides the first-person voice-over narration throughout the film. In fact, the film begins with such a narration from Sang-t'aek who states how he wants to revisit his memories. He informs us that the four boys have been friends since they were little, although he is not entirely sure how they became so close.

The first half of the film – covering the boys' early days in the 1970s and their troubled high school years in the 1980s – is therefore devoted to defining the characters and to establishing their bond. As small boys, they are inseparable, watching Western pornographic videos together, splashing around in the nearby sea, and arguing over who would be the faster swimmer – Asian Olympic medallist Cho Oh-ryŏn or a sea turtle. A few years later, in 1981, the boys are united again at the same high school. By this time, Jun-sŏk and Dong-su have firmly established their tough-guy status. Jun-sŏk is a born leader but the world of crime is the only world he knows; Dong-su is a leader-wanna-be who at once, albeit begrudgingly, respects Jun-sŏk; Sang-t'aek is a moralistic man and the group's peacemaker; while Jung-ho is everyone's sidekick. As the leader of the gang, Jun-sŏk looks after the timid bookworm Sang-t'aek who, in turn, provides him with some sort of normality. As teenage boys, they fight together, fall for the same girl, and form rivalries that will haunt them later in their lives. But most of all, they have become one another's bodyguards and, as the film's catchphrase illustrates, when they were together, they were not afraid of anything.

The happier first half of the film then makes way for a decidedly darker second half wherein the boys get involved in a particularly nasty group fight in

Figure 19 Boys in trouble: *Friend* (2001).

a cinema to defend Sang-t'aek from a rival gang, as a result of which Jun-sŏk and Dong-su are expelled from school, driving them further into the gang world. Soon, Jun-sŏk is a drug addict and Dong-su is in prison for reasons unknown, while Sang t'aek and Jung-ho become college students. A few years later, in 1993, while Sang-t'aek gets ready to study abroad and Jung-ho settles down to run a small restaurant, Jun-sŏk practically leads the gang that his father led until his death, while Dong-su has joined another gang, driven by the need to prove himself better than his old friend. Thereafter, the two old friends find themselves on opposite ends of a gangland conflict which ultimately leads to Jun-sŏk ordering the violent killing of Dong-su. Despite the efforts of everyone – including Dong-su's father, who urges him to deny any involvement – Jun-sŏk confesses in court that he is responsible for Dong-su's murder.

As a *jop'ok* film, *Friend* offers nothing particularly new or unpredictable in terms of narrative in its rather clichéd plot. What the film does present, however, as Anthony Leong describes, is 'male melodrama in gritty reality and raw emotion' (Leong 2002: 31). The film's sentimentality is often projected through the unlikely friendship between Jun-sŏk and Sang-t'aek. For instance, feeling indignant at the school's decision to expel his two friends while he is given only a temporary suspension, Sang-t'aek suggests to Jun-sŏk that they run away together with the money he stole from his parents. Although moved, Jun-sŏk turns down his offer and declares that Sang-t'aek should follow his own path. Later in the film, Jun-sŏk, recalling this incident, tells Sang-t'aek how he was proud of himself for sending Sang-t'aek home that night, hence not dragging him into the underworld. The sentimentality is epitomised in the line they alternately say to each other: 'there's nothing to be sorry about between friends'. Thus, for instance, when Sang-t'aek makes sarcastic remarks about Jun-sŏk's disciplinary attitude to gangster life, Jun-sŏk punishes his two subordinates who got caught staring 'disrespectfully' at his friend. The highly emotional encounter between the two friends when Sang-t'aek visits Jun-sŏk in prison at the end of the film is also designed to leave the audience with a lump in its collective throat.

In many ways, the film's highly sentimental treatment of male friendship is reminiscent of John Woo's Hong Kong titles, such as *A Better Tomorrow* (1986) and *Bullet in the Head* (1990), which prominently feature loyalty and male bonding. Similarly, the melodrama of this ultimately tragic tale of the rise and fall of friendship is accompanied by the specific gangster film iconography of dynamic action and violence. The most iconic scene in the film is when the four friends, dressed in their school uniforms, run through the streets of Pusan to the soundtrack of Robert Palmer's 'Bad Case of Loving You', illustrating the energy and vibrancy of the four youths. In addition, though not discernible to non-Korean speakers, the use of thick Pusan dialect throughout the film adds a quality of roughness.[7] Violence also prevails in the film. For instance, the scenes in which Jun-sŏk trains the new members of his gang how to kill with a knife are cross-cut with scenes of Dong-su and his men attacking Jun-sŏk's base and stabbing Jun-sŏk's right-hand man, as if to illustrate Jun-sŏk's off-screen instruction. Later in the film, when Dong-su is killed by an assassin sent by Jun-sŏk, the camera lingers on Dong-su's bleeding body as it is being stabbed repeatedly. The stabbing, in fact, stops only when Dong-su, drenched in rain and blood, mutters to the assassin that he has had enough. Here, Dong-su's quiet yet commanding remarks (to the assassin that he can now stop) add the raw immediacy of emotion. The drama of this sequence is also heightened by use of slow motion.

The tremendous popularity of *Friend* is, however, not entirely due to its fetishisation of visceral action. With its strong evocation of the past, the film also offers a powerful nostalgic yearning for the simplicities and certainties of the past. Indeed, much attention is paid to details that bring Pusan of the 1970s and 1980s to life. For example, the opening title sequence features children chasing passing fumigating trucks, the white disinfectant fumes of which momentarily smother the world around them. The sequence recreates the familiar summer images of the 1970s, capturing the havoc such public disinfections caused for adults who had hurriedly to cover their food and goods, while providing the children with an instant fairground. The sequence would immediately take audience members back to those days, especially the so-called 3-8-6 generation who might have participated in or witnessed the children's chase. The sequence's slightly sloweddown speed and sound, as well as its hazy visuals, also add a sense of distance that accompanies memory or recollection. Another scene that makes specific references to the late 1970s is the one in which Jung-ho brags about a new gadget his mother brought from Japan that copies television programmes. The gadget, of course, is a video-cassette recorder but his friends do not believe him because television broadcasters would go out of business if such a machine exists. In the next scene, all sit wide-eyed in front of the VCR, watching a porn video. Here, Jung-ho 'educates' his friends that a more sophisticated name for a woman's vagina is the 'menstruation'. Soon, they are out on the street, making cash by selling pages out of porn magazines as 'menstruation pictures' to equally curious neighbourhood boys.

The film also presents a version of the national past to evoke a nostalgic regard for institutions and social systems, which were often oppressive and divisive. As indicated earlier, the film 'reconstructs' the lives and the life-style of those who grew up in the 1970s, went to secondary school in the early 1980s, and who would be in their thirties at the time of the film's release – that is, the director's generation. For instance, creating a credible high-school environment in the 1980s, one of the classroom sequences depicts a group of students being punished by a rather sadistic teacher for not achieving decent grades. As a way of emphasising their filial duties as sons, the teacher ritually asks each pupil what their father does for a living before brutally slapping them as punishment for neglecting their fathers' efforts to educate them. When it comes to Dong-su's turn, the audience already knows how painful it is for him to say in front of the class that his father is an undertaker, but it gets even more explosive when Jun-sŏk has to acknowledge that his father is a gangster. In any case, his honest answer only infuriates the teacher who takes it as a rebellious dare and starts kicking and ranting at him about how great it would be for him to have a gangster father. Bouncing back from the floor, however, Jun-sŏk shouts back at him that he never said it was great, before storming out of the classroom with Dong-su.

In its portrayal of the insensitive and brutal teacher, the sequence clearly criticises the violent and authoritarian education this generation had to go through. Classroom violence, however, is but a meek imitation of gangland violence. In fact, the film's presentation of the past is highly ambivalent. As Andrew Higson points out in his discussion of British heritage films, nostalgia is 'a profoundly ambivalent phenomenon. It can . . . be used to flee from the troubled present into the imaginary stability and grandeur of the past. But it can also be used to comment on the inadequacies of the present from a more radical perspective.' Nostalgia, as Higson continues, is 'always in effect a critique of the present, which is seen as lacking something desirable situated out of reach in the past. Nostalgia always implies that there is something wrong with the present' (Higson 1996: 238). The present in the case of *Friend* is, indeed, a troubling one, especially after the 1997 IMF crisis when the International Monetary Fund had to bail out a South Korean economy facing bankruptcy. The 'humiliation' of accepting the IMF's funds and yet still enduring continued economic uncertainty exposed South Korean 'nationhood' as extremely vulnerable. With rampant unemployment, the problem of maintaining South Korean manhood became particularly acute.

The revival and popularity of the *jop'ok* cycle in the post-IMF period can be seen as a consequence of, and a response to, the national economic crisis. It spawns a tendency to extol the virtues of a traditional Korean culture (stoic, communal) and nostalgia for an era, especially the 1970s, when the effort for modernisation on a national scale provided a sense of progress and unity. The cycle also appears to reflect the desire to recover the nation's pride and to promote a particular vision of nationhood and manhood. As the most successful *jop'ok* film, *Friend* does showcase an 'imagined' past in which communal values and social propriety contrast with the individualistic and materialistic values of the present. In particular, the strong bond among friends, regardless of their backgrounds and, to a lesser extent, the hierarchy of the gang syndicates, appear to present the filial relationships the society as a whole has lost. Furthermore, the film celebrates and romanticises gang culture and gangsters as the bearers of counter-culture. The gangsters never meet the conventional standards for proper heroes but they certainly demand that the viewer rework the criteria of heroism. Dangerous and charismatic, these heroic outlaws recover what cops, soldiers, teachers and fathers could never secure: dignity and self-respect.[8] The film therefore offers catharsis to Korean men suffering from political and economic depression.

As South Korean feminist critic Gina Yu points out, however, 'films like these aim to feed male fantasies by depicting ideals like men's loyalty to each other under extreme circumstances and emphasising their toughness. But in doing so, they often isolate the female gender, even downright abusing them' (quoted in Kim 2001: 57). There is a rather extraordinary scene in which Jun-sŏk 'offers' Jin-suk, a pretty lead singer in a high-school pop band, to Sang-t'aek as a token of friendship. Critics also object to the scenes in which Jun-sŏk, now a drug addict, verbally abuses Jin-suk, his lover, for not properly greeting his pals when Sang-t'aek and Jung-ho – now college students – visit him. Indeed, the role of women is underdeveloped in *Friend* and women remain firmly in the background. Jin-suk is the only female character of note, but her role is barely more than a sketch. Although the focus of the film is clearly on the four friends, their relationships with women could have helped round out their characters. Jin-suk's troubled partnership with Jun-sŏk certainly does shed light on his character although even this strand is left undeveloped.

TAKE CARE OF MY CAT

In contrast to male-on-male relationships in *Friend*, Chŏng Jae-ŭn's first feature film *Take Care of My Cat* resolutely centres on female protagonists – five twenty-year-olds who formed a circle of close-knit friends during their vocational high-school days in Inch'ŏn, an industrial port city on the west coast, twenty-five miles from the capital Seoul. In terms of narrative, however, *Take Care of My Cat* offers an interesting parallel to *Friend*. Just like the four friends in *Friend*, the five friends (although the inseparable twins can be counted as one) in *Take Care of My Cat* are from varying backgrounds and represent certain types. Hae-ju (played by Yi Yo-wŏn) is the pretty one, and she works in a brokerage firm in Seoul as an office assistant and dreams of becoming a successful career woman. Spirited T'ae-hŭi (Bae Du-na) works unpaid at her family's sauna business and in her spare time works as a volunteer typist for a young poet afflicted with severe cerebral palsy. Quiet Ji-yŏng (Og Ji-yŏng) is a brooding orphan living unhappily with her frail and poverty-stricken grandparents in a run-down flat in a shanty town. She dreams of studying textile design abroad but, in reality, she cannot even find a decent job to help supplement the meagre family income. The other two girls are happy-go-lucky half-Chinese identical twins, Bi-ryu (Yi Ŭn-shil) and On-jo (Yi Ŭn-ju), who sell their hand-made trinkets on the streets around Inch'ŏn, preferring independence to running a shop.

Just as the two close friends in *Friend* turn into enemies, one-time best friends Ji-yŏng and Hae-ju gradually fall out with each other in *Take Care of My Cat* as their lives diverge along different paths after graduation. In fact, most of the tension of the drama derives from their escalating animosity. Unlike other girls who stay on in Inch'ŏn, Hae-ju works in a smart office in Seoul and continually tries to better herself. Hae-ju also realises that she is in a dead-end position, however, even though she is an efficient worker; it slowly sinks in that she cannot advance much further without a university degree. When away from the office, Hae-ju's insecurity is reflected in a preoccupation with her looks, conspicuous and excessive clothes' shopping and gaining and playing the upper hand with the other four girls, especially with Ji-yŏng, who does not seem to know how to deal with the harsh reality of their post-high-school lives. Their relationship starts to become somewhat strained when Hae-ju insensitively crushes Ji-yŏng's wish to go abroad to study textile design by saying that studying abroad is for the people who have money. The situation gets worse when Hae-ju returns the kitten Ji-yŏng gave her as a birthday present with the excuse that she cannot find time to look after it. Hae-ju then casually invites Ji-yŏng to meet her near her workplace for lunch but, when she comes, Hae-ju turns up only after Ji-yŏng is on her way back home, having given up after waiting for her for over an hour. Hae-ju's further self-absorbed attitude leads Ji-yŏng only to feel more isolated and hurt, while Hae-ju herself feels frustrated by Ji-yŏng's pride and stubbornness.

Witnessing how Ji-yŏng and Hae-ju drift apart, T'ae-hŭi acts as a peacemaker, keeping close ties with both of them. In the process, however, T'ae-hŭi gradually gains Ji-yŏng's trust, and a deeper friendship develops between them instead. In many ways, T'ae-hŭi's friendship sustains Ji-yŏng when things get even worse for her. For instance, when Ji-yŏng gets home after leaving a sleepover get-together with the girls at the twins' place, she finds that the sagging ceiling of her house has collapsed, killing her grandparents. Of her friends, it is only T'ae-hŭi who is present at her grandparents' quiet funeral. And when the police take Ji-yŏng in for routine questioning, it is also T'ae-hŭi who looks after Ji-yŏng's cat (Titi), and later visits Ji-yŏng in the juvenile prison where she is sent for refusing to speak to the police. (When the police point out the uncomfortable fact that she is now liberated from the duty of looking after her grandparents, she reacts to the situation with mute rebellion.) Ji-yŏng, however, slowly comes to terms with her reality, finally confiding to T'ae-hŭi that she has no strong desire to get out of prison; she has nowhere else to go. At the end of the film, however, T'ae-hŭi picks Ji-yŏng up on her release and suggests that they travel together; she has taken the equivalent of a year's wages from her family. The final image shows the two girls at the airport and a plane taking off, implying that they leave Korea altogether. As such, the film ends without following up the two girls' journey, closing with an optimistic yet highly uncertain picture of their futures. Yet the close bond formed between them (the most kind-hearted and open-minded one in the group and the utterly dejected one) fits in well with the structural demands of a buddy film narrative. It also provides a dramatic finale and the sense of one chapter ending but another one beginning.

The film, however, amounts to more than a case of incidental cross-dressing of the male buddy film. Thematically, though it is not exclusively designed and marketed as a feminist film, *Take Care of My Cat* answers the feminist call for on-screen female camaraderie to parallel the male buddy films. While privileging the subjectivities of its female protagonists, the film's attention to female

Figure 20 Female camaraderie: *Take Care of My Cat* (2001).

friendship also reflects the thematic preoccupations of its director/writer Chŏng whose earlier short films centralise the close relationship between young girls or sisters. For instance, Sŭng-jin and Chi-sŏn in *Girls' Night Out* (*Durŭi bam*, 1999) are high-school girls who secretly enjoy their nights out, aimlessly roaming the streets and just hanging out together. They are close friends but they want different things in life. Sŭng-jin wants to be a photographer and carries around an instant camera (she cannot afford a proper one), whereas Chi-sŏn is bored with her comfortable life. Out of boredom, she seduces her cousin and succeeds in having sex with him, but this does not make her any less lonely. Both girls slowly realise that they cannot have everything they want. Chŏng's other short film, *Yujin's Secret Codes* (*Dohyŏng ilgy*, 1999), also focuses on the imaginary and real world of Yu-jin, a primary-school girl, whose alcoholic poet father comes home one night, completely drunk, and dies, leaving her to look after her younger sister. Fearing that they will be sent to an orphanage, Yu-jin does not tell anyone about her father's death, but does her best to keep her younger sister happy, while imagining herself in the world of the American television series *The X-Files*. None of Chŏng's films provides concrete resolutions to the girls' stories, but the films are interested in exploring the ways in which girls/women interact.

Take Care of My Cat is not a radical or angry feminist film either but it registers the feminist theme of identity quest which is explored through the character of T'ae-hŭi in particular. T'ae-hŭi feels stifled by a seemingly stable family life that is governed by her father's materialistic values. For instance, her father does not have much regard for her voluntary work. In fact, for him, it is rather presumptuous of her to help anyone else when she cannot even help herself (i.e. she does not have a proper job). T'ae-hŭi's frustration is also clearly reflected in the scene in which the family goes to a new American restaurant. As they are trying out the new restaurant for the first time, everyone is baffled by the unfamiliar menu, but her father, taking no notice of T'ae-hŭi's effort to understand and choose what she wants, boastfully orders the waitress to bring the most popular dish in the restaurant for everyone. Although completely dismissed, T'ae-hŭi is no quiet victim of patriarchal domination: she wistfully remarks that removing a person's right to choose is also a form of violence.

The film, however, does not caricature T'ae-hŭi's father as a tyrannical patriarch. Despite his philistine values, he is portrayed as a well-meaning father who is just insensitive to his daughter's needs. At one point, T'ae-hŭi clearly remarks that it is not because of her father that she wants to run away. She dreams of going elsewhere and wandering around the world; her work in the family business offers her no prospects for fulfilment, even though she is well aware that simply running away from home is not going to solve anything, and it is, in any case, 'too tacky' and 'teenager-ish'. When noticing an advertisement for new recruits for sailors, T'ae-hŭi steps into the all-male space of a seamen's lounge to inquire if she can be on a ship, too. A bemused sailor patronisingly reminds her that the ship is not for a cruise, before ignoring her reply that she is not interested in going on a cruise. Here, the man's total disregard for T'ae-hŭi and her interest clearly demonstrates the 'impossible' gender boundaries that exist for a young woman to transgress. On another level, the sequence also hints at T'ae-hŭi's dissatisfaction with the conventional gender roles available to her, and foreshadows her eventual escape from the social structures that confine her. Indeed, the symbolism is played heavily when T'ae-hŭi cuts herself out of a family portrait, before embarking on a journey with Ji-yŏng. In effect, she is offering herself to form an alternative family with Ji-yŏng, who has lost everything. The big bundle of books she takes with her also indicates her serious attitude towards the journey.

Another symbol that also links the girls' divergent lives is the kitten Ji-yŏng finds and calls Titi. The kitten is then given to Hae-ju as her twentieth birthday present but it is given back to Ji-yŏng who, in turn, asks T'ae-hŭi to look after it when the police take her in. Finally, the twins become the last to take care of the cat, as T'ae-hŭi leaves it with them before taking off. It is perhaps most suitable that the twins are the last of the friends to possess the kitten. Their independence – having their own place and business – and the 'inseparable' ties between them will provide the stable and loving home the kitten needs.[9] As well as intertwining each of the main narrative threads, the cat is also a fitting symbol for the vulnerability and resilience of the young women. Director Chŏng explains: 'I had hoped for the girls to be like cats – flexible, independent, complex, to have the tendency to leave if they are not happy with their owner' (Jeong 2002). Just like cats, T'ae-hŭi and Ji-yŏng venture out into the world at the end of the film. (In fact, the whole film anticipates a road movie that would follow their adventure together.)

Chŏng also posits that it was the word 'nomad' that she thought of most while filming: 'I wanted my characters to be girls who possessed nothing permanent and therefore were able to leave. Their relationships change and the girls continue to walk. I believe that if something is not moving, the energy weakens and it needs to be filled with things that are moving.' Indeed, throughout the film, we see all five girls constantly on the move, roaming the streets, taking the bus, and catching the last train. In addition, the places the girls go to – Inch'ŏn Airport, Inch'ŏn harbour, subway stations, etc. – are all places of motion, accompanied by the restless camera. The characters' nomadic traits are also related to the film's setting, Inch'ŏn, an old port city that was one of the first to open its doors to foreign cultures. The foreignness in the film is personified in the male labourers (or sailors) from South Asian countries (e.g. Myanmar) whom the girls briefly encounter in Wŏlmido, a resort island near Inch'ŏn. Chŏng also explains that she was attracted to the fact that Inch'ŏn is 'a city full of wanderers' with many more immigrants than native settlers (Jeong 2002). For instance, an early scene shows T'ae-hŭi and Ji-yŏng at the chaotic Inch'ŏn harbour, handing out T'ae-hŭi's fliers to the stream of people arriving. Most of them are preoccupied with managing their huge amounts of luggage and getting to the next destination as fast as they can. Amid the noise and the chaos caused by the mass arrivals, the girls' fliers mostly end up on the ground, stamped upon and torn apart. Here, the camera positioning, in addition to the soundtrack, work to display the disorientation and vulnerability of the girls who could be swept away by the crowd. Similarly, in the Wŏlmido scene, the girls are seen in slow motion, battling their way forward against the strong wind, offering an iconic image that symbolically projects the girls' struggle against a harsh reality.

The solid presence of Inch'ŏn as a place also gives substance to the social conditions of modern Korea. The film starts with the girls in their school uniform, giggling around and taking photographs together at the dockside. With its off-hand, off-centre frames and extreme close-up shots, the hand-held camera of this pre-opening credit sequence has a home-movie quality, as if to project the girls' happy and carefree schooldays, but the harsh industrial backdrop to the photos they take provides a frame that surrounds them. In one of the film's many outdoor scenes, Ji-yŏng and T'ae-hŭi come across a wandering mad woman who briefly chases them, threatening to attack them. Running away from her, Ji-yŏng expresses her fear that she herself might end up homeless and crazy, while T'ae-hŭi says she often wants to follow such people to find out what they do all day and where they go. Again, the deep-staged, bleak industrial landscape offers gritty, yet unexpectedly beautiful, frames for the girls to reveal their deep-seated anxieties and wishes. A connection can also be forged between the girls' outsider/marginalised status and the city of Inch'ŏn that is situated on the outskirts of the capital Seoul. In addition, the girls are vocational high-school graduates, which has a secondary status in South Korea compared to the mainstream high-school that leads to university education – the social dilemmas of which are reflected in Hae-ju at work.

With its episodic, de-dramatised narrative mode, *Take Care of My Cat* stands stylistically in direct contrast to the energetic, goal-driven extravaganzas of the *jop'ok* genre. The emphasis is on character rather than on story and on the accretion of everyday detail, which affiliates the film with the European or US art and independent cinemas. Indeed, the film has an introspective quality that frames the thoughts and concerns of the young women. Nothing is dwelt on too long in the film, though. Instead, writer/director Chŏng uses simple observation of events, offering glimpses of the characters' everyday lives and dilemmas. The film, however, resists easy solutions. The girls have problems of their own that cannot be shared or resolved by friendship itself. The film offers, for instance, a snapshot of the complicated family relations of the ever-cheerful twins when they visit their Chinese grandparents who would not even let them inside the house, denying their mother's existence. Although underplayed, Hae-ju's dysfunctional family, especially her parents' turbulent marriage and their eventual divorce, also provides an insight into her desire to escape from her rather provincial Inch'ŏn roots. Most foregrounded are Ji-yŏng's problems – her poverty and orphan status. At one point, however, we see Ji-yŏng buying a sleek new mobile phone with the money she borrowed from T'ae-hŭi, instead of using it for more practical and immediate concerns. While avoiding didacticism, the scene provides a subtle yet compelling picture of the consumer society that governs the girls' lives.

As well as providing a narrative motif, the girls' obsession with mobile phones also provides a memorable visual motif for the film. When the girls type text messages to each other, floating text appears in bus windows or on building walls, as the words are punched into their phones, filling the impersonal space with intimate messages such as T'ae-hŭi's concern for Ji-yŏng's well-being. The most memorable element of the film, however, is the girls themselves. The film shows Chŏng's deep affection and respect for her characters, even for arrogant and self-centred Hae-ju who can test the patience of her friends. Avoiding didacticism and the clichéd depiction of sex and drugs in regular teen movies, *Take Care of My Cat* offers 'a clear-eyed post-feminist assessment of what it's like to be young and female in contemporary Korea' (Felperin 2003: 64). The film, indeed, offers a rare picture of how young Korean women think, what they worry about and how they enjoy themselves. These young women are defined not by men but by themselves and with each other.

As suggested earlier, in institutional terms, *Take Care of My Cat* belongs more to the art-house tradition, its association with international film festivals and art-house circuits positioning it as an 'art film'. The film does not necessarily break out of dominant conventions, however, as it remains rooted in the generic and narrational norms of the buddy film structure. Nonetheless, it negotiates or revises generic constraints by developing the progressive 'new' subject matter of female friendship while shifting the woman's film out of its melodramatic mode. In this respect, the film can be situated in the gap between experimental and classical modes, subtly broaching issues of vision and representation without alienating a popular audience. But more than anything else, *Take Care of My Cat* is a feminist film that transcends the very genre restrictions that make today's male-themed and male-targeted movies financially successful but politically unsatisfying. *Take Care of My Cat*'s poor box-office performance reveals a problematic strategy for feminist films that attempt to cross from counter-cinema to mainstream. It provides, however, one of the most prominent examples of a female- and feminist-addressed film that creates a new space for women's film in the mainstream, blending explicitly feminist themes and alternative cinematic directions with popular, mainstream interests.

REFERENCES

Elley, Derek (2001) '*Take Care of My Cat*', *Variety*, 26 November: 27–8.
Felperin, Leslie (2003) '*Take Care of My Cat*', *Sight and Sound*, 13, 2: 62–4.
Higson, Andrew (1996) 'The Heritage Film and British Cinema', in Andrew Higson (ed.) *Dissolving Views: Key Writings on British Cinema*, London: Cassell: 232–48.
Jeong, Jae-Eun (2002) 'Interview with Jeong Jae-Eun on *Take Care of My Cat*', *Kino International*. Online: http://www.kino.com/takecareofmycat/cat_dir.html.
Kaplan, E. Ann (1993) 'Melodrama/Subjectivity/Ideology: Western Melodrama

Theories and Their Relevance to Recent Chinese Cinema', in Wimal Dissanayake (ed.) *Melodrama and Asian Cinema*, New York: Cambridge University Press: 9–28.

Kim, Mi Hui (2001) 'Tough Going Becomes Seoul Consideration', *Variety*, 11 June: 57.

Leong, Anthony C.Y. (2002) *Korean Cinema: The New Hong Kong*, Victoria: Trafford Publishing.

Paquet, Darcy (2004a) 'Box Office', *Korean Film News*. Online. http://www.kofic.or.kr/english/database. 21 February.

——(2004b) '*Taegukgi* Crosses 10m Admissions', *Korean Film News*. Online. http://www.kofic.or.kr/english/database. 16 March.

Seo, Hyun-Suk (2002) 'To Catch a Whale: A Brief History of Lost Fathers, Idiots and Gangsters in Korean Cinema', *The Film Journal*. Online. http://thefilmjournal.com/issue2/whale.html.

NOTES

1. Interview with Kwak Kyŏng-t'aek, featured on the Ultimate Edition of the *Friend* DVD.
2. The record has now been broken by veteran director Kang U-sŏk's (Kang Woo-suk) 2003 blockbuster *Silmido*, the first Korean film to reach 10 million admissions. The Korean War blockbuster *T'aegŭkgi* (*Taegukgi*, dir. Kang Je-gyu, 2004) is the second film that crossed 10 million admissions in March 2004. At the time of writing it is likely to break the record set by *Silmido* (Paquet 2004a and 2004b).
3. There was a well-publicised campaign to save *Take Care of My Cat* in Seoul, led by veteran (male) singer/celebrity Cho Yŏng-nam. The film also attracted a lot of interest from foreign film festivals and art-house circuits, and it was distributed internationally by Warner Bros.
4. The cycle has been regarded by some as a remedy for spectacle-driven blockbusters, which became a popular formula after the phenomenal success of *Shiri* (*Swiri*) in 1999. The production and marketing costs of blockbusters, however, have turned out to be increasingly difficult to recoup.
5. All catchphrases and descriptions of the two films are from my own translations of cover notes for the DVDs and for the films' posters.
6. In 2002, *Take Care of My Cat* was invited to the following film festivals: Rotterdam, Berlin: Forum, Fribourg, Creteil Women's, N.Y. First Film, Hong Kong, Paris, Seoul Women's, Singapore, Washington DC, and the Buenos Aires Indie Film Festival. It had also been unspooled at the 2001 Pusan Film Festival.
7. To achieve a more 'authentic' Pusan dialect, the main cast, who are not from Pusan, practised their lines by listening to the audio tapes that the film's director recorded for them.
8. In 'To Catch a Whale: A Brief History of Lost Fathers, Idiots and Gangsters in Korean Cinema', Hyun-Suk Seo (2002) argues that the 'outsider status of the *jop'ok* reserves a space for mental integrity and ethical purity that incapable fathers, distrusted cops, and other fragile icons of the military era could never fully assume'.
9. One of the deleted scenes reveals that they were born Siamese twins, but were separated when they were babies.

9. 'JUST BECAUSE': COMEDY, MELODRAMA AND YOUTH VIOLENCE IN *ATTACK THE GAS STATION*

Nancy Abelmann and Jung-ah Choi

Attack the Gas Station (*Juyuso sŭpgyŏksagŏn*, 1999, dir. Kim Sang-jin) is a violent comedy: despite the considerable violence that runs the entire course of the film, the film has been widely appreciated as hysterically funny. In the words of one critic, 'This is the first truly comedy-like South Korean comedy action film that I've seen in a long time'.[1] The plot is this: four young men attack a petrol station, holding its 'president' (*sajang*) and workers hostage. Viewers laugh hard, for example, at radical role reversals: at the petrol station 'president' who offers to relinquish his presidency the moment he is instructed to 'bow down, head down!' because he is the 'president'; or at the dumbfounded response of petrol-station customers who are told that 'today is a cash and full-tank-only day'. This humour aside, there are moments that make us wince – when the violence, some of it misogynistic, is simply too ruthless to laugh away: for example, when the attackers lock a defiant woman in the boot of her car and proceed to hack at the boot (the film ends having left her and another customer locked away); or when, time after time, one of the attackers smashes the painstakingly repaired telephones that he had commanded the 'president' to fix. A box-office success, *Attack the Gas Station* ranked second among domestic films in 1999 (garnering slightly less than one-half of the viewers of history-making *Shiri* [*Swiri*] – 962,000 in Seoul by its eleventh week) and third overall (only slightly overshadowed by the American film *The Mummy*) (see www://koreanfilm.org).

In this chapter, we are broadly interested in the film's popularity, most particularly in its appeal to youth audiences. We wonder how it is that the film's violence does not somehow manage to detract from its humour. We argue that it is style in the film and the film's style – both the new-generation style of the attackers and its MTV-like aesthetics – in combination with its melo-dramatic approach to lives and recent history that destined the film for success. On the one hand, the film celebrates 'difference' (i.e. in the style and margin-ality of the youth attackers) while, on the other hand, the film offers conven-tional narration of personal histories (i.e. those of the youth) and of social inequalities in South Korea. We assert that it is precisely this combination – the ruse of style, and the comfort of convention – that makes the film appeal. It is the attackers' melodramatic personal histories (portrayed mainly through dreamy flashbacks) that manage somehow to sanitise their considerable vio-lence; plucked are the heart-strings of the viewers who learn about the trials and tribulations of their difficult youths. In the final analysis, *Attack the Gas Station* is a melodramatic comedy with political edge but perhaps little bite. While the attackers' parallel histories do not spur them to meaningful collec-tive action or to 'resistance', it does nonetheless index politics and history. To the so-called 'new generation', the film offers fleeting glimpses of the past, and passing reference to narrative coherence, but with the stylistic veneer of a 'just because' outrageous comedy/spectacle that can (seemingly) do as it pleases to please a youthful audience.

With its combination of new youth style (both the film and its protago-nists) and melodrama, *Attack the Gas Station* echoes a number of other recent youth pictures, among them *My Sassy Girl* (*Yŏpgijŏkin gŭnyŏ*, 2001, dir. Kwak Jae-yong), *Take Care of My Cat* (*Goyangirŭl but'akhae*, 2001, dir. Jŏng Jae-ŭn) and *Beat* (*Bit'ŭ*, 1997, dir. Kim Sŏng-su). All of these films sim-ilarly combine melodramatic narration of personal lives with new-generation film aesthetics. We note, however, that *Attack the Gas Station*, like *Beat* and *Take Care of My Cat*, and in contra-distinction to *My Sassy Girl*, is conven-tional not only for its telling of hard lives (i.e. of social marginalisation), but also for the particular way in which it maps those lives against the socio-historical landscape of South Korea's recent past; of particular note are the films' shared critiques of the class coordinates of educational opportunity in South Korea. (See Grossman and Lee's chapter in this volume for a discus-sion of a quite different film narration of South Korean schooling in *Memento Mori*.) As Abelmann and Curry (2003) argue, *My Sassy Girl* is interesting for the ways in which it refuses to have personal suffering index national, collective or historical trauma – it refuses to map personal trauma on anything other than individual history. Also, similar to the later-released film *Adaptation* (US, 2003), *My Sassy Girl* is consistently self-aware of its melodrama. This filmic meta-commentary serves as an effective social cri-tique of dominant narratives or 'structures of feeling' in South Korea – of how very difficult it is to narrate against the collective and historical melo-dramatic grain. (See Magnan-Park in this volume for a fascinating discussion of historical narration in *Peppermint Candy* [*Bakhasat'ang*, 2000].) We also note that *Attack the Gas Station* must be appreciated in the context of the recent surge of South Korean buddy/gangster films. Although less developed in this chapter – see Chi-Yun Shin in this volume for a sustained discussion of *Friend* (*Ch'in'gu*, 2001, dir. Kwak Kyŏng-t'aek)[2] – the appeal of the hooligan foursome in *Attack the Gas Station* must be appreciated in part as that of male buddies who are loyal to one another and put a premium on friendship-based solidarity. Indeed, beyond the attraction of their hard lives, it is their commitment to one another – epitomised in the film's final scene when they insist on departing in unison, despite considerable personal risk – that appeals to the buddy-film clientele.

AGAINST GRAND NARRATIVE: 'DIFFERENCE' AND 'JUST BECAUSE'

It is not an overstatement to say that 'just because' (*kŭnyang*) is critical to any reading of *Attack the Gas Station*. Shortly after establishing shots depicting four 'different'-looking youths who have attacked a petrol station late at night, print flits across the screen to ask: 'Why have they attacked?' 'Just because' and 'because we're bored' (*shimshim haesŏ*) are the answers we listen in on as the four youths lean against the counter at a convenience store. (See Nelson 2000 on youth and convenience stores in South Korea's contemporary urban landscape; and see also Hwang 1995/1997.) The attack, then, does not conform to standard narrative or plot demands. We submit that *kŭnyang* works perfectly to resist coherent narration; resisting cause and effect and the logic of 'History', *kŭnyang* speaks metonymically for South Korea in the era of 'posts' (post-authoritarian, post-Cold War, post-International Monetary Fund [IMF]). (See Abelmann 1996, 2003; Jager 1996, 2003; and Cho 2002 on the transformation of social and political sensibilities.)

The 1990s, a decade of democratic advances, consumption euphoria and the wane of Cold War politics, signalled considerable social transformation. (See Lett 1998 and Nelson 2000 on changing cultures of consumption in contemporary South Korea.) Implicated in Korea's colonial past (1910–45) and South Korea's decades of development mobilisation and anti-state activism (H. Y. Cho 2000; J. J. Choi 1993; Koo 2001) was a *collective* national subject – namely persons mobilised by collective projects, be they hegemonic or counter-hegemonic (e.g. anti-colonialism, nationalism). The 1990s initiated a publicly aired, deep-seated rejection of this collective logic; emergent were newfangled communities of consumption and boutique civil society movements that engaged issues of personal identity and well-being (e.g. sexuality, the environment). Both 'development' (and 'anti-Communism') and 'anti-state activism' were grand narratives, asking people to subordinate the personal – the indulgent – for the larger good. (See Abelmann 1996; Kwon 2000; and Song 2003 on the social critique of the collective subject.) The 1990s offered sudden, if partial, liberation from grand narrative. It is in this sense that we find *kŭnyang* so emblematic of changed times.

The rejection of the collective subject and of grand narrative also entails the celebration of 'difference' and the 'individual'. (See H. J. Cho 1998, 2000a, 2000b, 2002; Grinker 1998.) Indeed, the 1990s offered a decade of difference, albeit somewhat eclipsed by the IMF Crisis which momentarily asked South Koreans to recall the collective imperative in the face of economic crisis. (See B. K. Kim 2000 and Song 2003 on the IMF Crisis.) The *kŭnyang* logics of *Attack the Gas Station* are all the more dramatic (or un-dramatic, we might say) given the film's temporal status as an IMF-era movie. (See Song 2003 and K. H. Kim, forthcoming, on *Happy End* [*Haep'i endŭ*, 1999], Moon 2002 on *Friend*, and Baek 2003 on four recent blockbusters – as IMF films.) The youths in *Attack the Gas Station* work as visible icons of difference: their fashions, hairstyles, and even bodily comportment. In almost every antic, the youths defy the norms of social convention: Mudaep'o (for the 'staff' he always brandishes – marked in red ink with 'Korean', *taehan'gukin*), the attacker who commands 'head down' throughout the film, for example, flings his lanky body across the screen, while Ttanttara, another attacker who commands the 'president' to sing, is a bleached blond.[3] Paragons of an urban cool, each of the four youths makes his own fashion statement. (See Y. S. Chong 1998; H. J. Cho 1995 and 2000a on contemporary youth and their cultural expression.)

With these portraits of difference, *Attack the Gas Station* joins many other recent films with its celebration of youth gang culture (e.g. *Beat* and *Number Three* [*Nŏmbŏ ssŭri*, 1997, dir. Song Nŭng-han]). Indeed, the film offers its own gang wars, albeit ones that intermittently seem more like an MTV spectacle than anything else. The presentation of the attackers' marginality includes their dress and bodily comportment, and their crude idiom (strings of four-letter words), including many newly coined expressions.[4] These youths have, the viewer is assured, strayed far from the normative life-course in South Korea: they have left home, left school, and are destined for marginal lives. (See J. A. Choi 2002 on youth beyond home and school.) The film offers a glimpse of the sorts of public spaces that such youths inhabit, featuring an array of contemporary youth spaces: a petrol station, convenience stores (frequented by groups at night), and billiards rooms (*tanggujang*). Also featured are Chinese restaurant delivery men and so-called 'automobile guys' (*p'okjujok*) – the groups that can be considered to be the class and cultural neighbours of marginal youth.[5] Further, these spaces are offered as alternative spaces to those of mainstream, middle-class, college-bound youth. Juxtaposed with these spaces, home and school are portrayed as cold (i.e. not nurturing) and oppressive spaces; the youths retreat instead to convenience stores, petrol stations, and billiards halls. Against received hierarchies of achievement and success, these youths valorise physical prowess (e.g. of school gang leaders) and calibrate hierarchy according to the ability to fight. They look down on nerds and subservience. In one scene, Kkalch'i, a female part-time worker at the petrol station, looks on as one of the other part-time workers is studying his English vocabulary (in the middle of the attack!); as he mutters 'spe-cu-la-tion' she suddenly becomes agitated, and shouts in exasperation, 'Uhhhh, it is because of people like YOU that I hate school!' In this way, Kkalch'i intimates her interest in – or even attraction to – the attackers; both she and the non-nerd male part-time worker, Gŏnppang, can be thought of as a youth audience embedded in the film – an audience of normative, middle-class kids who are at once frightened by, and drawn to, the attackers.[6] Gang culture is celebrated in the film for its own meritocratic norms and values – ones that are deeply masculinised. We suggest that this film's portrayal of anti-normative youth culture works as a romantic fantasy. There are many instances of this counter-cultural code: 'No Mark' (Nomakŭ), the boss of the four attackers, is afforded respect and deference: Mudaep'o obeys 'No Mark' and, against great odds, Gŏnppang becomes 'number one' and begins acting like a tough guy. Loyalty and solidarity, cornerstones of the popular representation of gangster culture, are central to the attackers' drama; in the final scene, for example, 'No Mark' – willing to sacrifice himself – orders the other three attackers to run away. 'No Mark' makes this offer to the accompaniment of melancholic music. When his mates decide to stay with 'No Mark', viewers are made to identify with the gang's deep bonds. The romance of these elements of gang culture works against the relief of normative social life in which class marginality and difference (of all varieties) are punished. *Attack the Gas Station* offers a wonderful portrait of the ways in which South Korean adults gaze at and discipline 'difference'. The attackers are chided: for their appearance ('What the hell is that hair?'); their presumed lack of filial sentiment ('Do you want to bring shame on your parents?'); and their apparent low social standing (a policeman warns them, 'you had better know what will happen when your gang gets caught drunk'). Also, at many points the 'president' reminds the attackers that they have strayed (e.g. that they have forsaken their role as filial sons). The normative gaze is one that any South Korean youth (or person for that matter) could recognise; certainly there is something cathartic about the in-your-face way in which these youths wear and perform their marginality.

The film's violence must be appreciated in relation to this social critique. Although the attack transpires 'just because', the violence is, in fact, entirely socially legible: namely, it is meted out against the grain of South Korea's received structures of hierarchy (e.g. age/generation, gender, class, education). Interestingly, however, its primary targets are those at the apex of petty hierarchies: the petrol station 'president', the head of a high-school gang, and bumbling neighbourhood police. Also targeted are the petty wealthy – the unlucky customers who happen to frequent the petrol station under attack, and who furthermore happen to put on any airs (of superiority) at all. Woe to the customer who, for example, calls Mudaep'o 'ignorant' (*mushik*), a register for him of all that is unjust. The film's rituals of reversal (e.g. Gŏnppang fleetingly reigns over the gang-lord of his school, and the part-time workers are designated 'president') can be taken as a social critique that exposes the persistent inequalities and injustices of South Korean society into the age of democracy. Among other hierarchies, that of age is radically upset in the film. Older viewers could only wince at the attackers' use of non-honourific language (*banmal*) in addressing their elders.[7]

The film's social critique, however, is ambiguous throughout. On the one hand, the film's obvious reversals are cathartic. Here we suggest the film's nostalgic appeal to those reared in times with clear and visible enemies (e.g. the so-called 3-8-6 generation, in their thirties, having attended college in the 1980s, and born in the 1960s). On the other hand, however, because the agents of power in the film are, in fact, so petty, the salience or seriousness of the critique is tempered; instead it all seems absurd and hence works as comedy. Foremost, the 'president' of the petrol station – hardly an apt symbol of South Korea's upper class or for any of the ills from which the youths have suffered – renders the critique hollow. As the 'president' himself proclaims, sighing, 'How pathetic I am! How did I end up becoming the prey of these gangster-kids?' Via phone conversations with his family – we listen in on several rounds of a conversation with his kids about buying ice-cream – the 'president' emerges as nothing more or less than an ordinary father. Although much of the violence is serious and seriously misogynistic, some of it, like its objects, is decidedly petty. Indeed, much of the humour comes from the amateur antics, such as when Mudaep'o yields his stick, only to slam it down on his own foot (standard slapstick) or when he decides to exempt a 'pretty' woman from having to put her head down like everyone else (the sad-faced objections of Kkalch'i in this scene are also humorous). It is hard for viewers to take seriously a delinquent youth who is so amateurish and comical. But, the violence in the film is nonetheless very real. It is this violence and misogyny of the hoodlums – not to mention the film's humour – that interrupts at every turn any seemingly critical project.

If the film's social critique is muted, so is any serious consideration of the real problems of adolescents and adolescent gangs in South Korea. (See J. A. Choi 2002 on high-school drop-outs.) Because in this film, and elsewhere, gang culture – for example, in *Beat, Friend, Number Three, The Gang Class* (*Kkangpae suŏp*, 1996, dir. Kim Sang-jin), and *My Wife is a Gangster* (*Jop'ok manura*, 2001, dir. Cho Chin-gyu) – is celebrated under the guise of difference, its lower-class origins and its hypermasculinity are obscured.

MELODRAMATIC SYMPATHY: THE VIOLENCE OF HARD LIVES

Attack the Gas Station features four short flashbacks, one for each attacker. The flashbacks interrupt with their style, sensibility and generic features. While the camera of the film's present is skittish and playful (at several points the camera is canted or features the image upside-down), the flashback scenes are slow and steady. Also the *mise-en-scène* (i.e. costumes, make-up, sets, props, lighting and character gesture) are all much more muted and conventional in the flashbacks. This said, however, the film's present is also melodramatic in its use of deep focus. In parallel, the music of the present is fast paced and youthful while that of the flashbacks is sad and dark. It is clear that the flashbacks appeal to audience sympathy for these marginal men; each flashback is palpably legible to a South Korean audience. Indeed, these portraits of the dispossessed border on the hackneyed.

Each flashback establishes a turning point: a reason for each of the four youths having veered off the straight and narrow, the normative South Korean path. And each flashback illuminates long-standing ills of South Korean society. This film offers a veritable ethnography from below of the 'school crisis' (*gyosil bunggoe*) that has been widely proclaimed in South Korea in recent years, including school gangs, violence between peers, bribes, and authoritarian and discriminatory teachers.

In the first flashback, Ppaeint'ŭ (an artist with long bleached hair, and draped in velveteen shirt, jacket and pants) is at home in what appears to be a middle-class abode. We find his father *violently* smashing canvases over Ppaeint'ŭ's head while his mother screams to defend her son. The viewer is to understand that Ppaeint'ŭ has defied the normative educational path, opting instead for the unproductive arts. The flashback happens at an apt moment in the film: Ppaeint'ŭ is destroying the framed political slogans at the petrol station (one for each recent presidency, they are leaned up against one of the walls). Glancing at them, Ppaeint'ŭ curses their Chinese characters (*hanmun*) ('People who use big words should be killed'), signs of book learning (and of élite educational capital). The frames must have reminded him of his father's assault. The flashback ends with his cry, 'I will kill myself'.

In the second flashback, 'No Mark', the clear leader of the four, is being absurdly punished by a high-school coach; we witness the coach's *violent* discrimination against him for being an orphan and for being unable to pay up on the requisite bribes (offered to coaches). Widely understood in South Korea are the many ways in which the educational system and its actors discriminate against youths from poorer or deviant families. (See Cho 1995 and Seth 2002.) When it is clear that 'No Mark' is about to defy the coach's order, the coach insults him all the more: 'You think baseball is a joke? You should be grateful to me even letting you be on this team. You had better know how many parents kneel before me with envelopes of money [i.e. bribes] begging that their sons be able to join the baseball team.' 'No Mark's' flashback happens just as he is filling up the car fuel tank of a famous baseball player who has just given him a signed ball.

In one of the film's sub-plots (in the present) we see that 'No Mark' has not abandoned the romance of family. In a seemingly uncharacteristic moment he allows the nerd to go home and give his sick mother medicine (i.e. a classical filial plot). Furthermore, he drapes the nerd in his own jacket for the trip – the nerd has promised that he will return (the other attackers tell 'No Mark' that he is crazy to trust him). It is important that 'No Mark's' tattered family photograph is in the pocket of that jacket – a mishap that drives the final scenes of the film. In another scene, 'No Mark' scolds the 'president', 'Don't you care about your kids? Whether they are well fed or not? What kind of a father are you?'

The third flashback is Ttanttara's who is kicked out of his room in a bar (that doubles as his studio) for being behind in the rent; we watch the attackers *violently* smash his instruments. In the final flashback, Mudaep'o is tormented by a high-school teacher who minces no words in telling him that nothing will come of him, that he is destined for a life in the working class; we watch on as the teacher violently commands him to touch his head to the ground. If there is a single corporal signature to *Attack the Gas Station* it is that: 'head to the ground' (knees off the ground, and hands behind the back – a painful pose to hold). Throughout the film, Mudaep'o wields his stick to command 'heads down'. It is only after we watch his flashback that we understand why he so enjoys commanding 'heads down' to his hostages. In the film's final scene, Mudaep'o commands 'heads down' to a large crowd of people, including policemen.

In each flashback, the youth leaves the field (i.e. the metaphorically un-level playing field) – in some cases, quite literally walking off the screen. In the case of 'No Mark', he obeyed the coach's first and second command to run around the playground while the others were playing ball but, at the coach's third order, he exploded in exasperation, 'I won't play baseball any more!' The audience sympathises with the attackers: they have been mistreated for being marginal or different. Bared are naked class prejudice, the ugly workings of patriarchy, narrow-minded systems of value and the violence of family norms. Viewers sympathise because they are acutely aware that there is virtually no legitimate space in South Korea for youths who have been cruelly rejected by their families and schools.

As we have asserted above, we understand that these flashbacks work variously in the film's narrative and scopic economy. On the one hand, they win the audience's sympathy which helps the viewer make narrative and historical sense of the attack (i.e. its rationale); this sympathy, in turn, mitigates the youths' violence. We argue, however, that the attack and its social critique do not entirely make sense either. As reviewed above, the film's predominant comic (and anarchic) mode flies in the face of these neat promises of narrative coherence, reference and meaning. It is important that the flashbacks happen in private – bared only for the viewer; they do not work as points of connection or political alliance among (or beyond) the attackers.

The film's flash-forwards that play across the scene of the end titles, namely the five-/ten-years-on futures of each of the youths, take up where the flashbacks left off: each youth re-enters the field he had longed to join, resolving or sublimating his earlier pain: Ppaeint'ŭ takes up an amateur art career; 'No Mark' becomes a baseball player; Ttanttara is pictured as a performer at private parties; and Mudaep'o has become an amicable guard at an apartment complex where he is devoted to keeping kids on the straight and narrow. Against the generic blurring of the body of the film and the prevailing comic mood, these scenes of resolution ring unreal, both to the sensibility of the film, and the likely futures of these youths. Buried in the end titles, however, they do little to mar the film's humour.

WHITHER POLITICS: 'NEW-GENERATION' SENSE AND SENSIBILITY

If not with the narrative coherence and closure of its flash-forward melodramatic resolutions, where does *Attack the Gas Station* leave its viewers? In the penultimate scene described above, the attackers simply drive away, having held the motley crowd (the kid gang, the delivery-boy gang, the police, etc.) hostage to the flick of a lighter. In keeping with the film's 'just because' logic, we have little sense of 'what next'. In that last scene, the work and workings of power are at their most absurd, and there is little logic or rationale to the attack. The petrol station – its stretch of urban concrete – has become more and more stage-like over the course of the film. In a sense, the film's stage has become a literal metaphor for the film itself – a consumer spectacle.[8] Indeed, at one point, the stretch of concrete literally doubles as the backdrop for 'wannabe' rock stars (one of them actually played by a famous South Korean pop star). In the final scene, we are made acutely aware of the confines of this space. Before we witness the four walk away, off-screen, we have begun to witness the petrol station from the bird's-eye view of 'No Mark' who has been commanding the show from above. In the end, all four attackers ride off in the haze of dawn (an ironic citation of the Western) while the members of the crowd have their 'heads down' fearing an inferno. This penultimate scene teeters on the edge of the film's generic mix of comedy and melodrama. We know that 'No Mark' is biding his time, waiting for Kkalch'i to fetch the weathered photograph of his parents; the film gazes painfully and nostalgically at him – at the look and feeling of his painful past. The absurd comedy and the straight melodrama are at their respective apex in this scene. It is against this tension, that the credit flash-forwards make so little film sense – dissolving the film's tension entirely.

We take this final scene as emblematic of the film's project. The scene is simultaneously absurd and entirely melodramatic: against the back-drop of the hostage scene, we meet the excesses of a family melodrama. The film eclipses with the lighter and a family photograph. Neither has the film managed to subvert conventional socio-historical modes of telling lives, nor has it managed to offer a sustained social critique. Enabled in the film is a masculinist romance of resistance with muted political bite. The narrative of the dispossessed is registered but dissolves in humorous violence precluding any serious attention to alienated youth in contemporary South Korea. Here, by way of a contrast, we can recall the 1988 film *Ch'il-su and Man-su* (*Ch'ilsuwa Mansu*, 1988, dir. Park Kwang-su) in which, instead, the meaningless respite of two billboard painters (they are perched on the scaffolding smoking and enjoying a soft drink) is taken for a social protest. In keeping with 1980s' logic, the social gaze at these workers – a gaze that has posited them as protesters about to throw a Molotov cocktail – politicises them, making social activists of them. (See Abelmann 1996 on this film.) In *Attack the Gas Station*, however, the petrol station works as no more than an escape. Viewers meet a comical spectacle – one with fleeting overtures to history and resistance – that comes to little. The comfort of the familiar (and the familial) helps, we submit, to anchor, if ironically, the film's stylistic veneer: its 'just because' antics.

We would, however, also like to note that *Attack the Gas Station* is distinguished for the way in which its protagonists speak to family, school and daily life. Unlike standard gang films in which gangs occupy insular social space and act either like Superman or pariahs, those in this film inhabit entirely recognisable social spaces and practices. In this way, the film perhaps effects the identification of its youth viewers. Although its political bite is deflected with its 'just because' logic, comedy and masculinised solidarity (i.e. versus political comradeship), nonetheless, a political sensibility has been communicated. Arguably, this is the film's accomplishment. Further, this speaks perhaps to new ways of speaking of difference: it is for each viewer to decide whether seemingly individual plights have been politicised or whether seemingly social products have been depoliticised.

REFERENCES

Abelmann, Nancy (1996) *Echoes of the Past, Epics of Dissent: A South Korean Social Movement*, Berkeley: University of California Press.
——(2003) *The Melodrama of Mobility: Women, Class, and Talk in Contemporary South Korea*, Honolulu: University of Hawai'i Press.
Abelmann, Nancy and Curry, Ramona (2003), 'Melodrama with a Twist: The Personal, Patriarchy, and Meta-Narration in *My Sassy Girl*'. Paper presented at the 'Aesthetics and Historical Imagination of Korean Cinema' conference, Institute of Media Arts, Yonsei University, 29 September–1 October.
Baek, Moonim (2003) 'Traumatic State in Contemporary Korean Films: On What is Described and Unuttered'. Paper presented at the 'Aesthetics and Historical Imagination of Korean Cinema' conference, Institute of Media Arts, Yonsei University, 29 September–1 October.
Cho, Haejoang (1995) 'Children in the Examination War in South Korea: A Cultural Analysis', in Sharon Stephens (ed.), *Children and the Politics of Culture*, Princeton: Princeton University Press: 141–68.
——(1998) 'Constructing and Deconstructing "Koreanness"', in D. C. Gladney (ed.), *Making Majorities: Constituting the Nation in Japan, Korea, China, Malaysia, Fiji, Turkey, and the United States*, Stanford: Stanford University Press: 73–91.
——(2000a) *Hakgyo rûl ch'annûl ai, airûl ch'annun sahoe* [Children in Search of School, Society Waiting for Children], Seoul: Ttohanaûi munhwa.
——(2000b) '"You are Entrapped in an Imaginary Well": The Formation of Subjectivity Within Compressed Development – A Feminist Critique of Modernity and Korean Culture', *Inter-Asia Cultural Studies* 1, 1: 49–69. Trans. M. Shin.
——(2002) '*Sopyonje*: Its Cultural and Historical Meaning', in David E. James and Kyung Hyun Kim (eds), *Im Kwon-Taek: The Making of a Korean National Cinema*, Detroit: Wayne State University Press: 134–56.
Cho, Hee-yeon (2000) 'The Structure of the South Korean Developmental Regime and Its Transformation: Statist Mobilization and Authoritarian Integration in the Anticommunist Regimentation', *Inter-Asia Cultural Studies*, 1, 3: 408–26.

Choi, Jang Jip (1993) 'Political Cleavages in South Korea', in Hagen Koo (ed.) *State and Society in Contemporary Korea*, Ithaca: Cornell University Press: 13–50.

Choi, Jung-ah (2002) *Classed Schooling, Classless Identity: Schooling Stories of Alternative High School Students in South Korea*. Unpublished doctoral dissertation. University of Illinois at Urbana–Champaign.

Chông, Yusông (1998) *Chongsonyôn munhwa ûi kyoyukjok ûimi: sangsil kwa waegok esô suyong kwa ch'angjoro* [Educational Implications for Youth Culture], *Kyoyuk ch'ôlhak*, 21: 143–70.

Grinker, Richard Roy (1998) *Korea and Its Futures: Unification and the Unfinished War*, New York: St Martin's Press.

Hwang, Dongil (1995/1997) '24 sigan ûi pyônûi, 25si chibaechônsul' [Twenty-four Hours' Convenience, Twenty-five Hours' Controlling Strategy], in Kang, Naehûi and Yi, Sông-uk (eds), *Munhwa punsôk ûi myotkaji gildûl* [Several Paths for Cultural Analysis], Seoul: Munhak kwahaksa.

Jager, Sheila Miyoshi (1996) 'A Vision for the Future; or, Making Family History in Contemporary South Korea', *positions: east asia cultures critique*, 4, 1: 31–58.

—— (2003) *Narratives of Nation-Building in Korea: A Genealogy of Patriotism*, Armonk: M. E. Sharpe.

James, David E. (2003) 'Allegories of Uncertainty: Reflexive Structures in *Chihwaseon* and Other Recent Korean Art Films'. Paper presented at the 'Aesthetics and Historical Imagination of Korean Cinema' conference, Institute of Media Arts, Yonsei University, 29 September–1 October.

Kim, Byung-Kook (2000) 'The Politics of Crisis and a Crisis of Politics: The Presidency of Kim Dae-Jung', in K. Oh (ed.), *Korea Briefing 1997–1999: Challenges and Change at the Turn of the Century*, Armonk: M. E. Sharpe: 35–74.

Kim, Kyung Hyun (forthcoming) 'Lethal Work: Domestic Space and Gender Troubles in *The Happy End* and *The Housemaid*', in Kathleen McHugh and Nancy Abelmann (eds), *Gender, Genre, and Nation: South Korean Golden Age Melodrama*, Detroit: Wayne State University Press.

Koo, Hagen (2001) *Korean Workers: The Culture and Politics of Class Formation*, Ithaca: Cornell University Press.

Kwon, Insook (2000) *Militarism in My Heart: Women's Militarized Consciousness and Culture in South Korea*. Unpublished doctoral dissertation. Clark University.

Lett, Denise Potrzeba (1998) *In Pursuit of Status: The Making of South Korea's 'New' Urban Middle Class*, Cambridge, MA: Harvard University Asia Center.

Moon, Seungsook (2002) 'Consuming Celluloid Masculinities: Responses to the Crisis of (Middle-Class) Masculinity in (South) Korean and Japanese Films'. Paper presented at the University of Illinois, Urbana, 6 December.

Nelson, Laura C. (2000) *Measured Excess: Status, Gender, and Consumer Nationalism in South Korea*, New York: Columbia University Press.

Seth, Michael (2002) *Education Fever: Society, Politics, and the Pursuit of Schooling in South Korea*, Honolulu: University of Hawai'i Press.

Song, Jesook (2003) *Shifting Technologies: Neoliberalization of the Welfare State in South Korea, 1997–2001*. Unpublished doctoral dissertation. University of Illinois at Urbana–Champaign.

www.cineseoul.com

www.koreanfilm.org

NOTES

We are especially grateful to Ramona Curry, whose comments on an earlier draft of this chapter had a large impact on the nature and tone of many of our arguments. (See Abelmann 2003 for a discussion of Curry's impact on the thinking in this paper.) Additionally, we would like to thank Chung-kang Kim for a helpful reading of the chapter.

1. On the movie's popularity, see www.cineseoul.com, *Chosun ilbo* 10.22 (1999), *Donga ilbo* 12.12 (2000).
2. *Friend*, released in 2001, attracting 2, 579, 950 in Seoul alone, represents the height of the buddy-gangster film in South Korea.
3. 'Ttanttara' is a derogatory reference to a musician who performs vernacular music.
4. We note, however, that the attackers are, in fact, not so young; one imagines that they are in their thirties. This raises questions as to the reception of the film. We can query to what extent the attackers are, in fact, understood to be 'young people'. We are grateful to Chung-kang Kim for suggesting this point.
5. We are grateful to Jinsoo Ahn for his observation about the film's disdainful gaze at the delivery boys who are actually truly marginal figures in South Korea's social landscape.
6. *Friend* also offers an interesting instance of inter-class relations in a buddy film. (See Chi-Yun Shin's chapter in this volume.)
7. In an attempt to appeal to non-Korean speakers, the subtitled version of the film offers exaggerated translation of the dialogue, often inserting four-letter words and sexually explicit language where there is none in the original.
8. See David E. James (2003) and Abelmann and Curry (2003) on reflexive structures in recent South Korean film.

10. ALL AT SEA? NATIONAL HISTORY AND HISTORIOLOGY IN *SOUL'S PROTEST* AND *PHANTOM, THE SUBMARINE*

Chris Berry

INTRODUCTION

The border between North and South Korea is notoriously impermeable. As Chen Kuan-Hsing (2005) argues in a recent article, the Cold War is far from over in East Asia. He begins his disturbing analysis of the numerous ways it continues to structure developments in Taiwan with a moving account of the rare family reunions that filled Korean television screens in August 2000. This chapter examines some ways in which the ongoing Cold War on the Korean peninsula is shaping North and South Korean cultural developments and differences and, in particular, images of nation and national identity. As well as blocking communications between family members, the Cold War has barred cultural exchange between the North and South for almost fifty years. Therefore, the most fundamental difference between Taiwan and Korea is that, while different Chinese and other ethnic groups inhabit the same space in Taiwan, Koreans have been rigorously separated and their cultures have developed with little contact on the popular level.

At about the same time that the 'sunshine policy' pursued by former President Kim Dae Jung from the South enabled family reunions, however, it also opened the door for cultural and sporting exchanges. On 24 August 2001, the North Korean film *Soul's Protest* (*Sarainnŭn ryŏnghondŭl*, 2000), directed by Kim Ch'un-song, was screened in Seoul. It presents the North Korean perspective on an historical tragedy. Fifty-six years earlier to the day, the 4,730-ton *Ukishima*

Maru was carrying Koreans, who had been brought to work in Japan, back home at the end of World War II. Off the Japanese port of Maizaru, first one explosion and then a second rocked the ship and it sank quickly with great loss of life. Unsurprisingly, how many people died and who was responsible for the tragedy are disputed. The Japanese maintain that the ship was carrying 4,000 Koreans, and that 524 died together with twenty-five Japanese crew. Survivors say at least 7,000 Koreans were on board, that 5,000 died, and that the circumstances were suspicious (Choe 2001). *Soul's Protest* follows the survivors, presenting the sinking as a Japanese plot. The sinking is probably one of the few historical events that North and South Koreans could agree upon.

In his article, Chen Kuan-Hsing analyses two Taiwan films to produce greater understanding of the rifts among the island's inhabitants. He shows how the memories of those who were on the island during Japanese occupation and those who came later are incompatible, producing different structures of feeling based on memories of different kinds of suffering. Taking a leaf out of Chen's article, I set out to find a South Korean film to compare with *Soul's Protest*. As it happens, a South Korean boat film was released at about the same time. *Phantom, the Submarine* (*Yuryŏng*, 1999), directed by Min Byŏng-ch'ŏn, is a nightmare of nationalistic paranoia and resistance set in the immediate future, in which rival South Korean submarine officers struggle to launch or avert a nuclear war of vengeance against Japan.[1]

Both films use the boat as a symbol of the nation, and both boats end up at the bottom of the sea. *Soul's Protest* is based on historical fact, however, and looks forward to recovery. As I explain below, it is an exemplary piece of national history. *Phantom, the Submarine* is clearly a different type of text. Like *Mystery of the Cube* (*Gŏnch'ukmuhan yukmyŏngagch'eŭi bimil*, 1998), *2009: Lost Memories* (*2009 Losŭtŭ memorijŭ*, 2002), and other recent South Korean films, reviewers call this fiction piece an 'imaginary history' (*gasang yŏksa*), and it distinguishes the perspectives of state and citizenry.[2] I describe it here as 'national historiology'.

Initial comparison suggests that the North Korean film may be more optimistic than the South Korean one. Not only are there survivors, but also the event is depicted as a trauma that the nation struggles back from and overcomes. In contrast, the South Korean film looks forward towards a disaster in which all on board die. As I go on to explain, however, this comparison holds water only so long as films are (mis)understood as straightforward reflections of social reality. If films are understood instead as stories mediated through textual conventions, intertextual connections, and contexts of production and consumption, a more complicated picture emerges. Beneath the seeming confidence of *Soul's Protest*, there is anxiety. On the other hand, *Phantom, the Submarine*'s voyage to the bottom of the sea may represent a desire to purge certain social and political structures in order to save Korea, not destroy it. Finally, I conclude by returning briefly to Chen Kuan-Hsing's essay, to ask what the juxtaposition of national history and historiology in *Soul's Protest* and

Phantom, the Submarine can tell us about the impact of the continuing Cold War on Korean cultures and senses of national identity, compared with those prevailing on Taiwan.

NATIONAL HISTORY IN *SOUL'S PROTEST*

The link between cinema, modernity and powered vehicles is widely acknowledged. Lynne Kirby (1997: 39–46) points out that the railway passenger looking at what he or she thinks is the passing scenery when in fact the technology is passing the passenger by *it* is not unlike the movie-goer, given the impression of command over all that he or she surveys but, in fact, dependent on the technological, social and economic apparatus we call the cinema. (In her discussion of early Soviet, American and French films in the later parts of the book, Kirby also demonstrates the relevance of the railway for visualising projects of nationalism and modernity.) Of course, cars also feature heavily in the movies, figuring the plot as literally driven by the protagonist, although of course the plot places both driver and car. The figure of the car driver is particularly apt for narratives about the production of the individual subject imagined as autonomous, a type of narrative common in Euro-American film narratives and given much attention by Euro-American film theorists, especially those eager to undermine the seeming naturalness of this individual (Williams 1995).

For a national narrative, a boat may be better than a car or even a train. Like a train, a big boat – a ship – can hold and transport a human collectivity. But where a train has to distribute them in compartments, on a boat their symbolic national status is manifest when they gather on deck, at the same time as its below-decks stratification from first-class cabins to steerage produces a class structure. In *Soul's Protest*, the *Ukishima Maru* makes the nation visible. Japan's defeat at the beginning of the film sends celebrating Korean workers on to the streets of Japan, praising the then leader of the resistance fighters and future leader of North Korea, Kim Il-sŏng. The news of the *Ukishima Maru's* departure for Korea mobilises the crowds and gives them direction, turning them from milling masses to streams of humanity moving down the hillsides towards the port where the ship is anchored.

The *Ukishima Maru* also visualises the emergent status of the Korean nation at the end of World War II. Its passengers – the symbolic Korean national people – are shown emerging from the territory of Japan, where they had been held captive and exploited, much as Korea itself was consumed by the Japanese empire and exploited as a colony. The ship promises to transport them towards the homeland and a promised freedom that symbolises the realisation of full national sovereignty for Korea by bringing together people, territory and collective self-determination.

This linear progression from suffering to future Utopia is produced in the film through the distribution of flashbacks and fantasy among the four main characters – Ch'a Myŏng-jin; his mute buddy Yi Ch'ŏn; Yi's Japanese girlfriend,

Tomie, who has smuggled herself on board; and Myŏng-jin's fiancée from home, Hae-yŏn. Unbeknown to him, she has followed him to Japan and searched for him. Now they are both on the *Ukishima Maru*. Flashbacks show the horrors of the time in Japan. For example, Myŏng-jin recalls how Yi Ch'ŏn became mute. Horribly exploited by the Japanese as a forced labourer, Yi escaped only to be recaptured and punished by having his tongue ripped out. In another flashback, Hae-yŏn recalls how, when she refused to submit to his sexual advances, a Japanese officer ran over her with his motorbike, leaving her crippled.

Eventually, Hae-yŏn finds Myŏng-jin on the ship. In wonderment, Myŏng-jin asks how their reunion and this joyous journey home could be possible. She tells him everyone is saying it is all due to General Kim Il-sŏng. 'Yes,' he responds, 'if he had not restored the country to us, this meeting would have been impossible.' [All dialogue quotations are drawn from subtitles.] He tells her they should hurry back to their home town, where they will fix her leg and live happily. After a montage of passengers singing the national song 'Arirang', a medium shot of Myŏng-jin and Hae-yŏn authorises a fantasy sequence of a future Utopia. After a happy village marriage, we cut to a little boy – presumably their son – running into Hae-yŏn's arms. She no longer depends on crutches.

This idealised narrative of the voyage to full nationhood as a linear progression towards a state of perfection is characteristic of national history as the collective *Bildungsroman* of a polity born with and into modernity itself. It is not how the movement of time and human events is envisaged in many other polities. On this distinction, Benedict Anderson's work remains the key recent text. He notes that the nation-state casts its members as a citizenry with shared characteristics, culture, rights and duties, bounded by territorial borders. In contrast, the other social forms are hierarchical and defined territorially by the loyalty of their peoples to symbolic central palaces, thrones or religious sites such as Mecca or the Vatican. Whereas the nation-state envisages its history as a linear progression upwards towards some ideal state, dynastic histories, for example, tend to be cyclical and cast the passing from one dynasty to another as a quasi-organic process of growth, flourishing, withering and finally death (Anderson 1983 [1991]: 17–40).

In her discussion of Chineseness, Rey Chow (2000: 4–5) makes a useful comment for understanding some further characteristics of national history as manifested in *Soul's Protest*, when she states that Chineseness is often imagined according to 'the logic of the wound'. The flashbacks in the film not only show suffering in Japan, but also an Edenic village life in Korea before the Japanese demand for labourers. The first flashback in the film after the voyage begins starts with a close-up on Myŏng-jin's face. We see his courtship of Hae-yŏn, their betrothal, and then the arrival of the Japanese and Myŏng-jin's decision to go to Japan in Hae-yŏn's father's place. The sequence ends with another close-up, this time on Hae-yŏn's face. Myŏng-jin does not know she is on the ship and she has not been able to find him yet, so this organisation of the flashback suggests they are independently having the same memories at the same time. The sunny village scenes of smiling farmers in this flashback are very similar to the idyllic marriage fantasy discussed earlier, positing the wound in national history as a fall from an original state of grace, and the future Utopia as a healing of the wound.

This logic can be related to a contradiction that theorists have discerned underlying the modern nation-state. In 'Narrating the Nation', Homi Bhabha (1990: 1) cites Benedict Anderson (19) on the contradiction between the newness of nation-states as modern inventions and their claim to be eternal and transcendent: 'If nation states are widely considered to be "new" and "historical", the nations to which they give expression always loom out of an immemorial past and . . . glide into a limitless future'. This contradiction begs the question of where to start a linear national narrative, and how to stabilise the contradiction. The 'logic of the wound' provides an answer. It accommodates the idea of the eternally pre-existing nation and its disruption by some kind of trauma or injury, thus demanding the diagnosis and remedy that imply a progress narrative. Many national histories and foundation myths follow this formula, from the anchoring of the modern Zionist narrative in the biblical flight from Egypt to 1066 and the Battle of Hastings in English history.

This progressive model does not account for the tragic ending of *Soul's Protest*, however. Why does the film depict the frustration of an attempt to heal the wound? Facing the ongoing division of the Korean peninsula, the project of overcoming the wound must be figured as incomplete. No Korean narrative of national history can have a happy ending at the moment, and the tragedy of the *Ukishima Maru* is only too apt for portraying the truncated project of Korean nation-building.

NATIONAL HISTORIOLOGY IN PHANTOM, THE SUBMARINE

Grounding *Soul's Protest* in the narrative of national history is the assumption that the nation-state is singular, unified and coherent. There is absolute division between Koreans and Japanese. The exception that proves the rule is Tomie, who is conveniently eliminated by a Japanese crew-member as she runs towards Yi Ch'ŏn. There is complete unity among the Koreans, all of whom revere Kim Il-sŏng. Most importantly, there is no question of any distinction between the perspective of the Koreans on the *Ukishima Maru* – the people of the nation – and that of General Kim Il-sŏng and the proto-state that he symbolises. *Phantom, the Submarine* is much more complex. It is never clear that foreigners are the enemy and a source of threat. There are multiple divisions among the Koreans on the boat. And the protagonist's perspective and that of the South Korean nation-state are not securely sutured together.

These fundamental differences between the two films are clear in the differences between their opening sequences. *Soul's Protest* opens with a scene of the

Figure 21 Divisions amongst those on board: *Phantom, the Submarine* (1999).

elderly and wheelchair-bound Myŏng-jin revisiting the scene of the disaster. His voice-over narrates the beginning and closes the film with the hope that we will never forget the story. *Phantom, the Submarine* also opens in the present, but with a travelling shot through the sunken hull of the submarine. There is no sign of life, but a male voice says, 'I am floating over vast sands, and I am slowly sinking. I want to see the sky.' The voice is not identified until the very end of the film, when a shot from below a body floating face-down identifies it as that of protagonist Yi Ch'an-sŏk, and then his voice tells us nobody will know about what we have just seen and repeats the line, 'I want to see the sky'.

Soul's Protest is narrated from the space of survival, whereas *Phantom, the Submarine* is narrated from the space of death. With the benefit of hindsight, Myŏng-jin authorises an omniscient narration that continues throughout *Soul's Protest*. Not only does the basis of the film in historical events mean the ending is known, but also the film does not hesitate to show us the Japanese plot as fact. In contrast, the failure to identify the voice at the beginning of *Phantom, the Submarine* sets up a tone of mystery and suspense that continues throughout, placing the audience within the diegesis rather than in an omniscient position. Furthermore, where *Soul's Protest* presents its story as objective and known facts even though they are disputed, *Phantom, the Submarine* presents itself as contradictory and impossible, both speaking from the place of death and ending by claiming that no one will ever know what has happened, when the film has just shown us 'what happened'.

After the credits over the underwater wreck beginning *Phantom, the Submarine* comes documentary footage and titles identifying the date as 8 June 1999, during a Korean–US naval exercise. We find ourselves in the middle of a John Woo-style face-off on board a submarine where various characters have guns to one another's temples. The captain is convinced that other submarines in the drill are enemy submarines coming to destroy his ship and wants to torpedo them. When he will not desist, an officer – who turns out to be Ch'an-sŏk – shoots him. Despite saving so many lives, he is court-martialled and sentenced to death. We witness his execution. But, in the next scene, it turns out that Ch'an-sŏk is still alive. Another officer, 202, tells him he is now known as '431', and he joins the mission of the top-secret nuclear submarine, *Phantom*.

In these opening scenes, the inability to distinguish friend from foe, divisions among Koreans, and disjuncture between the state and even its most loyal citizens are all emphasised. Because we do not hear the evidence presented at his court martial, it is not even clear whether Ch'an-sŏk's execution of the captain was really justified. Is he a hero persecuted and exploited by his own government? Or a trigger-happy and dangerous officer, also exploited by his own government for these very characteristics? Knowing little more than Ch'an-sŏk, our position of partial knowledge and some confusion is aligned with his. This continues throughout the film, forcing him and us to make sense of things retrospectively and casting doubt on his judgement and ours.

While Ch'an-sŏk is recovering from his 'execution' and adapting to his new identity as '431', he has a flashback to himself as a little boy witnessing men in Korean naval uniforms kill his father, also a naval officer. In *Soul's Protest*, the logic of the wound binds the Korean nation together as victims of the foreigner. In *Phantom, the Submarine*, the logic of the wound undermines the Korean citizen's bond to the Korean nation-state, construed as a site of conflict forcing its citizens to make impossible choices.

A perspective distanced from the nation-state and the presentation of a story about Korea as futuristic fiction rather than as historical fact leads me to see *Phantom, the Submarine* as national historiology rather than as national history.

Johannes Fabian (1998: 88) uses 'historiology' to distinguish popular and inventive tales about the experience of colonisation and modernity that express the felt experience of the colonised and those whom modernity is visited upon from the official historiography of both the coloniser and the post-colonial nation-state.

If the nation is pictured as a large patriarchal family, the opening scenes of *Phantom, the Submarine* signify intra- and inter-generational homicide, with the protagonist killing his commanding officer and his own execution on the command of the court. This murderous logic structures the entire narrative, both in terms of individual relations and those between nation-states. For example, when 202 explains the project of the *Phantom* to Ch'an-sŏk, it is in terms of a need to keep up with Japan, which is rumoured to be building its own nuclear submarines.

In these scenes, 202 appears rational compared to the heavy-drinking captain, and the film seems to be suggesting an alliance between Ch'an-sŏk and 202 against the older generation represented by the captain. Things become murkier once the *Phantom* goes to sea, however. The captain confides to Ch'an-sŏk that he knew his father, and tells him to stay faithful to his beliefs. In a scene Ch'an-sŏk has no knowledge of, 202 tells other officers that a bomb placed by the captain has been discovered. They kill the captain and take over the ship in a move that seems similar to Ch'an-sŏk's heroic quasi-patricide in the opening scenes.

Almost immediately afterwards, however, 202 tells Ch'an-sŏk that, although the submarine is officially unarmed, there are enough nuclear missiles on board to destroy Japan. 'Our country hands over its pride and dignity for money,' he claims, 'but this time it's different.' Ch'an-sŏk sets out to foil 202's plot, eventually locating other bombs that the captain had brought on board and using them to sink the ship while Japanese submarines descend upon it. In a final stand-off, 202 tells him, 'the *Phantom* is sinking not because of a torpedo but because of our fear of gaining power. If we don't become stronger, we'll get trampled on.' He descends into a nationalistic rant. Ch'an-sŏk responds, 'Despite your reasons, it's imperialism nonetheless.' After the sublime white light of final explosions, we reach the scene of Ch'an-sŏk's body and the place of death from which it transpires the whole movie has been narrated.

TEXT, INTERTEXT AND CONTEXT

Although *Soul's Protest* depicts a national tragedy, it renders it as the foundation for identification and mobilisation around the nation-state. *Phantom, the Submarine*, however, seems a deeply pessimistic vision of the future for Korea, or at least for South Korea. This holds, however, only if a film reflects the society and culture that produces it. In other words, it assumes *Soul's Protest* reflects a shared national determination to overcome the traumas of the past by building the Democratic People's Republic of Korea (DPRK), whereas *Phantom, the Submarine* reflects a shared conviction among its population that the Republic of Korea (ROK) is hell-bent on self-destructive infighting. If, instead, we under-stand a film as shaped by the intertextual references it draws upon and by the industrial and social context of its production and reception, a more compli-cated picture emerges.

The context of production and reception for *Soul's Protest* means it may tell us nothing about the thinking of ordinary North Korean people, and only about the thinking of the regime itself. As Hyangjin Lee points out, in North Korea, 'art is no more than a revolutionary instrument' and 'Kim Jong Il has supervised every aspect of the film industry since he was appointed as the direc-tor of film art in 1968' (2000: 31). Socialist states assume no division between people and ruling party but, without this assumption, film in the DPRK can be understood only as manifesting the regime's public line, and not even necessar-ily what the regime's members may think.

Furthermore, the intertext of *Soul's Protest* manifests anxiety. Despite North Korea's alleged isolation, *Soul's Protest* is an answer to the Hollywood block-buster *Titanic* (US, 1997), complete with on-board doomed romance and special effects. In *Titanic*, Rose Calvert survives but her lover Jack Dawson dies. The gender roles in *Soul's Protest* are reversed, with Myŏng-jin surviving and Hae-yŏn drowning. This accords with the gendered logic of national history, whereby men are agents of nation and history and women symbolise the nation-as-object to be fought over, or in the name of (Yuval-Davis 1997: 45). Rose Calvert has kept the 'Heart of the Ocean' diamond necklace since the *Titanic*'s wreck, and returns it to the ocean at the conclusion of the film. As befits a socialist film, the love token in *Soul's Protest* is a more modest red ribbon. At the beginning of the film, but the chronological end of the story, when elderly Myŏng-jin is brought to Maizaru again, he pulls this ribbon out of his jacket pocket and drops it into the sea. Then we see it sink in an underwater shot, much as the necklace sinks in *Titanic*. Piecing together the information from later scenes in *Soul's Protest* reveals that Myŏng-jin gave this ribbon to Hae-yŏn when they were young, that she kept it with her in Japan and that, when the ship went down, he tried to find her but found only the ribbon floating on the water.

Also like *Titanic*, *Soul's Protest* includes underwater photography and other noticeable special effects. These are emphasised from the very beginning, when the title 'Maizaru, Japan' over the ocean is followed by a special-effects flower falling into the sea. Other special-effects shots occur later. Leading into a scene where the Japanese officers on board plan the destruction of the ship is a gra-tuitous shot of the bridge from outside. This appears to be a model. The camera then 'flies' into the dark interior and down into the ship, where the plotting is going on. Others can decide whether the special effects in *Soul's Protest* match those in *Titanic*. The effort suggests, however, not only anxiety but also implicit submission to the standards of success set by the United States, troubling the otherwise confident surface of *Soul's Protest*.

Phantom, the Submarine seems more likely to be linked to the general public than *Soul's Protest*, even if, in South Korea, the public is understood as possibly distinct from the state. Although cinema in South Korea was 'ideologically controlled by its government' (Lee 2000: 45), censorship has been greatly reduced in the 1990s and consumer demand has been mobilized as the primary driver in the fight back against Hollywood imports (Berry 2003). While this may suggest a link to producer conceptions about the market-place, however, no reflection can be assumed nor can unified South Korean tastes and perceptions. Turning to the intertext may provide further insight.

At least two intertexts are relevant to *Phantom, the Submarine*. One is the long series of submarine films including *Das Boot* (Germany, 1981), *Crimson Tide* (US, 1995) and *The Hunt for Red October* (US, 1990), all of which would be well known in South Korea. (Most recently, 2002's *K-19: The Widowmaker* (US) has continued this series.) What links these relatively recent submarine films is the metaphor of plumbing the murky depths to explore hidden complexities beneath the state's version of the truth and tensions between the state and its citizens and soldiers. In *Das Boot*, the horrific conditions in the World War II U-boat dislodge any Nazi jingoism in the crew, and, although the captain may be patriotic, he has no loyalty to the Nazis. In *Crimson Tide*, a radio communications failure causes problems in understanding an order on a US submarine: while the captain believes he has to launch nuclear missiles against Russia, the first officer disagrees and leads a mutiny in the name of a higher good. Finally, *The Hunt for Red October* is about a Soviet submarine captain's plan to defect. In each case, ethics trump politics. To understand how this operates in *Phantom, the Submarine*, it may help to consider the local intertext.

Phantom, the Submarine can also be placed in the long series of 'masculinity in crisis' films of the South Korean cinema, discussed by Kyung Hyun Kim (2004). In particular, it fits with those that have questioned the legacy of forced modernisation projects and macho nationalism associated with the military dictatorship that ruled until democratisation. By far the best-known example of this is *Peppermint Candy* (*Bakha sat'ang*, 2000), discussed in greater detail in this volume by Aaron Han Joon Magnan-Park. In *Peppermint Candy*, an executive ruined in the 1997 economic collapse reviews his own life-history which includes brutalisation as a conscript and a career as a police torturer, before throwing himself in front of the symbolic vehicle of national history – a train. What is being symbolically killed (and mourned) in *Peppermint Candy*? Is it all Korean men and the South Korean nation as a whole, or is it the legacy of military dictatorship?

In this intertext, *Phantom, the Submarine* might be considered as a 'masculinity at the margins' (Silverman 1992) film that manifests a wish for the critique and purging of nationalist patriarchy, symbolised in the dead-but-still-alive voice-over and the hero who survives his own execution. Its hyberbolically homicidal deployment of the oedipal metaphor that grounds nationalist patriarchy itself exposes the instability of that structure. The star image of Chŏng U-sŏng, who plays Ch'an-sŏk, is of a James Dean-like rebel who refuses to obey authority, further emphasising this point.[3]

This oedipal metaphor is also implicit in Chow's use of 'the logic of the wound', which not only alludes to the individual subject but also to its instability and inherent contradiction. In psychoanalytic theory, the wound refers to castration anxiety. This notorious phenomenon is allegedly stimulated in the infant male by misrecognition of the female genitalia as a wound (Freud 1977 [1909]). The little boy's anxiety is a symptom manifesting a return of the repressed knowledge of modern individual subjectivity, which misrecognises itself as autonomous and invulnerable rather than bound by relationships and necessarily vulnerable. In other words, the misrecognition of the female genitalia as a wound is a projection of the little boy's fearful fantasy about himself, generated by knowledge that he is unwilling to admit. In Freudian psychoanalysis the little boy responds to the threat of castration in two ways: he either pretends there is no threat or he destroys that which symbolises threat. If he follows the latter option, the process of projecting fears on to external objects and then eliminating them is one that repeats itself.

In the case of the collective modern subject or nation-state, Benedict Anderson's earlier-cited reference to attempts to project national identity back into an 'immemorial past' and project it into a 'limitless future' can certainly be understood as an example of the method of allaying anxiety by disavowing it. On the other hand, the national narrative that identifies the wound with the action of an outsider corresponds to the second method, in which the threat is identified and destroyed. As Prasenjit Duara puts it, 'national history secures for the contested and contingent nation the false unity of a self-same, national subject evolving through time' (1995: 4). Once again, this is a recipe for endless attack and counter-attack.

Such a larger critique of the nation-state and national history is in no way entertained by *Soul's Protest*, which assuredly implies that, but for foreign – in this case, Japanese – sabotage, the Korean Utopia would have been attained. Only in the intertextual anxiety about the United States marked in its effort to match *Titanic* is the on-going need to repeat the threat and counter-attack structure hinted at. In *Phantom, the Submarine*, in contrast, the entire male community of the film seem to be at each other's throats. Including Ch'an-sŏk's own father, the commander of the submarine in the opening sequence, the original commander of the *Phantom*, and 202 when he takes over the command of the *Phantom*, four captains are murdered in the film. Furthermore, 202's lethal plot to 'wipe out Japan' and Ch'an-sŏk's opposition stage the fight against this on-going patricidal and fratricidal logic as simultaneously an exposure of the danger of, and fight against, nationalism. Here is the particular South Korean local logic of ethics trumping politics that characterises this type of submarine film.

We should restrain ourselves from any easy binarism, however, whereby *Soul's Protest* is not only state national history but also invested in nationalism and therefore ideologically 'bad', whereas *Phantom, the Submarine* is not only popular national historiology but also determined to purge nationalism and therefore 'good'. First, we should acknowledge the very real power and importance of nationalism in resisting colonialism, which continues to be inscribed in *Soul's Protest*, however problematically. Second, we must also acknowledge ambiguities in *Phantom, the Submarine* that make its position on nationalism less than crystal clear and so may accommodate differences among South Korean audience members.

At one point in the film, 202 reveals to Ch'an-sŏk that his father was killed because he and other officers were trying to build a nuclear submarine. The United States and Japan discovered the effort and put pressure on the South Korean government to eliminate Ch'an-sŏk's father. Furthermore, his father is shown executing his wife – Ch'an-sŏk's mother – before he himself is killed. Presumably, he might have attempted to kill Ch'an-sŏk, too. Yet, Ch'an-sŏk hangs on to his father's watch. The film invokes two incompatible patterns here; oedipality and Confucian filiality. The original captain of the *Phantom* not only trusts Ch'an-sŏk and tells him to stick to his beliefs, but also reveals that he was a friend of his father. So, is Ch'an-sŏk's opposition to 202 an attempt to be loyal to his father – who was as committed to nuclear vengeance as 202 – or a rejection of both men and all they embody?

Ch'an-sŏk's condemnation of 202's plot as 'imperialism' at the end of the film would seem to suggest the latter. But, earlier on, in conversation with 202, he agrees that nuclear weapons would give South Korea 'full sovereignty'. At another point, he does not contest 202's idea of a war of vengeance outright, but suggests that South Korea may not be ready for this 'yet'. This suggests an ambiguity about whether Ch'an-sŏk rejects nationalist patriarchy altogether, only a particular version of nationalist patriarchy, or the suitability of its most aggressive form at the moment. This ambiguity is underlined by another plot line. All sailors on board the *Phantom* are known by numbers only and are not allowed any ties to their former lives, including photos. When Ch'an-sŏk discovers the cook on the submarine has a photo of himself with his wife and children, instead of reporting him, Ch'an-sŏk bonds with him. While this does suggest a rejection of warrior patriarchy (for now at least), does the fetishisation of the family suggest the rejection of patriarchy altogether in favour of the allegedly female realm of the home or only the rejection of warrior patriarchy in favour of a more domestic, civilian variety? Here, *Phantom, the Submarine* hedges its bets.

Instead of seeing *Soul's Protest* and *Phantom, the Submarine* as two neatly fitting contrasts within Korean cinema, perhaps we need to think of them as the products of autonomous entities, engaging local issues and circumstances. This makes their status quite different from the Taiwan films Chen Kuan-Hsing discusses. Both of those are examples of national historiology produced in one society and one industry, differentiated by the incompatible memories they invoke. In other words, different communities in Taiwan share the same society and culture but are separated by their own distinct structures of feeling, whereas North Korea and South Korea are not only separated geographically by the on-going Cold War but also by entirely different cultural and cinematic modes and practices, suggesting a different but no less distressing and difficult incommensurability.

References

Anderson, Benedict (1983 [1991]) *Imagined Communities: Reflections on the Origin and Spread of Nationalism*, London: Verso.

Berry, Chris (2003) '"What's Big About the Big Film?" "De-Westernizing" the Blockbuster in Korea and China', in Julian Stringer (ed.) *Movie Blockbusters*, London: Routledge: 217–29.

Bhabha, Homi (1990) 'Introduction: Narrating the Nation', in Homi Bhabha (ed.), *Nation and Narration*, London: Routledge: 1–7.

Chen, Kuan-Hsing (2005) '*A Borrowed Life* in *Banana Paradise*: De-Cold War/Decolonization, or Modernity and Its Tears', in Chris Berry and Feii Lu (eds) *Island on the Edge: Taiwan New Cinema and After*, Hong Kong: Hong Kong University Press: 39–53.

Choe, S. (2001) 'Payment, Film Revive WWII Ship Tragedy', *The Seattle Times*. Online. http://seattletimes.nwsource.com/html/nationworld/134333314_koreaboat25.html. 25 August.

Chow, Rey (2000) 'Introduction: On Chineseness as a Theoretical Problem', in Rey Chow (ed.), *Modern Chinese Literary and Cultural Studies in the Age of Theory: Reimagining a Field*, Durham, NC: Duke University Press: 1–25.

Duara, Prasenjit (1995) *Rescuing History from the Nation: Questioning Narratives of Modern China*, Chicago: University of Chicago Press.

Fabian, Johannes (1998) *Moments of Freedom: Anthropology and Popular Culture*, Charlottesville: University of Virginia Press.

Freud, Sigmund (1977 [1909]) 'Analysis of a Phobia in a Five-Year-Old Boy ("Little Hans")', in *The Pelican Freud Library*, Volume 8: *Case Histories I, 'Dora' and 'Little Hans'*, Harmondsworth: Penguin Books: 167–305.

Kim, Kyung Hyun (2004) *The Remasculinization of Korean Cinema*, Durham, NC: Duke University Press.

Kirby, Lynne (1997) *Parallel Tracks: The Railroad and Silent Cinema*, Durham, NC: Duke University Press.

Lee, Hyangjin (2000) *Contemporary Korean Cinema: Identity, Culture, Politics*, Manchester: Manchester University Press.

Silverman, Kaja (1992) *Masculinity at the Margins*, New York: Routledge.

Williams, Linda (1995) 'Introduction', in Linda Williams (ed.), *Viewing Positions: Ways of Seeing Film*, New Brunswick: Rutgers University Press: 1–20.

Yuval-Davis, Nira (1997) *Gender and Nation*, London: Sage.

Notes

1. *Phantom, the Submarine* (also known as *Phantom Submarine*) is available as an English-subtitled DVD from online stores specialising in Asian films. *Soul's Protest* is more difficult to find, but not impossible. I suggest locating the shops in your country specialising in North Korean publications to see if they stock the video-tape.
2. Thank you to Choe Youngmin for this point.
3. Thank you to Cho Eunjung for this point.

PART III

SOCIAL CHANGE AND CIVIL SOCIETY

11. *PEPPERMINT CANDY:* THE WILL *NOT* TO FORGET

Aaron Han Joon Magnan-Park

The nation is a narcissistic entity for it celebrates rather than questions its past. Underlying this narcissistic sense of itself as a national self is the necessity *not* to remember certain aspects of its own history. This holds especially true when these historical moments would question the nation's ability to live up to its full national promise to those who constitute the nation as well as to retain its honourable status within the community of other nations. This double imperative – simultaneously to remember and *not* to remember – is a key factor in theorising the nation. In 'Qu'est-ce qu'une nation?' Ernest Renan stipulates:

> *L'essence d'une nation est que tous les individus aient beaucoup de choses en commun et aussi que tous aient oublié bien des choses . . . Tout citoyen français doit avoir oublié la Saint-Barthélemy, les massacres du Midi au XIIIe siècle.* (Renan, quoted in Anderson 1991: 199)
> [The essence of a nation is that all of the individuals have many things in common and also that they have already forgotten many things . . . All French citizens must have forgotten Saint Bartholomew and the Midi massacres of the thirteenth century.] (My translation)

In *Imagined Communities*, Benedict Anderson concurs with Renan by drawing attention to Renan's insistence on having 'already forgotten what Renan's own words assumed that they [the French have] naturally remembered!' (Anderson 1991: 200) Anderson does this by highlighting Renan's use of the 'peremptory syntax of *doit avoir oublié* [have already forgotten] instead of *doit oublier* [must forget]' (ibid.) when discussing the nation's darkest past history. Homi Bhabha continues this line of thinking in 'DissemiNation' where he agrees with both Renan and Anderson and furthers the imperative to forget by stressing that there is an 'obligation to forget' (Bhabha 1990: 310. My italics). This imperative to wilful national amnesia, to 'have already forgotten' what Renan's own words assumed the French had naturally remembered and, by extension, what all other nationalised individuals are required to partake in forgetting, is especially pronounced when the historical event involves an internal purge wherein one part of the nation decides to eliminate a part of itself through state-sanctioned violence. This holds especially true when official history – that which is perpetuated by, for, and of the state rather than the people – seeks to repress, deny, and silence those moments of a nation's life when it betrayed itself.

An alternative ethos of national engagement involves not an obligation to forget but rather the very opposite – an obligation *not* to forget. By choosing *not* to forget, one embraces the limitations of the nation as practised, its grandiose aspirations along with its unglamorous crudeness, such that the national ideal can, indeed, live up to its full potential by acknowledging its very shortcomings for what they are; an historical actuality of the nation's traumas of its own fears of disappearance that does not then have to over-determine the future prospects of the nation – but if and only if it can insert these moments of nation-induced trauma as part of, rather than separate from, the nation's official history. In *Peppermint Candy (Bakhasat'ang*, 2000), writer/director Yi Ch'ang-dong (Lee Chang Dong) embraces this alternative ethos of national engagement by returning to cinematic memory aspects of South Korea's recent history that were formerly repressed by the state. Yi's will to remembrance, his wilful act *not* to forget, is courageous on the individual level and coincides with the government's relaxing of its rigid hold over official history. It celebrates South Korea's political passage from military to full civilian rule, and a collective desire to redress those repressed aspects of its military-dominated past as a means to acknowledge the present for what it is – a present that cannot have a viable future unless it is first willing to face up to its complete and unadulterated past.[1] For without this unbiased *rapprochement* with itself, that is a self-inscribed cultural Sunshine Policy of full disclosure, the nation exists as a spectre, a hollow shell that falls short of its full national promise.[2] Specifically, Yi Ch'ang-dong's depiction of national betrayal and shared national trauma focuses on three key events that the film's protagonist Kim Yŏng-ho partakes in. They are the Kwangju Massacre of May 1980, a regimen of quotidian police interrogation and torture, and the consequences of the 1997 IMF (International Monetary Fund) crisis that was compounded by the country's lack of a social-welfare safety net. Yi's *auteur* insistence *not* to forget, despite the pain and the shame, serves as a cathartic elixir to insure South Korea's idea of its nationhood is enhanced by repositioning it as a remembering national community that is worthy of continuation.[3]

My analysis of *Peppermint Candy* and its ethos of *not* forgetting addresses the film's invocation of a psycho-temporal critique in its reverse chronological narrative and its dual enigmatic 'beginning'/'ending' of Yŏng-ho's unexplained suicide in the spring of 1999 and his fatalistic gaze in the autumn of 1979 at the very railway bridge where he will commit suicide a full twenty years later. I will argue that *Peppermint Candy* provides the possibility of re-imagining South Korea as a nation and as a self-inscribed collective self because of, rather than in spite of, its unflinching insistence on *not* forgetting South Korea's traumatic national past. Michel de Certeau's notion of the 'mnemic trace' and his division of the space of memory between psychoanalysis and historiography will frame my analysis.

Peppermint Candy directly challenges the linear basis of temporal and narrative causality by adopting a reverse chronological narrative structure that 'begins' in spring 1999 and 'ends' in autumn 1979. It is Yŏng-ho's final wish, just before he is about to be overrun by an oncoming train, to 'go back' in time to rectify all that has gone amiss in his tormented life. He screams, 'I *want* to go back again!' and the film grants him his dying wish.[4] The film doubly fulfils our own spectatorial desire to understand the chain of events that led to his 'inevitable' suicide. Ergo, two decades of Yŏng-ho's life progressively recede back in time in seven distinctive vignettes to question the very fact of narrative causality and the inevitability of his suicide. The vignettes, in their order of occurrence within the film's reverse temporal *dénouement*, include:

1. 1999 Spring, Picnic
2. 1999 Spring, 3 days prior, Camera
3. 1994 Summer, Life is Beautiful
4. 1987 April, Confessions
5. 1984 Autumn, Prayer
6. 1980 May, Visiting Camp
7. 1979 Autumn, Picnic

As each vignette elaborates upon Yŏng-ho's life and the issues that compound themselves as they get embroiled within the linear structure of the cause-effect chain of narrative and human existence, the spectator cannot help but wonder what, if anything, could have been done differently such that, when these seven vignettes are placed in their proper chronological order, they are not fated, predetermined, and obligated to end up with Yŏng-ho's suicide. In fact, we cannot help but ask, 'What was the Ur trauma that completely undermined Yŏng-ho's life from the potentiality of happiness that is present in the autumn of 1979 but is completely absent by the spring of 1999? What exactly brought about Yŏng-ho's absolute absolutely wretched state of affairs?' The film's reverse chronological narrative continually peels back into the further reaches of Yŏng-ho's past in order to question the very teleological assumptions which insist that A must lead to B which will then lead to C and so on down the line (or in our case vignette 7. to 6. and all the way to 1.).

The opening vignette complicates matters by creating a mystery under which Yŏng-ho arrives at a river-bank school reunion inappropriately attired in his

Figure 22 Was he fated to kill himself? *Peppermint Candy* (2000).

business suit. His classmates are surprised because they had lost touch with him for twenty years. Amid the re-introductions and the general gaiety of the outing, Yŏng-ho engages in an impromptu slam-dance routine and a heart-rending off-key karaoke performance. In keeping with his unexpected and irregular behaviour, he rushes into the river screaming his anguish and begins to advance towards the railway bridge. Amid his friends' confused reaction and polite avoidance of his pain, we next encounter Yŏng-ho already on top of the railway bridge. His first attempt at suicide is humorously side-stepped by the fact that the train is on the opposite track. The second train, however, is on the track that he is occupying. Here, as Yŏng-ho ends his life, we identify not so much with Yŏng-ho but rather with his diminutive male classmate who is concerned enough with Yŏng-ho's distraught state that he dares to follow him to the foot of the railway bridge. It is from his diegetic and powerless position that we gain proximity to Yŏng-ho's final moments.

In coming to terms with Yŏng-ho's suicide and the film's unique narrative structure, there are five narrative elements that help to link each vignette to the rest. They include the diegetic inclusion and/or references to trains, his ex-girlfriend Yun Sun-im, peppermint candy, the camera, and Yŏng-ho's leg wound. The multiple diegetic presence of trains and their inclusion within the film's construction connotes a dual function. First, the inclusion of trains delineates one vignette from the next. In keeping with granting Yŏng-ho's death wish to go back, and the interrogation of linear causality, the train sequences that divide one vignette from the next are screened in reverse chronological order such that what appears to be a shot of a train moving forward along a rail track is, in fact, that very sequence projected in reverse.[5] This narrative device acts as a cognitive tonic to allow what occurred in the previous vignette to settle in before the next vignette unfolds. These interludes between vignettes provide a rhetorical pause that grants us a contemplative moment to ponder the necessary inevitability between the historical events and their eventual outcome – Yŏng-ho's suicide. Therefore, instead of passively accepting these links as sacrosanct and pre-ordained, the film provides each historical segment as a moment when the 'inevitability' of the trajectory could be, and should be, altered before the 'eventual' suicide. This point is driven even deeper by the inclusion of a visual and/or aural train presence within each of the seven vignettes that reminds us of the linear predisposition of causality and a plea to Yŏng-ho to reverse his causal trajectory before it becomes too late.

The film's psycho-temporal critique favours a return of the repressed scenario where the disguised past returns to bite the present again and again in what Michel de Certeau identifies as the 'mnemic trace'. Except for Yŏng-ho's leg wound, the other three narrative elements (Sun-im, peppermint candy, and the camera) are present throughout the seven vignettes since they are also present at the earliest historical moment in vignette 7. Together, these four narrative elements exist as a disguised past that doggedly returns repeatedly to re-engage the present that is Yŏng-ho's life. In this respect, *Peppermint Candy*'s reverse chronological narrative and the inclusion of these four repeating narrative elements bring into play Michel de Certeau's observation on the interaction between history and the type of memory that is allowed and constitutes Yŏng-ho's personal set of mnemic traces. De Certeau states this dynamism as one where:

> History is 'cannibalistic', and memory becomes the closed arena of conflict between two contradictory operations: forgetting, which is not something passive, a loss, but an action directed against the past; and the mnemic trace, the return of what was forgotten, in other words, an action by a past that is now forced to disguise itself. (De Certeau 1986: 3–4)

In *Peppermint Candy*, regardless of Yŏng-ho's desire to forget his past, the events of his past cannot help but haunt his present and continue to haunt him into the future. Put another way, Yŏng-ho cannot live his life or create a future for himself unless he can directly address these four mnemic traces and come to terms with them given that his attempts at forgetting only prompt their very return.

De Certeau's mnemic trace governs Sun-im's narrative position across all seven vignettes. It is Yŏng-ho's failure to consummate his love for her that then delineates her into a mnemic trace – the element of his past that he attempts to erase from his memory but which continues to return in disguise again and again to re-inscribe his present as his most unfinished and unfulfilled wish. Sun-im is *the* critical part of the recoverable past that Yŏng-ho desires to embrace but one that is compromised by the fact that he has denied for himself this possibility the first time around. Sun-im is present in the picnic of vignette 7. She gives Yŏng-ho a peppermint candy, explaining that her job at the sweet factory requires her to wrap 1,000 of them each day. Yŏng-ho responds by giving her a flower and expresses his desire to become a photographer. This vignette establishes the potential lifetime of happiness based on their incumbent heterosexual union. By vignette 6, however, Sun-im begins her transformation from a corporeal to a spectral presence. Sun-im returns in vignette 6 twice. The first time is real in that she visits his military base and is about to gain entry to visit him only to have her efforts curtailed by his unit's sudden mobilisation. As Yŏng-ho departs his base on a truck, he sees her walking along the road but hesitates and therefore fails to call out to acknowledge his recognition of her. The second time involves a spectral subjective glimpse where Yŏng-ho imagines that the female student who gets caught in the open as the military stepped in to quell the Kwangju demonstrations is, in fact, Sun-im. While Yŏng-ho agrees to allow her to pass, her fervent expressions of gratitude compromise his act of generosity because his fellow soldiers return before she can leave the railway depot. In his desperation to hasten her departure, he accidentally discharges his rifle and discovers to his horror that his second gunshot has inadvertently killed her.

In vignette 5, Sun-im arrives to visit Yŏng-ho and presents a camera that she has saved up long and hard to purchase. She desires to help him fulfil his original career aspirations of becoming a photographer. Yet, because of his accidental killing of the surrogate Sun-im in the previous vignette and his fresh return from his baptism in police interrogation, he can only spite her and her conviction that his hands bespeak of his inner kindness by feeling up Hong-ja's skirt to Sun-im's personal shock. To add insult to injury, Yŏng-ho accompanies Sun-im back to the railway station and returns the camera to her just as the train begins to leave the station. After this separation, Sun-im's doubled inscription in vignette 4 cements her mnemic trace. First Yŏng-ho voices the fact that the site of his current police surveillance is the same neighbourhood that Sun-im resides in. Moreover, he befriends a café waitress who volunteers to become a surrogate Sun-im for the night. The two share an intimate night together and Yŏng-ho is given a chance to 'speak' with an open heart to 'Sun-im' but all that he can do is repeat her name. In vignette 3, Sun-im takes on an ethereal quality since Yŏng-ho's act of revenge against his wife's infidelity should not be enacted with his secretary Miss Yi but instead should direct him to relocate Sun-im. This is reinforced by his acceptance of the peppermint candy that Miss Yi gives him – the very material object that is enmeshed with the memory of Sun-im. By the time vignette 2 comes around, Sun-im is no longer a mnemic trace but re-corporealised in a comatose state in the hospital. Finally, her very absence at the reunion in spring 1999 leads Yŏng-ho to sing out accusingly, in karaoke mode, that she has unfairly left him behind to be all alone before taking his own life. In effect, despite her death, Sun-im serves as the inescapable past that returns repeatedly throughout all seven vignettes, disguised at times but still very present, until she can no longer be denied in vignette 1. It is this direct refusal to deal with his own past or to make amends to redress his past that ultimately compromises Yŏng-ho. A similar sustained present/absent account is applicable for peppermint candy and the camera.

Peppermint candy is directly linked with Sun-im since it is the first object that she offers to Yŏng-ho in vignette 7, continues to send individual pieces of it to him with each letter during his military service, and is directly linked to her occupational status as a labourer in a sweet factory. Thus Yŏng-ho diligently collects each piece that she sends to him with a letter. Cementing the taste of peppermint candy directly with Sun-im is the fact that he eats one in vignette 7 when Sun-im first offers one to him and he eats one for a second time in vignette 3 after having sex and then dinner with his secretary. Thus, peppermint candy serves as the flavourful mnemic trace that is the film's equivalent of Marcel Proust's famous memory-invoking *madeleine* (Proust 1920). In a final act of supplication for forgiveness, he purchases a jarful to remind Sun-im of that cherished memory when he visits her at her hospital deathbed.

In similar fashion, the camera stands as a rejected mnemic trace as a recall device of the past since it is an apparatus designed to capture a moment of the present in order to establish its reality of the past for the future. Unfortunately for Yŏng-ho, his participation in the Kwangju massacre in vignette 6 and his career as a formidable police detective, who is required to partake in the torture of suspected civilians in vignettes 4 and 5, are memories that are better forgotten. The horror of accidentally killing the female student whom he imagined to be Sun-im in 1980 and the similar traumatic experience of his first participation in torture in 1984 are reinforced by the graphic match that establishes both events as formally linked to each other. In both cases, Yŏng-ho occupies the centre of the frame. He is in a sitting position and embracing the body of his victim, which remains largely off-screen at the bottom of the frame. His colleagues flank Yŏng-ho in the background periphery – soldiers in the first instance and police detectives in the later. In both cases, Yŏng-ho raises his hands and stares in horror at the bodily discharge that he has prompted from his victims – blood in the first and faeces in the second. Yŏng-ho's radical departure from his youthful ideals is reinforced by this graphic match. Heightening this departure from himself and his will to forget, Sun-im inauspiciously arrives to present Yŏng-ho with a camera. Unfortunately, his twice-soiled hands refuse to engage in dealing with an apparatus designed to preserve time when his daily interaction with time is now one that is better not being remembered. Thus, by the time Yŏng-ho is reunited with this same camera in vignette 2, he pawns the camera and destroys the exposed roll of film. In effect, his refusal to re-engage with the past is almost absolute because it is a past that can only cause him grief.

In contrast to Sun-im, peppermint candy, and the camera, Yŏng-ho's leg wound is not present in vignette 7 but becomes a part of his life only in vignette 6 when he is accidentally shot in the leg during his deployment in Kwangju. It is an invisible wound that flares up on occasion. For example, when Yŏng-ho descends the hospital stairs after visiting Sun-im and when he attempts to chase down a wanted subversive. As a wound, it is inherently tied to his activities in May 1980 and it cannot help but recall the unintentional killing of the female student because both events are inherently linked to each other. This leg wound then serves as a personal and physical reminder of a past that cannot be erased as easily as Sun-im, peppermint candy, and the camera because the wound does not have to partake in the act of disguise that is required of the mnemic trace. Rather, it is a physical reality that returns at unexpected moments to remind him of a past that he is actively attempting to forget when the memory is ultimately unforgettable.

Yŏng-ho's elaborate coping strategy of forgetting the past and the continued return of mnemic traces of that past to confound his will to forget is linked to a psycho-temporal disparity between the contradictory conceptualisations of time that separate psychoanalysis from historiography. De Certeau delineates this difference as one where:

> Psychoanalysis and historiography thus have two different ways of distributing the space of memory. They conceive of the relation between the past and present differently. Psychoanalysis recognizes the past in the present; historiography places them one beside the other. Psychoanalysis treats the relation as one of imbrication (one in the place of the other), of repetition (one reproduces the order in another form), of the equivocal and of the quiproquo (What 'takes the place' of what? Everywhere, there are games of masking, reversal, and ambiguity). Historiography conceives the relation as one of succession (one after the other), and disjunction (either one or the other, but not both at the same time). (De Certeau 1986: 4)

Yŏng-ho's struggle with the memory of his past is exactly caught up in this temporal dichotomy between psychoanalysis and historiography. He wants his past to remain within the past, as required by historiography, but his life is filled with his past, as stipulated by psychoanalysis. The added burden of the multiple mnemic traces then reminds Yŏng-ho that historiography cannot ultimately triumph over psychoanalysis. Thus, Yŏng-ho's final wish (his scream of 'I *want* to go back again!') is to relinquish historiography in favour of psychoanalysis by breaking with linear time and accepting the presence of the past throughout time.

Yŏng-ho's personal tragedy serves as a microcosm of a larger national phenomenon that affects more than just one individual. In particular, *Peppermint Candy*'s national allegory and social engagement highlight the Kwangju Massacre of May 1980 (vignette 6), the regime of quotidian police interrogation and torture over its citizens (vignettes 4 and 5), and the consequences of the 1997 IMF crisis that was exasperated by the country's lack of a social-welfare safety net (vignette 2). First, in May 1980, after the assassination of President Park Chung Hee by his own chief of the Korean Central Intelligence Agency (KCIA) and the rise of Chun Doo Hwan to military and political dominance, political demonstrations calling for the return of civilian rule broke out in earnest in Kwangju – the regional capital of Southern Chŏlla province and the historical hotbed of political criticism of the central government in Seoul. Chun ordered élite paratroopers and other military units forcibly to quell the protest and this continued for a good ten days from 18 to 27 May 1980. The resulting bloodshed of a minimum of 500 individuals was suppressed within the Korean media but reported outside Korea (Cumings 1997: 377).[6] Second, police participation in suppressing anti-government movements and labour organisation with the regular use of torture to extract information was part of everyday life. The most critical cases of suspected anti-government subversion involved a 'trip to Namsan' (Cumings 1997: 366) – the KCIA's main detention building was located at Namsan (literally 'Southern Mountain') in the very heart of Seoul. Finally, there is the IMF crisis of 1997 and the economic devastation that befell the country. All three are nation-induced traumas from which the nation is still trying to heal itself. All three events qualify as the less-than-ideal moments of Korea's past that, within its official history, requires erasure as one of those many things that all Koreans are obligated already to have forgotten.

The only possibility of national bliss occurs in vignette 3. The economic prosperity, however, that should then herald an upsurge in all affiliated forms of happiness is compromised by the double act of marital infidelity and Yŏng-ho's abrupt departure during his house-warming celebration. In fact, economic prosperity cannot make up for, or erase, the traumas that led to the economic boom. Moreover, the economic upsurge cannot sustain itself indefinitely since an eventual downturn is part of the economic cycle, and even economic collapse, as happened in 1997, is a very real part of any economic future. By taking this position, it becomes impossible wistfully to forget these events as Renan, Anderson and Bhabha collectively highlight.

The importance of psychoanalysis's concept of time is that it breaks the ideology of positivistic progressivism that is inherent in historicism, especially when it is appropriated by official history. *Peppermint Candy*'s reverse chronological narrative structure directly challenges the progressive, linear and teleological construction of historicism and its incorporation within official history. Re-visioning the past, or the act of recognising the past in the present and its ability to inflect the future, requires a willingness to avert one's gaze from its future orientation and turn it 180 degrees as Yŏng-ho does just before committing suicide. Here, *Peppermint Candy*'s reverse chronological narrative structure invokes Walter Benjamin's 'angel of history' and, with it, the questioning of historiography and official history's teleological progressivism. In 'Theses on the Philosophy of History', Benjamin invokes his angel of history to critique the tendency of progressivism to turn a blind eye to the costs that must be endured, tolerated, perpetuated and eventually forgotten for the notion of positivistic progressivism to exist in the first place:

> A Klee painting named 'Angelus Novus' shows an angel looking as though he is about to move away from something he is fixedly contemplating. His eyes are staring, his mouth is open, his wings are spread. This is how one pictures the angel of history. His face is turned toward the past. Where we perceive a chain of events, he sees one single catastrophe which keeps piling wreckage upon wreckage and hurls it in front of his feet. The angel would like to stay, awaken the dead, and make whole what has been smashed. But a storm is blowing from Paradise; it has got caught in his wings with such violence that the angel can no longer close them. This storm irresistibly propels him into the future to which his back is turned, while the pile of debris before him grows skyward. This storm is what we call progress. (Benjamin 1968: 259–60)

For the Korean context, Yŏng-ho is our angel of history. At the moment of his suicide, '[h]is eyes are staring, his mouth is open, his . . . [arms] are spread'. Yŏng-ho invokes his past, and it is accompanied by a 'chain of events' that is but 'one single catastrophe' – that is/was his life. His desire to 'go back' is a parallel wish to 'make whole what has been smashed'. When his desire to go back *again* is coupled with his vocalisation of *déjà vu* in vignette 7, we locate Yŏng-ho as a tragic angel of history stuck within a temporal loop that could repeat itself *ad infinitum* and *ad nauseam* if he chooses actively to forget, rather than *not* forget, the very causal chain of events that compromises his life and 'inevitably' leads to his heart-rending suicide.

For Yŏng-ho and the Korean nation to break from psychoanalysis and regain historicism's linear temporal trajectory, the *déjà vécu*, that which has already been lived, requires direct acknowledgement rather than active repression. In short, for the nation to regain its forward momentum, a wilful remembrance of the past, no matter how compromising, is *de rigueur* if it has any hopes of ensuring that its future as a nation can and will be sustained for itself, by itself and of itself.

REFERENCES

Anderson, Benedict (1991) *Imagined Communities: Reflections on the Origin and Spread of Nationalism*, 2nd edition, New York: Verso.

Benjamin, Walter (1968) 'Theses on the Philosophy of History', in Hannah Arendt (ed.), *Illuminations*, London: Jonathan Cape: 255–66. Trans. Harry Zohn.

Bhabha, Homi K. (1990) 'DissemiNation', in Homi. K. Bhabha (ed.), *Nation and Narration*, New York: Routledge: 291–322.

de Certeau, Michel (1986) *Heterologies: Discourse on the Other*, Minneapolis: University of Minnesota Press. Trans. Brian Massumi.

Christian Institute for the Study of Justice and Development (1988) *Lost Victory: An Overview of the Korean People's Struggle for Democracy in 1987*, Seoul: Minjungsa.

Cumings, Bruce (1997) *Korea's Place in the Sun: A Modern History*, New York: Norton.
Proust, Marcel (1920) *À la recherche du temps perdu*, Paris: Gallimard.
Renan, Ernest (1947–61) 'Qu'est-ce qu'une nation?' in *Oeuvres Completes* vol. I, Paris: Calmann-Lévy: 887–906.

NOTES

1. There are two dates that mark the change from military to full civilian rule. The earlier date is 1988 with the inauguration of Roh Tae Woo. Roh's former ties to the military and to his predecessor Chun Doo Hwan, however, mark him as a transitional figure. Kim Young-sam's inauguration in 1993 marks the return of full civilian control over the presidency since 1963.
2. In 2000, President Kim Dae Jung reversed the traditional Cold War logic that had kept relations across the 38th Parallel icy and antagonistic since 1953. Known as the 'Sunshine Policy', this political *rapprochement* with North Korea earned Kim the Nobel Peace Prize.
3. Yi Ch'ang-dong entered the film industry as a screenwriter for Park Kwang-su's *To the Starry Island* (*Kŭ sŏme kago ship'da*, 1993) and *A Single Spark* (*Arŭmdaun ch'ongnyŏn Chŏn T'ae-il*, 1996). His directorial credits include *Green Fish* (*Ch'orok mulgogi*, 1997) and *Oasis* (*Oasisŭ*, 2002). He is currently South Korea's Minister for Culture and Tourism.
4. In Korean, Yŏng-ho screams, '*Nan da si dol a gal le*'. Gramatically, this phrase conveys a desire to go back rather than a definitive statement that he is going back as suggested by the English subtitles on the DVD release of *Peppermint Candy* which incorrectly translate this phrase to 'I am going back' (which would be '*Nan dol a gan da*').
5. While at first this reversed sequence is not noticeable, scenes of cars, kids running, a bird flying, and a man pulling his cart projected in reverse motion make this unapparent aesthetic choice very apparent.
6. Given that this is an official government figure based on an event that the government would prefer to play down, the official death toll appears lower than expected. A higher figure of 2,600 total deaths is possible based on the number of actual reported deaths for May 1980 of 4,900 as opposed to the average monthly death rate of 2,300 prior to the Kwangju Massacre. This larger figure is provided in a study published by the Christian Institute for the Study of Justice and Development (1988: 30–2).

12. THE AWKWARD TRAVELLER IN *TURNING GATE*

Kyung Hyun Kim

Kim Sŭng-ok, one of the most celebrated writers of the post-Korean War era, as well as being one of the first generation of writers to be educated in the national language after Korea's liberation from Japan, is perhaps most famous for his short story: 'Seoul: Winter, 1964'. Written only a few years after the 19 April student uprising of 1960 that toppled the corrupt Syngman Rhee government and the 18 May *coup d'état* of 1961 which ushered in a military dictatorship that ruled for three decades, the author's satiric perspective is mirrored in the two main characters, Kim and An, who meet at a street tavern. They are both failures: Kim flunked his military academy entrance exam and An was a student activist of futile political demonstrations. As they eat roasted sparrows and drink cheap alcohol, the two strangers trade lines that neither produce thematic significance nor forge a strong relationship. The conversation constantly trails off, producing awkward intervals. Breaking one of these silences, Kim randomly begins, 'Of the street lights that are lined up in front of the P'yŏnghwa Market, the eighth one from the east end is not lit . . .' All of a sudden, a look of delight appears on An's face. He responds, 'There were thirty-two people at the West Gate bus stop; seventeen were women, five were children, twenty-one were youths, and six were elders' (Kim Sŭng-ok 1993: 88–9). In great humour, they take turns to recite detailed descriptions of the streets in Seoul: the broken branches in front of the Red Cross Hospital; two chocolate wrappers in the waste bin in the alley next to the Tansŏngsa Theatre; the five prostitutes all named Mija at a bar in the third block of Ŭljiro Street; and a two centimetre-long fingernail scratch below the handle of the toilet door in the Yŏngbo Building. All of them are visual signs that constitute the residue of what they experienced throughout the day. They are images that reside only in the reservoir of memory, their purity and essence are undiluted. They are already immaterial, insubstantial and implausible; yet they are the only things that can re-connect the two characters fighting boredom in the vacuum of that cold, barren night in Seoul.

This difficulty of communication that is connoted by the ambivalence and fragility of friendship, pure signs of urbanity composed of the random experiencing of trivial things, and characters who are struggling against ennui, make up the atmospheric mood that sometimes overwhelms the plots of Hong Sang-su's (Hong Sangsoo) films. Hong's characters are sometimes forced to talk only to avoid the awkwardness of silence, not because there is a compelling reason for them to talk. The essence of the pure sign or the pure sound rendered in his films is therefore tempered by stripping it of reason, meaning and thematic motivation. The post-ideological fervour of the post-1980s – when the student protests in Korea were as intense, if not more so, than those that took place in 1960 – contextualises the sombre mood that has enveloped all of Hong's films since *The Day a Pig Fell into the Well (Twaejiga umule ppajin nal*, 1996).[1]

Every intense political movement in Korea during the twentieth century was followed by a cultural renaissance. Modernism was often a humble coda to a dramatic overture. During the 1930s, after the anti-Japanese nationalist movement of the 1920s, symbolised by the Kwangju Student Uprising (1929), had lost its steam, it was Yi Sang whose poetry startled literary circles and who became the bedrock of Korea's modernism. During the 1960s, once the democratic regime established through a student-led revolution in 1960 had come to an end, it was modernist writers, such as Kim Sŭng-ok and Kim Su-yŏng, who starred in the literary world that anchored post-war Korea's intellectual discourse. During the most recent post-political phase, Hong Sang-su emerged, not only as the film critics' favourite, but also as the literary critics' prodigal son. Critics saw in Hong's work a profound crisis of meaning in language that was intimately tied to the withering of subjectivity, a symptom in any 'post-political' model. Indeed, verbal miscues, miscommunication and awkwardness underscore the humour of Hong's narratives that leave contradictions and complexities between characters afloat without neatly disentangling them. Compounding the very essence of this linguistic crisis is Hong's characters who never veer too far from everyday ordinariness. People in his films are neither heroes nor villains; they are only slightly good and sometimes slightly selfish and callous. On one level, this portrayal of everyday banality pays attention to the discords and ailments that routinely annoy people (i.e. waiting, unwanted phone calls and nagging cold symptoms), but sublimates this experience in subterranean fashion to the social totality of the epoch.

In Hong Sang-su's film, *Turning Gate* (also known as *On the Occasion of Remembering the Turning Gate/Saenghwalŭi palgyŏn*, 2002), Kyŏng-su, an actor in the midst of a career-change from stage to film, finds himself caught between jobs. As the film opens, he receives a phone call from his director friend, who notifies him that he has been sacked. Kyŏng-su is told that he is being blamed for the box-office failure of the last film in which he had been cast. Upon visiting the production office, he receives 1,000,000 won (about US $1,000) as residual pay for his last film. Because the movie has flopped so badly, the director insists that it would be unethical for Kyŏng-su to take the money. The pay is legitimised by a clause in his contract but Kyŏng-su's personal friendship with his director becomes jeopardised the moment he accepts it. The director warns Kyŏng-su, 'It is difficult to be human, but let's try not to become monsters'. This satirical statement functions as one of the central themes of the film as Kyŏng-su struggles between 'human' and 'monster' throughout.

Ironically, by being dismissed, Kyŏng-su has earned himself some free time from his work. He travels to Ch'unch'ŏn, a three-hour railway ride from Seoul, to see an old friend, a writer, before visiting his family in Pusan. Kyŏng-su's nomadic identity allows the story to find some space in a modern world divided between routine drudgery at work, family responsibilities, and sleep. In other words, the narrative space of *Turning Gate* escapes conventional causality through Kyŏng-su's temporary relief from having to work. The film follows the aimless trajectory of its idealistic protagonist Kyŏng-su who, on the road, pursues the meaning of life. (The direct translation of the film's Korean title is 'Discovery of Life'.) By being released from work and from the metropolitan centre of Seoul, Kyŏng-su has time to indulge in a capriciousness and idealism that are amusing to the film's viewers, who are constantly being weaseled and baffled by the congested human traffic in urban centres.

The main characters of all the films Hong Sang-su has made to date are at some point humiliated, and Kyŏng-su is no exception. His idealism and obstinacy may be noble but, in practical reality, he is a person who – as a fortune-teller tells him – 'cannot easily blend with the others'. He resists love when it is offered to him, yet he clamours for it when it is denied. Kyŏng-su meets Myŏng-suk, a dancer in Ch'unch'ŏn, the first city he visits. Despite the fact that Sŏng-u, the novelist friend he is visiting, already fancies Myŏng-suk, he sleeps with her without guilt or love. Myŏng-suk has already seen Kyŏng-su in films several times, and she has fallen hopelessly in love with him. Her attempt to win his love comes to no avail. Kyŏng-su leaves town on a train, leaving Myŏng-suk behind, her eyes swollen from crying. The unrequited love Myŏng-suk feels for Kyŏng-su will soon be felt by Kyŏng-su as well. Continuing on his way to Pusan, he happens to meet Sŏn-yŏng, an attractive woman who is travelling home to Kyŏngju. Helplessly drawn to her, Kyŏng-su gets off at her stop and surreptitiously trails her to discover where she lives.

This unscheduled stop releases Kyŏng-su from the linear line of plot. Since he has no plan and only a vague idea of seduction, which may or may not happen, he has effectively freed himself from the chain of dramatic causality. In a conventional film, what will happen in the subsequent shot is sometimes more important than the present shot. Kyŏng-su is unconstrained by other external matters because the film has refused to develop characters beyond those whose function is to advance the narrative.

Kyŏng-su is not just a lonely traveller, he is also an outsider from the metropolis in a small town where he is not particularly welcome. He finds himself in

Kyŏngju, an ancient capital of Korea and a city in which he knows no one other than Sŏn-yŏng who, it will soon be revealed, is a married woman. Although he has found out where she lives, and will soon visit, surprising her and the rest of her family, he has yet to make up his mind about what to do next. He books into a cheap boarding-house. Alone, he takes a walk to a part of the city where tourists rarely visit and nonchalantly enters a restaurant. In this flimsy yet crowded barbecue restaurant, he orders some *kopch'ang* (beef intestines) to grill at the table and a bottle of *soju*, on which he will become slowly intoxicated.

'What were you looking at?' asks a young man dining next to Kyŏng-su, rudely awakening him from a reverie he has fallen into while eating and looking at a woman's lean, exposed legs. The male diner's thick, provincial accent clearly marks him as someone rooted in this traditional, conservative town. The man is upset that Kyŏng-su has been staring at his girlfriend's legs. Kyŏng-su immediately denies the charge, replying meekly, 'What . . . me? Nothing. I wasn't looking at anything'. Despite Kyŏng-su's denial – he protests that he had been examining a poster pinned right above the woman's head – the audience already senses Kyŏng-su's guilt. His feeble lie – the denial that he was not looking – exasperates the male diner. Irritation soon transforms into rage, producing obscenities and insults directed at Kyŏng-su, a stranger who has violated the code of ethics. 'Where are your fucking manners?' blurts out the angry diner who himself seems to have lost any sign of decency. Fortunately, the quarrel does not explode into physical violence after the female diner pleads to her boyfriend to calm down.

Though deeply textured with action and drama, this scene – shot in a single take – achieves a sense of emptiness by detaching itself from the rest of the narrative. Instead of further suturing the drama, this scene almost punts the audience out of it. Ironically, this scene exempts the audience from the narrative's structural tyranny, forcing them to explore the details of the space, the community in which Kyŏng-su finds himself, and the intricacies of drama to be found beyond the primary one. This shift in focus from the protagonist to other diners reminds us of the Jean-Luc Godard film *Masculine-Feminine* (France, 1966), in which minor characters seated in a café divert attention from the main characters. Unlike the Jean-Pierre Leaud character in the Godard film, however, Kyŏng-su stays in the frame even when his role is that of the voyeur and the eavesdropper, thus minimising the potential rupture to the drama that would be caused by introducing characters who have nothing to do with the main plot.

The visual composition of the shot – which places Kyŏng-su dining in the foreground, the male diner and his girlfriend in the mid-field of the frame and a crummy poster pinned up on an otherwise blank wall in the back of the frame – offers the eyes of the viewer an opportunity to wander the big screen. Though the focus of Kyŏng-su's concentration is on the legs of the woman, which means that at least some of the audience will follow the line of his gaze, the audience is also free to focus on other sections of the frame. The beauty of the woman's leg is hardly the matter that controls the mood and the impulse of the entire scene, though it is the main reason why Kyŏng-su gets into trouble. Had the scene, which is composed of one single long take, been broken up into fetishistic close-ups and conventional shot/reverse shots, it would be far more scandalous than it is now. The scene's long take not only leaps over the constraints of the narrative and proposes to divert the audience's gaze to different aspects of the *mise-en-scène*, it also serves as a temporal guide through the process of Kyŏng-su's awkwardness: first, the stage of initial desire (from looking at the woman's legs), guilt (for having peeped), and finally obsessive denial (for insisting that he was looking at a poster on the wall). The entire scene – shot in real time, in a simple long shot, with very little camera movement – is critical in diversifying the audience's gaze.

In this one single shot, the film goes beyond telling one single story or one single action. The characters in the background do not help Kyŏng-su realise his main objective in Kyŏngju, and will not appear again in the film. 'In a day made up of 24 hours, couldn't you possibly spare ten minutes to make one simple phone call?' asks the male diner in his thick accent before catching the suspicious sight of Kyŏng-su. The woman – also with a similar accent – replies, 'I was too busy . . . I am sure that you understand.' The tension between the couple reflects the all-too-common situation of a country boy who has been anxiously left behind while his girlfriend pursues her dreams in the metropolis.

As noted above, the scene is, at first glance, almost 'wasteful' in its failure to further the narrative. For instance, it says little about how Kyŏng-su will go about executing his plan to seduce Sŏn-yŏng, the reason for his sudden roundabout. Half the film is over, and yet we are still unsure what might be in store for us. In this moment, narrative time is temporally halted. By introducing these minor characters, the rigid conventions of a narrative structure are cracked open, serving to underscore the dreamy state Kyŏng-su is in and to awaken him from it. The excesses, the halting of the narrative time, the conversations between two characters that often trail off, all contribute to creating a mood of awkwardness that is now patented in Hong Sang-su's films.

Korean critics have long been fascinated by the way in which the audiences of Hong Sang-su's films become as awkward as his characters. (Though none of Hong Sang-su's films to date has been a major local box-office hit, they have all been highly praised by critics.) Equally important, however, is Hong's ability to release the tension between his characters, not through their reconciliation but through the acknowledgement of the impossibility of reconciliation. For instance, in the restaurant scene, the male diner's refusal to accept Kyŏng-su's excuse that he was looking at a poster causes the tension between the two to escalate. The threat of the fight is resolved, however, when the diner realises that Kyŏng-su is a fool and not even worth fighting. Kyŏng-su is still in a dreamy state, and cannot easily wake up. Here, he does not retreat from his insistence that he was looking at something else other than the woman. He walks up to the *ajumma*, the owner of the restaurant, and demands to know where he can actually purchase the poster that is little more than a giveaway advertisement for an alcoholic beverage. By refusing to give up, awkwardness is transformed into pitiable laughter. No matter what Kyŏng-su does to try to reclaim his integrity, he will be further ridiculed by the two diners and also by the audience. The more Kyŏng-su tries to protest, the more face he loses and the more distance he will create between himself and the world that fails to understand him.

This de-centering of subjectivity, through which the protagonist becomes humiliated, serves as an underlying theme in *Turning Gate*, which constantly places Kyŏng-su in awkward positions. He assumes the role of the *flâneur*, who meanders the city looking for things that are exciting, only to fall into a pit of paradox between the public and the private. Kyŏng-su's appetite for beauty finds him trying desperately to steal a look at a woman's legs and then even more desperate to deny ever having looked. Though he did not commit a crime, he is violating the couple's privacy and the code of decency that regulates people's behaviour in a public space. I use the word 'violation' to focus not only on Kyŏng-su's attempt to peek but also on our eavesdropping into the private conversation between the two diners.

The male diner who confronts Kyŏng-su is upset, not only because of Kyŏng-su's act of 'looking' but also because he has rudely violated the privacy of he and his girlfriend. Kyŏng-su is an urbanite, and he is already a threat simply by being there. But is Kyŏng-su to be morally deplored for appreciating the beauty of a woman's legs? What about the position of the tranquil camera? If the *mise-en-scène* is constructed as a long take, is the perception of the audience's gaze differently figured than the one that induces voyeuristic scopophilia? What about the act of eavesdropping on the private conversation between the two? Since the couple is external to the narrative, are not we – the film's audience – also implicated? And finally, if the diners do not want other people to hear them talk about their private lives, why are they sitting and talking in a restaurant where the rest of us can hear them? These questions open up the very interstices set forth by the film's paradoxes where the lines between the public and the private are constantly crashing and eroding.

Like Japanese director Ozu Yasujiro, whose films 'pick[ed] out the intolerable from the insignificant itself' (Deleuze 1995: 19), the simplistic quality of life Hong Sang-su depicts cannot easily be severed from anxiety and torment. Kyŏng-su, who is a transcendental, idealistic being, constantly finds himself struggling against the world. Kyŏng-su refuses to fall in love with Myŏng-suk, the dance teacher who desires him, only to commit a crime of passion with Sŏn-yŏng, a married woman who must be 'stolen' from her family. Yet, like his pathetic attempt to persuade others that he was looking at something other than a woman's legs, his effort to woo Sŏn-yŏng is not an easy one. He endures several days of waiting for Sŏn-yŏng to make up her mind.

During this waiting period, the film's theme of not 'turning into monsters' begins to act upon Kyŏng-su, transforming him. It is interesting that the film recounts a seventh-century legend of the turning gate as a prelude to Kyŏng-su's metamorphosis. As told by Kyŏng-su's writer friend when Kyŏng-su visits a temple in Ch'unch'ŏn, the story of the legend of the turning gate is derived from an ill-fated love affair between a common man and a princess of the Tang Dynasty in China. Upon learning that a man of ordinary rank has dared to seek his daughter, however, the Emperor Tae-tsung orders that the admirer's head be cut off. Unrelenting, the dead man is reincarnated as a giant serpent which wraps itself around the princess's body. Desperate to free herself from the 'man-who-has-become-a-serpent', she seeks advice from a priest who tells her to visit a temple in Korea. Once there, the princess begs the serpent that she will quickly enter the temple to get some food. The snake waits for the princess for a considerable time. Tired of waiting, he tries to enter the gate only to be turned away by well-timed thunder and lightning.

As if to resurrect the legend, the story in Kyŏngju delineates the process by which Kyŏng-su walks a perilous path and sinks to a form that is less than human. By the end of the film, Kyŏng-su bears little if any resemblance to Scott Nearing, a peace-activist and an author of a book that he is reading: *The Making of a Radical*. Instead, he has begun his transformation into a monster, a process of 'becoming' articulated by Gilles Deleuze and Felix Guattari when they write of 'the sense in which becoming is the process of desire' (Deleuze and Guattari 2000: 272). Kyŏng-su is not only a becoming-animal, he is also a becoming-Sŏng-u (he repeats the swaying movement when drunk and he sleeps with Sŏng-u's girl), a becoming-child, and not least a becoming-impotent when heavy drinking finally catches up with him. He is transforming, but only insofar as the plane of life on which he is traversing remains fundamentally unchanged. Every moment experienced in the past is reflected through the glass of the present, multiply overlaying the actual subject who is haunted by the phantom of his memory.

Turning Gate's theme of 'eternal recurrence' is realised through the use of 'repetition' as its central motif. Almost every event, critical dialogue and situation are repeated in the film, and every repetition constitutes a degree of difference. For instance, the phrase 'I love you' is a verbal utterance that crucially underpins the central irony of the film, and is therefore repeated several times.[2] It is first demanded by Myŏng-suk, and Kyŏng-su's unwillingness to say it ends up humiliating her. His stubborn insistence that 'love' is an awkward word to him is conveniently forgotten when he courts Sŏn-yŏng. He confesses to her his love on their first date during a sexual encounter that is visually explicit. The word 'love' is an inscription, a sign capable of anything but its real meaning. But what is – to borrow a Deleuze-ian term – the 'thing-ness of the sign' in *Turning Gate*? For instance, is there an essence of the image of Myŏng-suk in the photo she offers to Kyŏng-su? What about the tattered poster pinned up in the barbecue restaurant? The uncountable empty bottles of *soju* that are always there on the dinner table? The persimmon falling from the tree in Kyŏngju? The naked bodies of a man and a woman 'making love' without love in a private hotel room? And the ubiquitous duck-boats wherever there is a patch of water? By refusing to endow such objects with sentimental power, the film causes them to emerge as sites of melancholia and of difference. Difference is not something that is empirically produced between two different objects, but rather that which exists between the same objects or the recurring use of the same objects. To the question of whether there should not be some meaning that is attached to these recurrent signs, Hong Sang-su responds that they simply reproduce a praxis of everyday life, a substance that is material to his work of art.

All of these repetitions take place in a kind of double articulation of past and present that has been integral to the temporal rhythms of Hong Sang-su's films. If, however, earlier films such as *Virgin Stripped Bare By Her Bachelors (O! Sujŏng*, 2000) had tangled time by restaging the same event twice, *Turning Gate* brings Hong Sang-su's previous experimentation with time, that almost always forks into two different paths, to a halt. *Turning Gate*'s time remains linear but it constantly interweaves the past and also the future into the present. Repetition also plays a critical role. Equally interrogating is the Truth when repetition and memory contest the veracity of what really has taken place. For instance, when Sŏn-yŏng and Kyŏng-su engage in pillow-talk, Kyŏng-su confesses to Sŏn-yŏng that he had witnessed her husband dating another woman. His remembrance of the husband and the questioning of his moral integrity – despite the protest that he draws from Sŏn-yŏng – are only possible because Kyŏng-su has accidentally met with Sŏn-yŏng's husband twice before in the film: the first time in Ch'unch'ŏn, when his duck-boat bumps into another in which a stranger – accompanied by a woman – asks for a light; and the second time in Kyŏngju, when Kyŏng-su is loitering in front of Sŏn-yŏng's house and the same stranger walks up and is revealed as Sŏn-yŏng's husband. (Kyŏng-su hurriedly walks away to avoid confronting the husband, leaving a floating question, 'Can you speak English?'). But, like the viewers who have forgotten whether the stranger in the boat and Sŏn-yŏng's husband are, indeed, the same person (Hong Sang-su has deliberately cast a non-professional actor to play the role of the husband), Kyŏng-su's memory is unreliable. 'Perhaps I was mistaken,' he mentions before cynically adding that, 'all Koreans look alike.' Is it only in the area of physical appearances that Koreans are alike? What about other qualities, such as behaviour? Could this statement be reconstrued to imply that the gap between one Korean (the husband) and another (Kyŏng-su) is also indiscernible? Along with the question, 'was it really Sŏn-yŏng's husband out there in the boat?' the answers to all of these questions are left in abeyance.

Though *Turning Gate* raises the idea of a legend or a myth that directly refers to the exterior conditions that circumscribe the fate of its protagonist, the myth serves not to facilitate the transcendent meaning of life, it simply derives an objective social condition that suffocates any form of idealism and desire. Kyŏng-su's relentless pursuit of Sŏn-yŏng leaves the two in a state of limbo. To help her choose between the two alternatives, they visit a female fortune-teller. The fortune-teller draws a verdict like a blind prophet at the climax of a Greek tragedy, compelling Sŏn-yŏng finally to choose her husband over Kyŏng-su. The fortune-teller is a female *mudang* (a shaman who communicates with the local spirits) who is incisive in her decision in a situation in which there is no clear line between what is right and what is wrong. Kyŏng-su is 'truly' in love to the extent that he declares there is 'nothing else that I would want in a woman'. But it is unethical for him to love a woman who has a family with another man. The *mudang*'s analysis is simply too cruel for him. She finds Kyŏng-su's future to be cursed with vacuity, wandering and physical danger, while Sŏn-yŏng's husband enjoys a fate that will be filled with prospects of career advancement, wealth, and popular respect. It is intriguing that the *mudang*'s 'verdict' about the *present* is reached through her clairvoyance of the *future* after analysing the *past* – that is, the birthdays of Kyŏng-su, Sŏn-yŏng and Sŏn-yŏng's husband (who, of course, is absent during the fortune-telling session). Time again jumbles between present, past and future. Ironically, the supernatural and the pre-modern must be invoked in order to resolve a conflict between the ideal (love) and the practical (marriage) at a time when no other productive mechanism can be found to arrive at a decision. The powers of the supernatural, of clairvoyance and of the future nail down the coffin in which rests the ideal love aspired to by Kyŏng-su.

Though Kyŏng-su's ego is bruised, and his quest for the meaning of life can never succeed, his failure gives us a glimpse of what Georg Lukacs, according to Fredric Jameson, once pointed out as 'the most basic image of human freedom' – 'the *momentary* reconciliation of matter and spirit toward which a hero strives in vain' (Jameson 1971: 173. My emphasis). Kyŏng-su's obsession and stubbornness have at least *temporarily* made him a hero who will strive for the unity of transcendental ideals and a pragmatic life, despite the probability that he will fail miserably in its pursuit. In the process, he will have fallen short of 'becoming-human', a project that was cursed from the beginning and acknowledged as unrealisable. By portraying a man who has been thoroughly humiliated, however, the film succeeds in reverberating with the redemptive message that life still needs to be lived – even when its meaning remains undiscovered. After all, disappointment produces a pivotal moment in any given quest. 'It is difficult to be human, but let's try not to become monsters', pleads Kyŏng-su several times throughout the film. This repeated plea, which is just as well directed at him as at others, is at once comic and a critique. *Turning Gate* thus realises a theme that is extremely rare in stories today and almost extinct in contemporary films: that of a hero who achieves meaning only in opposition to his context and who is hurt when he seeks integration, whether into a society or into true romance. By portraying this awkwardness, Hong Sang-su draws out a story of human experience in which will and truth, however futile, are worth striving for.

REFERENCES

Deleuze, Gilles (1995) *Cinema 2: The Time-Image*, Minneapolis: University of Minnesota Press.
Deleuze, Gilles and Guattari, Felix (2000) *A Thousand Plateaus: Capitalism and Schizophrenia*, Minneapolis, University of Minnesota Press.

Jameson, Fredric (1971) *Marxism and Form: Twentieth-Century Dialectical Theories of Literature*, Princeton: Princeton University Press.

Kim, Kyung Hyun (2004) *The Remasculinization of Korean Cinema*, Durham, NC and London: Duke University Press.

Kim Sǔng-ok (1993) 'Seoul: 1964, Winter', in Marshall R. Pihl and Bruce and Ju-Chan Fulton (trans. and eds), *Land of Exile: Contemporary Korean Fiction*, Armonk, New York: M. E. Sharpe: 84–101.

NOTES

1. He has since then made *The Power of Kangwon Province* (*Kangwǒndoǔi him*, 1998), *Virgin Stripped Bare By Her Bachelors* (*O! Sujǒng*, 2000), *Turning Gate* (*Saenghwalǔi palgyǒn*, 2002) and *Woman is Man's Future* (*Yǒjanǔn namja-ǔi miraeda*, 2004).

2. See my chapter, 'Too Early/Too Late: Temporality and Repetition in Hong Sang-su's Films' (Kim 2004: 203–30). In it, I argue how the utterance of 'I love you' in Hong's films is often a signifier that is devoid of its meaning.

13. *MEMENTO MORI* AND OTHER GHOSTLY SEXUALITIES

Andrew Grossman and Jooran Lee

In an English-language anthology dedicated to the 'new' South Korean cinema, where issues of Western cultural imperialism and neo-colonialism will inevitably raise their heads, we encounter special difficulties as we address themes of alternative sexuality. Even if basic civil rights ideology derived from much-dreaded 'Western cultural imperialism' has recently swollen the ranks of Seoul's gay-pride '*Mujigae* Parade',[1] South Korea has yet widely to disseminate queerly contentious media, let alone foster something like a Westernised queer film movement. Therefore, when we consider Korea's few extant queer films, we are caught between condescendingly excusing the absence of a progressive queer theory in Korea, and engaging transnational or universalised readings that, with equal condescension, pretend Korean homosexual identities are not historically particular. But Korean sexual culture diverges not only from Western sexuality, but also from other East Asian sexualities.

While, in China, the records of the Han Dynasty glorified male homosexuality among the aristocracy, and while Japanese literature, from Murasaki Shikibu's *The Tale of Genji* to Saikaku's *Life of a Sensuous Man*, has traditionally included bisexuality as a regular facet of upper-class hedonism, Korea has no classical or canonised literature of same-sex love. True, it is well known that, in the Silla Kingdom (57 BC–AD 935), the Hwarang,[2] a military troop of handsome, aristocratic youths, made homosexual love (and occasional transvestism) a part of their martial ethos, and that, during the Koryŏ Dynasty (935–1392), homosexuality was tolerated among aristocrats and Buddhist monks. The rise of imported Neo-Confucianism during the Chosŏn Dynasty (1392–1910), however, actively repressed the liberal tendencies of Koryŏ Dynasty Buddhism, established heterosexist kinship as a state norm and effectively made homosexuality invisible, ghostly. It is perhaps no accident, then, that the two queer films we examine in this chapter, Kim T'ae-yǒng and Min Kyu-dong's *Memento Mori* (*Yǒgogoedam dubǒntchae iyagi*, 1999) and Kim Dae-sǔng's *A Bunjee Jump of their Own* (*Bǒnjijǒmp'ǔrǔl hada*, 2001),[3] fixate upon ghostly absences and presences. They also employ themes of sexual haunting and recovered identity to advance boldly – if confusedly – unearthly, immaterial and arguably post-modern queer sensibilities whose imaginary sexualities become *de facto* identity politics in a Korea where sexual identity remains strictly regulated.

Contemporary Western gay and lesbian politics have been structured around two revolutions: the civil identity politics that followed the 1969 Stonewall riots, and the post-modern queer theory that rejects all essentialist and binary identities – sexual or otherwise – to strike better at the heteronormative heart of late capitalist hegemony. In modern Korea, however, Neo-Confucian kinship structures became so embedded in both nationalist identity and the mass unconscious that anti-gay legislation and debates about homosexuality were historically deemed unnecessary. Therefore, queer Koreans lacked easy targets to oppose or prohibitive laws negatively to identify themselves against. Seo Dong-jin (Sǒ Dong-jin), one of Korea's foremost gay intellectuals, suggests queer Koreans have been at a loss to define themselves (either in terms of essentialist gay identity or post-modern queerness) precisely because alternative sexualities have been absent from the popular Korean consciousness: 'Homosexuality . . . seems to be an entity whose meaning has been endlessly deferred . . . "homosexuality" is a term without its own referent' (Seo 2001: 66). In 1994 and 1995, however, small but vocal gay and lesbian student groups at Yonsei (Yǒnse) University and Seoul National University began attracting media attention. Moreover, internet bulletin boards began affording queer Koreans secure, anonymous spaces in which to connect with one another and with queer political movements in the West. Soon, young, middle-class gay Koreans began politicising their identities, indignantly calling themselves *iban*, or 'second-class' citizens, as opposed to *ilban*, or the 'universal' or 'dominant' class of heterosexuals (ibid.: 69). Partly at the behest of Korea's vociferously anti-gay Protestant community, government reactionaries quickly enacted many homophobic policies. These included a 1997 Youth Protection Act describing homosexuality as 'harmful to youth', and a preposterous 2001 Ministry of Information and Communications ban on youth access to even non-pornographic gay websites.[4]

Korean gay activism has been steadily gaining ground, however. The Youth Protection Act's anti-gay language was revised, the internet ban was repealed in April 2003, and sex-and-gender issues are finally being aired in Korean cinema. Kim Yu-min's graphically sexual *Yellow Hair* (*Norang mǒri*, 1999) has been hailed by Korean critics for its feminist politics, and his *Yellow Hair 2* (*Norang mǒri 2*, 2001) has notably focused on transgender issues. Meanwhile, director Kim In-shik has advanced his *Road Movie* (*Rodǔ mubi*, 2002) as Korea's first realistic foray into explicitly gay sexuality, though he easily overlooks *Broken Branches* (*Naeillo hǔrǔnǔn kang*, 1995), Pak Chae-ho's optimistic, landmark treatment of an inter-generational gay Korean romance.[5] Equally notable is director Lee Hong See-il, who has recently become Korea's first 'out' film-maker with his gay-themed shorts *Always Like Sunday* (*Ŏnjena iryoil ch'ŏrŏm*, 1998), the award-winning *Sugar Hill* (*Shyugŏ hil*, 2000) and *Macho Hunter* (*Mach'o sanyangkkun*, 2002). Yet, if *Road Movie* and Lee's shorts broach the material, social spaces of queer visibility, the marginality of queer themes in Korean cinema then shifts from an understanding framed in terms of space to one of linear, hierarchically ordered time. That is, as English-language scholarship on Korean cinema is still in its early stages, we accept implicitly that queer themes should, and will, be temporarily, if politely, shunted aside – after all, these remain subordinate concerns conveniently extricable from Korea's post-industrialism, post-modernisation and other, more 'universal' themes. Only *after* we exhaust these obligatory avenues are we permitted to plunge into allegedly more 'personal' and 'self-interested' – but, in fact, altruistic – investigations of alternative sexuality.

Culturally minded queer theory has rightly argued that it is folly even to have these cultural (or 'superstructural') debates without first critiquing the coercive heterosexism that undergirds the post-industrial family and, by extension, all social interactions. If some have yet to adopt, wholesale, queer theory's assertions that sexuality is, as Wilhelm Reich suspected, a liberating and not strictly anatomical force, and that shifting human desire is, to reverse and subvert Darwin's terms, an ultimate rather than proximal goal, queer theorists have their own obscurantist jargon partially to blame. But post-modern jargon aside, in Asian film studies the discussion of sexuality as a controllable cultural phenomenon is often subsumed by a merely sociological examination of the effects of gender roles wherein patriarchy, Neo-Confucian or otherwise, is chastised but underlying assumptions about gender remain unquestioned. The resulting cry for liberal gender egalitarianism thus evades the agendas of queer theory and radical feminism which argue that heteronormative men desperately need queer liberation from their own narrow false consciousness. (Straight people are potentially queer, too; they just don't know it.) For example, when Hyangjin Lee (2000: 87) criticises North Korean directors Yu Wŏnjun and Yun Ryonggyu's Marxist version of *The Tale of Chunhyang* (*Ch'unhyangjŏn*, 1980) for its 'total removal of sexuality from its discussion of gender relations', we can do little but blandly consent to a well-intended, uncontroversial sentiment. But if North Korea's Communist film-makers neuter female heterosexual desire with the totalitarian scissors of socialist realism, what kind of totalitarianism is responsible for 'temporally' removing gender from the discussion of sexuality? The queer metaphysics of *Memento Mori* and *Bunjee Jump*, however, transcend both regional politics and the more conservative aspects of Korean film studies, allowing international viewers to imagine how emerging queer identities can operate in any culture that subjugates even feminine heterosexual identity.

As tales of reincarnation that sublimate their homosexual impulses through images of ghostliness, one might presume *Memento Mori* and *Bunjee Jump* follow the puerile Western horror tradition of making homosexuality a ghoulish metaphor for moral decadence while secretly exploiting it so as to explore titillating taboos. Of course, marginalised queer audiences have long appropriated these taboos as liberating identifications, seeing themselves as the subversively queer monster rather than the nobly straight hero commissioned to destroy it. As Harry Benshoff notes, 'the cinematic monster's subjective position is more readily acceded to by a queer viewer – someone who already situates him/herself outside a patriarchal, heterosexist order and the popular culture texts that it produces' (1997: 12). But what happens when the queer monster of a 'popular culture text' is not a freakish fascination, an agent of the antiquated, heterosexist female-to-female fantasies promulgated by Jean Rollin and Hammer Studios, or even a subject of alternating erotic identification and abjection, like the vampiric pederast of Ulli Lommel's odd queer horror film *The Tenderness of Wolves* (West Germany, 1973), but is the heroic, subjective centre, as she is in *Memento Mori*? Additionally, while ghost-story genres safely compartmentalise stunted fears in the secularised West, in East Asia, where ghost genres have a higher literary pedigree, and where notions of fate (and fatalism) have not yet been fully supplanted by rationalism, empiricism, neo-pragmatism, existentialism or nihilism, portraying erotic desire in supernatural forms remains a method of intensifying eros rather than of stigmatising it.

Memento Mori – originally titled *Yŏgogoedam 2* to pose commercially as a sequel to Pak Ki-hyŏng's more conventional 1998 horror film *Whispering Corridors* (*Yŏgogoedam*)[6] – is basically a romantic, queer ghost story for

Figure 23 A queer ghost story for adolescents: *Memento Mori* (1999).

adolescents. While its intense lesbian themes alone would merit an 'R' (Restricted) rating in an increasingly reactionary and paranoid United States, remarkably, the film secured from illiberal Korean censors the '12' certificate its producers wanted. Although the directors voluntarily snipped a homo-erotic bathing scene from the shooting script, this apparently liberal censorship ruling may more directly result from a simultaneous backlash over the banning of Jang Sun-woo's much-hyped, sado-masochistic *Lies (Gŏjinmal,* 2000), and thus does not necessarily reflect a public acceptance of homosexuality. Indeed, a recent sociological survey of Korean social-work students found that they are about twice as likely to be homophobic as their American counterparts (Lim and Johnson 2001). Regardless, through the ironic contingencies of both market-place demographics and censorship, *Memento Mori* emerges as a unique example of a queerly centred mainstream film aimed squarely at an adolescent (female) audience. This, in a sense, makes *Memento Mori* more progressive than 'unrated', independently produced American films, such as Todd Solondz's *Storytelling* (2001) and Michael Cuesta's *L.I.E.* (2001), which cynically frame teenage homosexuality in terms of anxious film-festival hipness, and reject as naïve the very prospect of an elegant, fantastically sincere queer love for adolescent delectation.

Memento Mori opens with a dream image of its two heroines, the jealous, suicidal Hyo-shin and the moody, impish Shi-ŭn, sinking to the bottom of a swimming pool – when Hyo-shin alone drowns, we fear martyrdom lies in her future. In an all-girls' school, where teachers are predatory neurotics and parents are non-existent, Hyo-shin and Shi-ŭn find solace in each other, an elaborately iconic picture-diary that memorialises their love, and, most curiously, a sexually charged telepathy that puts them specially in tune with one another. Their dialogues, too, bespeak emotional supplementation and symmetry: Hyo-shin asks, 'Look into my eyes', to which Shi-ŭn replies, 'I can only see myself'. Elsewhere, Hyo-shin says to the half-deaf Shi-ŭn, 'You have a bad ear and I keep hearing things . . . in fact, I heard a bell going off when I saw you for the first time'. When discordantly cutting the wires of the piano she mournfully plays, Hyo-shin philosophises, 'All people have their own tune . . . it can become a harmony or a dissonance . . . together we could make the perfect harmony'. They secretly tryst on roof-tops, at invisible yet ecstatically swirling heights, and the romantic but spectral images of their love captured by a purloined video-camera at once foreshadow the ghostly rampage to come and remove that love to an other-worldliness impotent to effect political, material change. Analogously, the projected images of *Memento Mori* itself may futilely struggle to normalise queerness in a still-homophobic Korea.

When Shi-ŭn is seduced (and possibly impregnated) by a handsome, predatory teacher, she assures Hyo-shin she will remain faithful to her. Nevertheless, Shi-ŭn is unprepared to make their lesbianism public, and regrets Hyo-shin passionately kissing her, bloody lipped from a homophobic teacher's slap, in the midst of a stunned classroom. 'You mean nothing to me – I'm ashamed of you,' sobs Shi-ŭn, prompting Hyo-shin suddenly to use the roof-top's height to free herself fatally from a life of unrequited lesbian love. When a third, rather awkward girl, Min-a, discovers Shi-ŭn and Hyo-shin's mock-religious, now discarded diary, she becomes intrigued by the girls' doomed lesbian connection, and the film refocuses on her journey of sexual self-discovery. Soon, Min-a gradually becomes possessed by Hyo-shin's restless, vengefully 'dissonant' ghost, who haunts the school's homophobic students in a climax reminiscent of Brian De Palma's *Carrie* (US, 1976). Hyo-shin's spirit revisits the abusive teacher to whisper deathly charms in his ear, maddening him until he slashes his wrists, her suicidal tendencies now properly transferred to one more deserving of them. In the film's coda, Hyo-shin's spirit has fully possessed Min-a, who confesses to Shi-ŭn, 'I lost your diary,' to which Shi-ŭn responds, ' . . . it's OK, we can always write a new one.' Just as the titular '*memento mori*' (a medieval conjuration of the plague-ridden dead) recalls to the eternal present unjustly condemned souls, Min-a will now embody and vindicate Hyo-shin's restless lesbian spirit in what will presumably be a cycle of eternal queer return.

At first, *Memento Mori* seemingly offers a quick solution to the evil, easily vanquished queer monsters Benshoff catalogues. *Memento Mori*'s sympathetic queer ghost leaves in her wake a beatified, transcendental queerness, and her generic terror, rather than symbolising the homophobia of a heterosexual filmmaker and his adolescent audience, is refreshingly redirected at homophobic characters in the film proper. *Memento Mori* thus emerges as the most significant Korean lesbian film since Kim Su-hyŏng's *Ascetic: Woman and Woman* (*Gŭmyok: yŏjawa yŏja*, 1976), an intense story of female bonding that queer Korean audiences now recognise as Korea's first lesbian-feminist film (Jooran Lee 2000). Our interview with *Memento Mori*'s directors, however, summoned new complications.[7] Kim T'ae-yŏng conceives of *Memento Mori*'s lesbianism not only as a welcome twist on the familiar ghost story he and co-director Min Kyu-dong were offered,[8] but as a parable of psychosexual development: 'As the *Bildungsroman* signifies the process by which one enters society, the progression from homosexuality to heterosexuality becomes a vital series of codes for adolescents . . . that reflect the inner struggle of the individual.' But the film's heroines give no indication of 'progressing' towards heterosexuality; on the contrary, the film's denouement suggests the mystical lesbian connection between Shi-ŭn and Min-a will continue beyond their teenage years and outside the homosocial spaces of their typical all-girls' high school. To a Westerner weaned on Freud, director Kim's comment might suggest that the heroines' homosexuality – or failure to progress into heterosexuality – can be understood in the Freudian terms of an arrested latent stage, where the same-sex attractions common among prepubescent youths are unnaturally continued beyond puberty. But Kim's rationale may also reflect the lingering influence of Neo-Confucianism, in which the continuing segregation of the sexes normalises homosocial bodily contact (girlfriends holding hands, young male friends draping their arms around each other's shoulders) that, in the West, would be viewed as deviant or suspicious. Therefore, if *Memento Mori*'s directors hesitantly – and somewhat unconvincingly – characterise the film's female love as more of a developmental 'stage' than authentic homosexuality, it may only be an extension of the Neo-Confucian belief that 'the natural place for deep and satisfying interpersonal relationships' is in voluntary same-sex bonding (Sohng and Icard 1996: 120), rather than the obligatory marital partnerships that inevitably lie in Korean girls' futures.

Regardless, the homosexual confusion that Kim T'ae-yŏng calls the 'inner struggle of the individual' is textually solved by exteriorising Hyo-shin's cosmic, saintly queerness and relocating it within Min-a's material body. Director Kim reiterates ideas of Freudian sublimation, however, when he explains what fears Hyo-shin's generically determined (yet queer) ghost represents: 'The fear of otherness. For example, South Korean society fears [North Korean] communism, but this is really the fear of being called a "communist," not a fear or hatred of communism itself.' But if the post-war label of Communism is the ultimate issue of national Korean otherness, the film's heroic lesbianism is undermined. The 'inner struggle of the individual' thus becomes the 'inner struggle' of a politically divided Korea longing to be reunified as an autonomous, 'individual' nation-state, and the film's lesbianism is metaphorically relegated to an infantile stage in a maturing Korean body still reeling from the polarising effects of civil war.

Director Min Kyu-dong also refuses to politicise the film's eros. 'If one defines it as lesbianism, one has a narrow view of love . . . we would like *Memento Mori* not to be seen as propaganda . . . The most effective way of making a film is making it in the least political way,' he says. While Min's balking at the possibility of being labelled a queer sympathiser – much like being labelled a Communist – is unsurprising in a still virulently homophobic Korea, Hyo-shin and Shi-ŭn's public kissing scene is transparently political and arguably the film's centrepiece. Indeed, Min tellingly confesses, 'When I saw *Memento Mori* in a cinema, I realised it was too political, and that I also had become too political.' He further reveals that he had fought to preserve the kissing scene when it prompted some of those present during the editing process to exclaim, 'Disgusting!' But Min's comment about 'narrowly' reducing the film's eros to lesbianism can also be interpreted in the 'correct' queer sense. Because lesbianism should be no more essentialised than heterosexuality, Shi-ŭn's implied sexual object choice in the film's coda is not represented by Min-a's materially female body *per se*, but the mystical queerness inhabiting it. Still, we may become suspicious when mainstream film-makers, Korean or otherwise, homophilically frame their queer subjects as radically innocuous allegories of liberal bourgeois humanism, much as pro-democracy Hong Kong film-makers did just before 1997.[9]

Whereas *Memento Mori* is a relatively optimistic text muddied by ambiguous authorial intentions, the more benign ghost story of *Bunjee Jump* offers expressly 'gay-positive' politics sabotaged by a climax that essentialises gender even as it disrupts the heterosexual object-choices that normally follow from gender essentialism. The story begins in 1983, as college student In-u bumps into his dream girl, T'ae-hŭi, amid the fateful, heavenly rain imagery that recurs throughout the film. In-u discovers T'ae-hŭi in a figure-sculpting class, where the teacher propounds, 'In reality . . . our bodies are not perfectly symmetrical', only seconds before he is struck by In-u's presence. 'That student's face has perfect symmetry,' he says, recalling the analogous dialogues about subjective 'harmony' in *Memento Mori*, while implicitly deducing that In-u is susceptible to phenomena as 'unreal' as the reincarnation drama about to unfold. But as artistic representations or incarnations of Platonic reality, the clay bodies T'ae-hŭi sculpts can represent her truthful soul no better than the materially gendered body her spirit will inhabit upon her untimely death.

When mountain-climbing, T'ae-hŭi reveals suicidal inclinations ('What will happen if I jump down?') more glibly than Hyo-shin in *Memento Mori*. Visualised from above by a heaven-sent crane shot, she muses, 'I want to go to New Zealand . . . I heard people [bunjee] jump off a cliff there.' Here, New Zealand's occidental otherness echoes Wong Kar-wai's occidentalist view of Argentina's orgasmic Iguassu Falls in *Happy Together* (Hong Kong, 1997), a film, incidentally, that *Memento Mori*'s directors cite as a model non-political gay film. We cut forward to 2000, where In-u now mourns the death of T'ae-hŭi, claimed (we learn at the end) in a bus accident. Now a high-school teacher, In-u explains destiny to his students in terms of infinitesimal probabilities – as infinitesimal, presumably, as T'ae-hŭi being hit by a bus and being reincarnated as In-u's seventeen-year-old male student, Hyŏn-bin. When In-u recites the story of his first romance to his teenage charges, Hyŏn-bin tartly claims love at first sight is falsely based on superficial appearances. Yet Hyŏn-bin's protests augur a special knowledge of the surfaces of love – and gender. In-u gradually becomes obsessed by elfin Hyŏn-bin, especially when drawings spied in Hyŏn-bin's sketch-book oddly remind him that representational art, whether drawn, clay-sculpted (or even filmed?) is just as removed from transcendental truths as are the deceptive appearances of gender. Soon, In-u can conceal his obsession for Hyŏn-bin no more than Hyo-shin could for Shi-ŭn in *Memento Mori*, and homophobic rumours about them circulate. In-u, fraught with sexual confusion, seeks the advice of a doctor who reassures him, 'I would say your curiosity in the same sex should be taken comfortably as a part of human nature', a comment that simply undoes *Memento Mori*'s Freudianism and its directors' digressions into sublimated Communist allegory.

Finally, In-u, overcome with raging infatuation, shouts his conviction that Hyŏn-bin is actually T'ae-hŭi reincarnated: 'T'ae-hŭi, how come you can't even remember me a little?' But, in an alternative series of flashbacks told from Hyŏn-bin's perspective, we discover it was not In-u but Hyŏn-bin who chose to participate in a 'three-legged' race that intimately bound the two at the ankles, and Hyŏn-bin now does, indeed, intuit the nostalgic meaning of a cigarette-lighter s/he once gave In-u. In a race-to-the-railway-station finale trite enough to make D. W. Griffith blush, Hyŏn-bin reunites with In-u just before his departure. But the image Hyŏn-bin reflects in the train's window shows not his biological exterior, but the image of T'ae-hŭi as she was seventeen years earlier. 'Better late than never', deadpans In-u, and the two journey to New Zealand to engage in life-affirming bunjee jumps that permit them rapturously to enjoy feigned deaths without being further inconvenienced by the gender-bending determinisms that real deaths, in this film, apparently entail.

While contemporary American psychiatry has de-pathologised the so-called 'gender inversion' that once marked the fatalistic era of Radclyffe Hall's novel *The Well of Loneliness* (1928), many psychiatrists, even after the 1973 de-pathologising of homosexuality, still describe the healthy, well-socialised gay male as one who conforms to stereotypical masculine behaviours in accordance with a 'Core Gender Identity'. Eve Kosofsky Sedgwick has outlined how these trends – under the phony auspices of gay rights – democratise and denaturalise sexual object choice but covertly renaturalise gender (Sedgwick 1993: 73). Though psychiatrists superficially appeased post-Stonewall civil rights with the 1973 decision, they still insidiously perpetuate the *status quo*, Sedgwick argues, by rewarding men for reproducing personalities that are aggressively masculine, competitive and, by extension, capitalistic. Gay men, who need to prove their masculinity and 'normality', must conform to these gender stereotypes all the more. Inarguably, *Bunjee Jump* is guilty of renaturalising gender when T'ae-hŭi's soulful, 'core' female identity is climactically reflected in the carriage window as clearly as a soulless vampire's image is not. Some queer Korean audiences, and even the directors of *Memento Mori*, have therefore criticised *Bunjee Jump* for foolishly believing homosexuality results from gender misidentification. *Bunjee*, however, innocently romanticises, rather than demonises, the incongruity between interior (natural) gender and exterior (social) sexual object-choice. Furthermore, the film's sunny climax suggests that Hyŏn-bin will be able to experience life better as a man without a masculine core identity than he ever could as a man with one.

Just as *Bunjee Jump*'s plot optimistically reverses common perceptions about core gender identity, so does T'ae-hŭi subvert the traditional idea of Buddhistic reincarnation by actively reclaiming and recontextualising his former feminine identity, rather than blindly accepting the male identity into which fate delivers him. But, if the gender essentialism nevertheless lurking beneath *Bunjee*'s homophilic skin reflects the unintended double-meaning of the English word 'homophobia' – literally a fear of sameness, but figuratively a fear of otherness – it is largely a function of the very subject–object duality both *Memento* and *Bunjee* attempt to challenge metaphysically. It is true, however, that neither film's metaphysics go far enough in this regard. Hypothetically speaking, had Hyo-shin's vengeful ghost in *Memento Mori* possessed the predatory male teacher's body and then used it to intermediate a transitively lesbian, but materially heterosexual, love with Shi-ŭn, we would have not a multi-faceted queerness but merely a lesbianism as essentialised as T'ae-hŭi and In-u's basically heterosexual odyssey in *Bunjee Jump*. But, had Hyo-shin possessed Shi-ŭn's body rather than

Figure 24 A heterosexual odyssey . . . or what? *A Bunjee Jump of their Own* (2001).

Min-a's in *Memento Mori*, subject and object would have been miraculously unified in a single body more truly 'harmonious' than any of the subject–object splits either film actually offers.

Memento Mori's obscure metaphysics may allow its directors to make films in the 'least political way' (to use Kim T'ae-yŏng's phrase) but *Bunjee Jump*, filled with unfortunately banal depictions of high-school homophobia, is clearly attempting to exist in the most political way. Nevertheless, because both films are fascinated with how erotic bodies can be represented by, and mediated through, video-cameras (in *Memento Mori*) and sculpture (in *Bunjee Jump*), they prompt us to question further how representations of queer love can be legitimised in a mainstream cinema as homophobic as Korea's. *Memento Mori*'s 'telepathic lesbianism', somewhat unsatisfactorily represented in the film through voice-overs, has the singular luxury of currying erotic sensibilities not only irrational but unrepresentable, and thus beyond politics. *Bunjee*, however, more clearly addresses how unconventional sexualities can – and cannot – be represented by cuing major tonal shifts in its narrative. Specifically, early scenes of T'ae-hŭi and In-u's confidently heterosexual romance, replete with awkward first meetings and schmaltzy sunset dances, and the romantically scored climax where the two belatedly reunite, tonally clash against In-u's dark, anxious mad scenes in the middle of the film, where he doubts his heterosexuality. Though it is debatable whether these hackneyed sunset scenes are really intended to parody heterosexual romance, they do call into question how deviant sexual desires can be represented in a commercial film culture so rigid and narrow that heterosexuality itself has become little more than the mobilisation of generic cues, such as sunset dances and romantically inflated, hack soundtracks. Because the traditional formula has sublimated this problem of representation by childishly positing a binary of heroically heterosexual sunsets (text) pitted against ghostly homosexual shadows (sub-text), when *Bunjee* cues In-u and Hyŏn-bin's climactic expression of love with the romantic music generally reserved for heterosexual romance, it can be seen as a subversive or even optimistic gesture. *Memento Mori*'s non-political ambitions and allegorical deflections, however, offer no such gestures. Given that even a film as unapologetically commercial as *Shiri* (*Swiri*, 1999) trades in South Korea's fears of Communism and wishful dreams of national reunification, it is ironic that the less-commercial *Memento Mori* should rationalise its problem of erotic representation by placing fairly mundane Communist fears in a ghostly sub-text, whereas less socially expressible fears about homosexuality rest in heroic text. For director Kim T'ae-yŏng, who bitterly muses that 'East Asia itself could be a subculture of America', such ironies may be the inevitable result of rejecting 'out' Western identity politics.

If these films' transmigrating queer identities ultimately question how unconventional sexuality can be represented in conventional media, and prompt us to think about sexuality in pure, abstract terms, we still must ask pragmatically whether the noun 'sexuality' can exist unmodified by descriptive prefixes such as hetero-, homo-, bi-, or trans-. Though framed here in the obligatory terms of post-modernism, this debate is no different from the idealistic quarrel of Plato's *Gorgias*, wherein Socrates doubts philistine Callicles' claim that pleasure, as a categorical noun, can exist in the abstract, apart from specific or descriptive human experience. In our discussion here, we have connected the spiritual, anti-materialistic queer ghosts of *Memento Mori* and *Bunjee Jump* to the anti-materialistic, anti-biological tendencies of Western queer theory to investigate how the material existence of gender might be cleverly overcome in arch-conservative mainstream cinema. Though we may be disappointed that *Bunjee Jump* unwittingly reduces queerness to essentialised gender role-playing, and that *Memento Mori* fails to disrupt subject–object distinctions as radically as it might have, both films, neither oppositional enough to qualify as *passé* modernism nor Utopian enough to pass as politically correct post-modernism, resist easy categorisation. Drifting somewhere 'in between', these films ultimately force us to consider a neo-pragmatic viewpoint, where short-term, modernist identity politics and long-term, post-modernist, post-identity politics become only tools in which their relative values depend on the historical contexts in which they are currently deployed. In the political context of Korean cinema, we might place ourselves in the minds of Korean queer audiences, who will not be likely to perceive these films as Freudian parables, sublimated fears of Communism or even mixed-up, perhaps unintentional parodies of gender essentialism but, paradoxically, as metaphysical films of which their own material, public existence *as films* becomes incipiently political in a culture where gay identity politics and post-modern fancy remain largely unavailable.

REFERENCES

Benshoff, Harry M. (1997) *Monsters in the Closet: Homosexuality and the Horror Film*, Manchester and New York: St Martin's Press.

Gatto, Robin and Polinacci, Yanis (2001) 'Interview with *Memento Mori* Director'. 2 February. Online. www.filmfestivals.com/rotterdam/2001/interviews/shtml.

Lee, Hyangjin (2000) *Contemporary Korean Cinema: Identity, Culture and Politics*, Manchester: Manchester University Press.

Lee, Jooran (2000) 'Remembered Branches: Towards a Future of Korean Homosexual Film', in Andrew Grossman (ed.), *Queer Asian Cinema: Shadows in the Shade*, Binghamton: Harrington Park Press: 273–81.

Lim, Hyun Sung and Johnson, Miriam McNown (2001) 'Korean Social Work Students' Attitudes Toward Homosexuals', *Journal of Social Work Education*, 37, 3: 545–54.

Sedgwick, Eve Kosofsky (1993) 'How to Bring Your Kids Up Gay', in Michael Warner (ed.), *Fear of a Queer Planet*, Minneapolis: University of Minnesota Press: 69–81.

Seo, Dong-Jin (2001) 'Mapping the Vicissitudes of Homosexual Identities in South Korea', *Journal of Homosexuality*, 40, 3–4: 65–79. Trans. Mark Mueller.

Sohng, Sue and Icard, Larry D. (1996) 'A Korean Gay Man in the United States: Toward a Cultural Context for Social Service Practice', *Journal of Gay and Lesbian Social Services*, 5, 2/3: 115–37.

NOTES

1. *Mujigae* is Korean for 'rainbow'. The parade was inaugurated in 2000.
2. The *Hwarang* was a sixth-century military society highly influential in the development of Korean martial arts. *Hwarang* literally means 'flowering manhood', and is commonly translated as 'flower knights'. Translators who refer to the *Hwarang*'s homosexual tendencies, however, often use the effeminised rendering 'flower boys'.
3. The film's credit sequence carries the mistranslated, yet commonly used, English title *Bunjee Jumping of Their Own*.

4. For further information on queer Korean life, see the bilingual website for Korea's foremost gay rights organisation, *Ch'in'gusai* ('Between Friends'), at www.chingusai.net.

5. Other relevant films include the transvestite-themed *The Man With Breasts* (*Gasŭmdallin namja*, 1993), the transgender-themed *A Hot Roof* (*Gaegat'ŭn nalŭi ohu*, 1995), *My Boss My Hero* (*Dusabuilch'ae*, 2001), the lesbian-themed *Romance Guy* (*Yŏnei sosŏl*, 2002), and *Hera Purple* (2001), which features an openly gay actor in a gay role.

6. *Whispering Corridors* (also set in a girls' school) indicts Korea's oppressive educational system, and thus South Korean modes of capitalistic socialisation. It contains no queer themes.

7. All comments and quotations from directors Kim T'ae-yŏng and Min Kyu-dong are taken from our August 2002 interview, conducted in Korean and translated by Jooran Lee, with emendations by Andrew Grossman.

8. Min Kyu-dong also cites his own lesbian-themed short film, *Her Story* (1995), as an inspiration for *Memento Mori*. (See Gatto and Polinacci 2001)

9. For example, Shu Kei's *Hu-du-Men* (1996) and *A Queer Story* (1997) exploit queerness as a universalising allegory for democratic freedoms in the face of impending Chinese Communism.

14. INTERETHNIC ROMANCE AND POLITICAL RECONCILIATION IN *ASAKO IN RUBY SHOES*

Hye Seung Chung and David Scott Diffrient

'Home' has become such a scattered, damaged, various concept in our present travails. There is so much to yearn for. There are so few rainbows any more. How hard can we expect even a pair of magic shoes to work? They promised to take us *home*, but are metaphors of homeliness comprehensible to them? (Salman Rushdie, 'At the Auction of the Ruby Slippers')[1]

The above words – drawn from Salman Rushdie's short story about the famous footwear worn by Judy Garland in *The Wizard of Oz* (US, 1939) – find the author in a reflective mood. No stranger to the kind of emotional upheaval and cultural displacement literally 'weathered' by Dorothy in her picaresque rite of passage from sepia-toned Kansas to kaleidoscopic Oz, Rushdie slips from reverie to rhetorical yearning, and evokes – in his description of a 'scattered' and 'damaged' home – a sentiment that has become increasingly salient in South Korean cinema. It should come as no surprise that this Holy Grail of movie memorabilia, this fetishised pair of magic slippers which first enticed the exiled writer as a young boy in Bombay, emblematically figures in a millennial film that similarly revolves around departure and return, migration and habitation. As suggested by its English-language title, *Asako in Ruby Shoes* (*Sunaebo*, 2000) is a 'hymn . . . to Elsewhere', one that plunders the iconography of a Hollywood classic so as to reformulate such perennial themes as alienation, desire and boredom in the context of another geospatial imaginary. Like *The Wizard of Oz*, *Asako in Ruby Shoes* is a film 'about the joys of going away, of leaving the grayness and entering the color, of making new life in the "place where there isn't any trouble"'.[2] Whether adorning the feet of a troubled teen or perched atop an auction block, the glittering slippers offer something seductive to city dwellers and country folk alike: the promise of adventure, the possibility of escape. But, unlike so many other symbols of mobility, they ensure the countervailing comfort of return. It is this tension between escape and return, superimposed on the broader dichotomy of Self and Other, that gives *Asako in Ruby Shoes* its emotional potency. Alongside other films sensitive to ethnic and racial 'otherness', *Asako in Ruby Shoes* lifts the epistemological anchorage that has long subtended conventional wisdom regarding Korean and Japanese identity.

Promoted as the first co-produced project undertaken by Korean and Japanese companies (respectively, upstart Koo & Film supplied 60 per cent of the funding while powerhouse Shochiku added the remaining 40 per cent), this unusual 'Good Neighbor' collaboration heralds a new chapter in the ongoing redefinition of East Asian relations, suggesting that positive cultural exchange between the two nations is taking place. Written and directed by E. J-yong (Yi Chae-yong), *Asako in Ruby Shoes* is as unconventional as the film-maker's acronymic *nom de plume*, subtly allegorising the political reconciliation between these eventual World Cup co-hosts in an interwoven and chronotopically fragmented fashion. Moreover, its story – concerning the belated romance of an ineffectual civil servant living in Seoul and a Japanese student who becomes 'Asako' in Tokyo's commodified world of cyberporn – poses a critical intervention in South Korean cinema's traditional approach to gender politics. Yet, by situating idealised images of Japanese femininity in spaces once occupied by Korean women, the film reflects yet another emergent trend – one that evidences not only the increased recognition of racial and ethnic minorities in a largely homogeneous society but also male anxieties amplified in the wake of the 1997 IMF (International Monetary Fund) crisis.

There's No Home-like Place: Departure, Diaspora and the International Date-line

Asako in Ruby Shoes tracks the lives of two lonely individuals who – though separated by physical distance and cultural barriers – share a sense of disenchantment with their immediate surroundings. Korean heart-throb, Yi Chŏng-jae, and Japanese television actress, Misato Tachibana, star as U-in and Aya respectively, the two main characters in this wistful, yet astringent, antimelodrama. Leaping from Tokyo to Seoul in the blink of an eye, from the crisp, clean lines and geometric symmetry of the middle-class Japanese household to the cluttered and abject-laden spaces of the Korean sequences, *Asako in Ruby Shoes* betrays a savvy awareness of borders, their permeability as well as their figurative relation to alterity. Although Aya's voice-over accompanies the luminous prologue of the film (an Alaskan snowscape that will return at the end), we are first introduced to U-in, a government employee who toils at a municipal office by day and downloads Internet porn in his empty apartment by night. A loner, whose gossiping co-workers are no friends and whose family is only distantly evoked through his intrusive, off-screen mother's phone calls and his brother-in-law's sudden appearance, this blank-faced public servant remains intensely private throughout, masking his motivations behind layers of accrued neuroses. U-in's daily tasks (telling people when to put out their rubbish, distributing tax notices and electricity bills, etc.) – though central to the maintenance of civic order – appear to be of little consequence, and underscore the tedium, repetition and banality of his lacklustre existence.

The deadening weight of his work no doubt hits a nerve with Korean audience members, many of whom are similarly drained office drones whose only sources of amusement are PC games, Solitaire and practical jokes to while away the hours. So bored are U-in's office-bound colleagues that the appearance of rain sends them flocking to the windows – brief respite from their menial tasks. In another early scene, a co-worker unwittingly staples U-in's finger to a wall. This motif returns in a later scene, when the desensitised protagonist fails to notice his bleeding little finger which is caught in a hotel window. Initially oblivious to his bloody digit, U-in's delayed reaction may simply be a sign of psychosomatic numbness, but it also connotes his resignation to being 'stapled in place'. Even at his comparatively comfortable home, he seems transfixed by the hypnotic glow of the computer screen. U-in is literally stuck in a groove, and his lack of physical mobility underscores social as well as emotional paralysis.

U-in's sexual frustrations are exacerbated by his failure to attract the attention of a young woman named Mi-a whom he surreptitiously spies on with

Figure 25 Mi-a, the spitting image of indifference, holds two eggs in a cooking class, self-reflexively showcasing her non-conformist sexuality as well as the film's double narrative structure: *Asako in Ruby Shoes* (2000). Courtesy of the Korean Film Archive

digicam in hand. A rebel without a pause, this red-haired object of U-in's misplaced affections breaks many of the conventions of Korean femininity. Interestingly, U-in first sees Mi-a when he happens upon a cooking class being taught in a building adjoining his office. Mi-a, the teacher's assistant, nonchalantly holds two eggs for the class to see. This image of the two eggs, besides illustrating her disinterest in traditional forms of female domesticity, connotes the double structure of the film which is equally divided between U-in's story and that of Aya (both characters, in a sense, have yet to 'grow wings' and fly away from their respective nests). Besides the eggs, there are several other instances that evoke the film's double structure, most notably a scene in which U-in takes photographs of a pair of Chinese–Korean twins. The twins, who are visually echoed by a pair of younger twins in Japan, additionally prepare us for the mirroring image of Mi-a and Aya's Asako – two redheads for whom U-in has made identity cards.

Significantly, it is in his capacity as a government worker that U-in gains knowledge about Mi-a, who claims to have lost her residence ID card. After he takes her fingerprint, creates her picture ID and learns her name ('Mi-a' is a Sino-Korean pun, meaning 'lost child'), U-in has all the necessary data to begin piecing together his ideal virtual partner online. Procuring a credit card for the sole purpose of gaining access to a 'Members Only' porn site, he designs the perfect cyber-girl – 'Asako in Ruby Shoes' – using Mi-a's age, astrological sign and physical traits as a template. We soon learn that his Frankensteinian creation, Asako, is played by Aya, who ultimately replaces Mi-a as an object of U-in's affections once he spots the Korean woman with her lesbian lover at a grunge club. The film subtly re-frames Mi-a's tomboyish demeanour within a queer lens, and suggests that the emergent discourse of homosexuality in Korean cinema is but a belated nod to perhaps the most marginalised group in a society that limits the expression of non-conformist identities.

Nearly ten years older than Aya, U-in seems to be in a state of suspended animation that could only come from months of monotonous work. And yet, even at the tender age of eighteen, Aya is no less a creature of circumstance and habit. Trapped in a dull existence, emotionally estranged from her spouse-swapping parents and her younger brother (who is too engrossed in *manga* or Internet porn to notice her), this pill-popping youth bears all the marks of an angst-ridden teenager. Having failed her college entrance exams, she attends a learning institute – an intermediary space that underlines the film's thematic emphasis on 'in-between-ness', on not fitting in. During a class lecture about the international date-line, the disinterested pupil prepares for her impending suicide by holding her breath. Choosing one's own death, she believes, is the ultimate freedom, and she intends to follow in the footsteps of her grandfather – a legendary globetrotter who, according to Aya's recently deceased grandmother (a once-famous geisha), is rumoured to have taken his own life by holding his breath. Like U-in, who is forced to go to the office for privacy once his brother-in-law and niece arrive, Aya seeks refuge at her dead grandmother's house (which her mother, a money-hungry socialite, is eager to sell), with only her grandmother's cat (improbably named Foucault) to keep her company.

Like Mi-a, who wants to be an ugly old hag so that her irritating admirers will stop pestering her, Aya has unconventional dreams. To achieve her dream of committing suicide on her birthday, she leaves school without her parents' consent, takes a part-time job at a sports centre and begins saving up her salary for a flight to Alaska that will cross the international date-line (a place, Aya muses, that 'is neither yesterday nor today'). After being sacked from her job (for breaking into the gym after hours) and spending her savings on a pair of expensive ruby shoes, Aya answers an advertisement for 'Internet modeling'. Her new employers – oily, entrepreneurial web cameramen – describe her job as a 'spiritual healer [for] men around the world tormented by loneliness', and take promotional shots of her against a blank backdrop that will later be matted with shots of an Alaskan landscape. Wearing red wig, ruby shoes and white fur, she embodies the fabricated image of virginal femininity ('Asako') that U-in consumed in an earlier scene. By retroactively shuttling between the Korean consumption and Japanese production of a surreally minimalistic strip-tease, the film deconstructs this male fantasy which is predicated on a simultaneous awareness of, and obliviousness to, the artificial nature of any sexual gratification induced by commercially fabricated, technologically mediated imagery.

This emphasis on image-fabrication extends to Aya's one true confidante – a co-worker named Rie – whose closets are lined with life-sized cut-outs of her own image as a professional woman. Besides illustrating her desire for upward mobility, the cut-outs recall a shot of promotional cardboard celebrities (including Hong Kong superstar, Jackie Chan) outside a travel agency, cut-outs which underscore the constructedness and transnational circulation of mechanically reproduced images. In reality, Rie – when not working at the health club – is a struggling night-club dancer who, like her mother, is pregnant with an illegitimate baby. Projecting an artificially cheery image, Rie is in a deeper panic than Aya, and can barely hide her slashed wrist from her friend. Just as Aya is obsessed with the romantic imagery of death in Alaska, so too is Rie fascinated with Egypt which she imagines as an exotic and mysterious place where passion and adventure await. In fact, Rie was initially attracted to her Iranian boyfriend, an illegal immigrant named Mohammad, because she mistook him for an Egyptian.

Before losing his job as a bouncer and being deported, Mohammad is shown searching for Rie's apartment in a direct allusion to Abbas Kiarostami's *Where is the Friend's Home? (Khane-ye doust kodjast*, Iran, 1987) – one of many cinematic citations throughout *Asako in Ruby Shoes*. Overhead shots of pastel umbrellas recall Jacques Demy's musical *The Umbrellas of Cherbourg (Les Parapluies de Cherbourg*, France, 1964). But perhaps the most blatant reference is to *The Wizard of Oz*. Because Aya is bound to a life of inertia, small things – such as the glint of a sequinned shoe – provide the only thrills in her

Figure 26 Aya transforms into 'Asako in Ruby Shoes' in the cyberporn world to fund her 'suicide trip' to Alaska. Courtesy of the Korean Film Archive

life. Unlike Dorothy's, however, Aya's ruby slippers do not completely alleviate her frustrations – a point illustrated when, walking home, Aya steps on a piece of chewing-gum, which sticks to the bottom of her newly purchased shoes. Just as Dorothy's flight from the dustbowl realities of monochromatic Kansas signalled a spiritual and emotional maturation, so too does Aya's departure from the claustrophobic confines of home and school entail a transformation of self. And yet, unlike her Hollywood predecessor, who realises that 'there is no place like home', both Aya and U-in discover that home holds no place for them. By cyclically revisiting the prologue images of Anchorage, the film ends on a note of return, but also gestures towards a road about to be taken – not a Yellow Brick Road, but an untrammelled path of political and cultural reconciliation.

THERE'S NO WOMAN (LIKE THE OTHER WOMAN)

In her provocatively titled article, 'Disappearing South Korean Women', Kim Soyoung points out that North Korean, Swiss and Chinese women have begun taking centre stage in narratives of great national import, effectively 'effacing' the presence of South Korean women.[3] In *Shiri* (*Swiri*, 1999), North Korean sniper Yi Pang-hi disguises herself as a devoted South Korean fiancée to the very secret agent who is hunting her. In *Joint Security Area* (*Kongdong gyŏngbi guyŏk*, 2000), Major Sophie Jean, a Korean–Swiss officer, is dispatched to the Demilitarised Zone to investigate a border-shooting between South and North Korean soldiers. Ostracised as a racial, national and sexual other, she fails to comprehend the complex homosocial relationships among the men involved. In *Musa* (2001), a blood-soaked epic set in China during the Ming Dynasty era, a group of exiled Korean warriors sacrifice their lives to save a Chinese princess and refugees from Mongolian attack. In *Failan* (*P'airan*, 2001), an Inch'ŏn-based gangster experiences remorse after the premature death of his Chinese paper-marriage wife, an illegal immigrant whose simple, yet exquisite, beauty casts in comparative relief the film's only substantial Korean female character – a middle-aged laundress. In *Musa* and *Failan*, South Korean women are literally invisible or desexualised, whereas traditional Chinese femininity is privileged as an object of the male gaze.

One could argue that increased male anxieties in the wake of the 1997 IMF Crisis, which resulted in massive lay-offs, bankruptcies and family upheavals, are responsible for this structured absence, this symbolic annihilation of women deemed threatening and aggressive – an anxiety best demonstrated by such titles as *My Wife Is a Gangster* (*Chop'ok manura*, 2001) and *My Sassy Girl* (*Yopgijŏkin gŭnyŏ*, 2001). The 'disappearance of South Korean women', however, can be inversely translated into the 'emergence of racial and ethnic others' whose absence or marginalisation had been pronounced in Korean cinema until recently. It is indeed disturbing that women of different ethnicities and nationalities are mobilised to promote the virtues of traditional femininity (similar to the way in which Japanese women functioned in Hollywood's 'War

Bride' films produced during the 1950s). The presence of non-South Korean women in contemporary films, however, corresponds to their increased visibility in a society that has traditionally valued its racial and ethnic homogeneity. In recent years, the exploitation of immigrant women from mainland China and South-East Asia surfaced as a looming social issue (tellingly, exploitative working conditions are to blame for Failan's death). They took the place of rural Korean women from the 1960s to the 1980s as low-wage housemaids, factory girls and prostitutes. Just as Korean factory workers had been put to use as cheap foreign labour by American companies, *chaebols* (South Korea's family-owned industrial conglomerates) are now exploiting South-East Asian labourers and benefiting from the international division of labour. As a middleman between First World and Third World in the age of global capitalism, a Korean masculine subject-position is necessarily precarious because of its 'double consciousness' (both victim and victimiser, colonised and coloniser). This complex psychological split is projected on to the idealised bodies of foreign women whose need for protection neutralise masculine guilt and restore phallic power.

In *Asako in Red Shoes*, the relationship between South Korean and other women is more complex and multi-layered. In the first half of the film, U-in's voyeuristic gaze oscillates between the real space of Mi-a and the virtual space of Asako/Aya. At one point, he fuses the images of the two women by pasting Mi-a's face (from the ID picture he took earlier) over Asako's body on the computer monitor. Later, he reverses the direction of virtual-to-real substitution by buying a pair of ruby slippers for the Korean woman – his original object of desire who is eventually replaced by, ironically, her Japanese stand-in. Despite their resemblance and interchangeability, Mi-a and Aya represent radically different femininities. The cheeky-mouthed Mi-a is a 'castrating' woman whose toughness and queerness test U-in's already emasculated psyche. Quite the opposite, Aya is a non-threatening woman whose soft and passive femininity, in the guise of Asako, rekindles U-in's sexual drive. In addition to Aya and Mi-a, there is a third woman who attracts U-in's attention: Kuk-jŏng, an ex-classmate whom he accidentally bumps into at a bank. A Chinese immigrant who grew up in Korea, moved to Alaska, studied in Los Angeles and returned to Seoul as a hotel manager and fund-raiser for the Establishment of the New Chinatown in Korea, Kuk-jŏng is no doubt well informed in the ways of the world. Unlike Asako, both Kuk-jŏng and Mi-a make aggressive gestures towards U-in. Mi-a, when not ignoring U-in altogether, shoots derisive looks at him. Both a nymphomaniac and a mother-substitute, Kuk-jŏng infantilises her friend by repeatedly calling him 'cute' and by paying for his hotel room after their impotent sexual encounter.

U-in, unable to sustain an erection with Kuk-jŏng, conversely commands a degree of consumer power *vis-à-vis* Asako's commercialised cyber images. In response to his Barbie Doll-carrying niece's question about the site he is surfing, U-in calls Asako a 'doll' who comforts him in times of loneliness. Like a puppet,

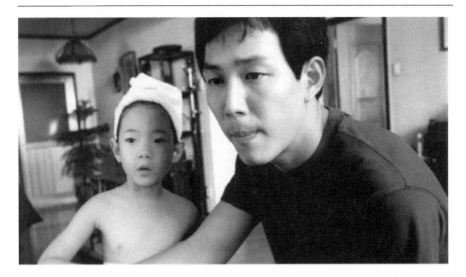

Figure 27 U-in idles away his free time consuming Aya/Asako's cyber images while his curious niece peeps in. Courtesy of the Korean Film Archive

Asako obediently follows the soliloquised instructions ('stand up', 'come closer', etc.) of U-in, whose manipulation of the website's panning and zooming controls simulates the directorial powers of the cameramen filming Aya in Japan. U-in's illusion of controlling the female image restores his masculine confidence and foreshadows his active pursuit of Aya in the penultimate airport scene. In the final scene, as the couple stands side by side on a hill overlooking an Alaskan forest, U-in displays a protective, slightly paternalistic gesture towards his young companion, covering her bare shoulders with his jacket. This ultimate ascendancy of Japanese femininity and Korean masculinity is achieved at the expense of South Korean women who are effectively expunged from the narrative. Mi-a disappears from the film after her sexual orientation is divulged. U-in's mother is a disembodied, telephonic voice literally disconnected by her apathetic son. And finally, U-in's philandering sister undergoes the most emphatic erasure of all. As the object of her detective-husband's investigation, the missing woman might very well be an off-screen extension of the adulterous heroine in E. J-yong's directorial début *An Affair* (*Chŏngsa*, 1998) – a film which broke many conventions of Korean maternal melodramas by highlighting a mother and wife deserting her family without fear of repercussions.

Like the heroine at the end of *An Affair*, who boards an aeroplane alone for Rio de Janeiro, Aya has become 'unhoused' in her trek to Alaska, and her momentary exemption from the rigours and responsibilities of gendered work puts her in league with other seemingly emancipated women – the 'Madame Freedoms' who buck tradition and set off on their own. Aya will presumably take her place beside U-in as wife, however, and thus fulfil a traditional role that could be less enabling than the ones she left behind. Leading up to this 'radical conservative' image of combined freedom and constraint are several moments when Aya appears unfettered by family expectations whether riding her bike, floating alone peacefully in a swimming pool or leaping into the air after purchasing a pair of ruby slippers. As this last example testifies, however, female emancipation often hinges on the socio-economic leverage underpinning middle-class aspirations, as well as a kind of willing victimage to commodity fetishism.

IMPROBABLE, YET INEVITABLE: 'INYŎN' AND THE OXYMORONIC-SYNCHRONIC

Having disentangled some of the intertextual and extra-cinematic references in *Asako in Ruby Shoes*, we now turn to its crucial source of literary inspiration: P'i Ch'ŏn-dŭk's canonical 1980 essay, 'Inyŏn'. Halfway through the film, a seemingly capricious, staged interlude from this melancholic essay appears, momentarily interrupting an otherwise 'realistic' outdoor scene in which daydreaming U-in listens to his lower-class colleague complain about work. Set to the lilting arpeggios of Debussy, an overhead shot shows a man dressed in antiquated business attire and a woman wrapped in a kimono bowing repeatedly to each other as snow begins to fall. The man, who appears to have wandered into the frame from another, colonial-era film, is actually U-in. The woman, dressed in traditional Japanese garb, would accordingly seem to be Aya, given the nationalistic coding of her clothes. Close inspection, however, reveals that the woman is played by the same actress who stars as Mi-a (Kim Min-hŭ), a case of interethnic masquerade that further compounds the slipperiness of identity in the film. Their bowing is cut short by the startling, off-screen screech of an alley cat, which catches the attention of the two fictitious characters and realigns the narrative within a realistic mode.

Because this puzzling insert-shot is not narratively motivated, spectators not well versed in Korean literature may be dumbfounded by its inclusion. Indeed, the shot in question speaks specifically to audience members who can recognise the allusion to 'Inyŏn', an autobiographical story similarly revolving around a Korean man and a Japanese woman named Asako.[4] This privileging of a specific spectatorial reading position problematises the film's bipartisan appeal to Japanese and to Korean sensibilities, tipping the scales towards the latter. Written by P'i Ch'ŏn-dŭk, 'Inyŏn' recounts three meetings between the celebrated author and the daughter of a social worker, Mr Miura. At the age of seventeen, P'i first met Asako in Tokyo as a temporary lodger in Miura's house. Only a first-grader at the time, Asako presented the young tenant with a handkerchief and a ring, as well as a kiss on the cheek upon his departure. Nearly fourteen years later, the author revisited Japan and met Asako again, who was a college junior majoring in English at the Sacred Heart Women's University. Having rapturously chatted about Virginia Woolf's *The Years* (1937) late into the night, the two parted once again; this time with a friendly handshake. When P'i met Asako for the last time in 1954, she had become the wife of a

Japanese–American officer. Like strangers, the two silently say their goodbyes through several awkward bows. It is this final genuflectory parting that is visualised in the film's fleeting fantasy shot.

The film's incorporation of their reverential, yet distant, bowing simultaneously disturbs and brings order to the text. As a 'text within the text', this moment is a small-scale model of the film, one erected not simply for aesthetic reasons but principally for its evocation of the colonial past. While this irruption of the past – of a *theatrical performance* of the past – into the present is nostalgically framed as an object of consumption, a kind of tableau vivant in which history and literature are translated into light and shadow, it evaporates the borders between reality and fantasy, mimesis and semiosis. Rather than simply function as a kind of 'decoder ring' for the film, 'Inyŏn' opens up the hermeneutic possibilities of the text to the legacy of Korean–Japanese relations, lending the film a depth of meaning as well as an historical sweep. Book-ending P'i's autobiographical story is a reference to his immediate departure to Ch'unch'ŏn, a romantic lake city three hours drive away from Seoul where a sister campus of the Sacred Heart University is located – a transnational connection which sparks his sentimental recollection. Near the end of the essay, the author – who could not consummate his feelings for Asako because of colonial circumstances – muses: 'Sometimes one cannot meet someone he or she yearns for after the first encounter, sometimes one does not meet again someone he or she cannot forget. I met Asako three times. It would have been better had I not met her the third time.'

As this extract suggests, a sense of belatedness and sorrow hangs over the essay. Delayed by historical upheavals, P'i Ch'ŏn-dŭk's third meeting with Asako arrived after her marriage to another man. This thematic fixation on perpetual postponement is a component of several films revolving around interethnic couples. In the tear-jerking finale of *Failan*, for example, a hoodlum receives letters from his dead Chinese wife 'too late' and belatedly mourns the happiness he could have had with the one person who regarded him with respect. In Kim Ki-dŏk's *Address Unknown* (*Such'wiin pulmyŏng*, 2000), a letter from the United States arrives 'too late' to a Korean woman who wrote repeatedly to her husband – an African-American GI who had deserted her. The long-awaited reply never reaches its addressee, this downtrodden woman who – in a moment of insanity following the suicide of her 'tragic mulatto' son – took her own life. The tragic finales of *Failan* and *Address Unknown* result from a double temporality which allegorises the unequal industrial and economic development of the nations represented by the couples. South Korea's 'lateness' in relation to the United States and other advanced nations contrasts with its forward-marching status *vis-à-vis* mainland China and South-East Asian countries. The men and women in these films miss one another because of this temporal and national schism.

In marked contrast, the symbiotic time–space in *Asako in Ruby Shoes* evokes an historical and cultural reconciliation between Japan and South Korea.

Although diplomatic relations were normalised by a treaty of 22 June 1965, there have been large obstacles to surmount on the path to reconciliation, above all the enduring pain of Japan's colonial domination of Korea. Unresolved issues, such as the plight of comfort women, the Dok-do/Takeshima territory debate and Japan's whitewashing of colonial atrocities in history textbooks, continued to anger the Korean public even after 1998 summit meetings between President Kim Dae Jung and Prime Minister Keizo Obuchi, which resulted in a joint declaration of their 'new partnership' and confirmed South Korea's commitment to opening its ports to Japanese popular culture. Much has been written about the politico-economic dimensions of this watershed period but it is worth pointing out that the co-operation between these two historically divided nations – though mutually enriching as a source of cultural exchange and technology transfer – did not completely remedy the trade imbalances that have long defined East Asian relations. If not a seismological shift in the history of the Pacific region, the Open Door Policy proved to be a pivotal step towards market liberalisation and government deregulation, setting the stage for a greater diversification of industrial, generic and narrative modes in South Korean cinema. The 1998 lifting of the ban made possible not only the theatrical screenings and video releases of Japanese films but also the casting of Japanese actors in Korean films.[5] In addition, it increased the viability of the pan-Asian co-production.

Although touted by film reps as the first Korean–Japanese co-production, *Asako in Ruby Shoes* actually follows in the wake of earlier ventures such as Kim Su-yong's *Apocalypse of Love* (*Saranguí muksirok*/*Ai no mokusiroku*, 1995) and Pak Ch'ŏl-su's *Kazoku Cinema* (*Kajok sinema*, 1998). Despite the fact that *Apocalypse of Love* – a biopic about a Japanese woman who married a Korean man and dedicated her life to the care of Korean orphans – was made with a Korean work-force and primarily featured Korean locales, the South Korean government prohibited its release on the basis that it was a 'Japanese film' (produced by a Japanese company and starring Japanese actors). Based on Yu Miri's autobiographical novel, *Kazoku Cinema* is a Japanese-language co-production about a Korean family living in Japan, with only subtle references made in passing to Korean cuisine. Neither of these two films manages to balance Japanese and Korean resources (in terms of funding, locales, languages and creative personnel) as judiciously as *Asako in Ruby Shoes* which broke new ground in utilising two separate crews under the guidance of cameramen Hong Kyŏng-p'yo and Masashi Chikamori. While all of these films bombed at the box-office, they herald a new trend in multinational collaborations, and attest to a growing willingness on the part of South Koreans and Japanese alike to enter into a bilateral trade relationship driven as much by cultural interests as by economic imperatives. The significance of Japanese–Korean co-productions thus lies more in their symbolic function as the material embodiment of the two nations' cultural reconciliation than in their commercial appeal.

The inter-ethnic coupling in *Asako in Ruby Shoes* is therefore based on a temporal synchronisation that resonates with South Korea's desire to gain an equal political and economic footing with Japan. This symbiotic relationship is implicated in an e-mail letter that U-in sends to Aya. He says, 'Tokyo is the same time as Seoul'. In fact, until the film's cross-cut synchronisation of the two cities during Aya's live 'adieu performance' (which U-in watches in real time), their temporalities had been disconnected and disjunctive. The two characters' encounter in Alaska brings to fruition this movement towards chronotopic synchronisation. In contrast to the three meetings in P'i Ch'ŏn-dŭk's essay, Aya and U-in meet only twice in *Asako in Ruby Shoes*. Their first meeting is indirectly implied in a still photograph taken during Aya's class trip to Seoul. Before her departure to Alaska, Aya accidentally stumbles upon a picture that shows her in school uniform posing beside U-in (wearing a banner promoting South Korea's 'Smile Movement'). The back of the photograph reads: 'With a Korean guy at Kyŏngbok Palace, 1998'. Two years later, Aya and U-in miraculously meet one another again in Anchorage. In voice-over, Aya ponders, 'I feel like I've met him before somewhere. Where could it have been?' U-in's voice follows: 'She said her name was Aya . . . Aya.' The film ends with the newly formed couple harmoniously merging two languages and voices, simultaneously saying, 'This is how our story began'. This ending suggests a will to uproot their future relationship from the grievances of the past, architecturally inscribed in the space of their first encounter: Kyŏngbok Palace, an historically contested site partially destroyed by the Japanese colonial government which deliberately built its Governor General's Hall in the vicinity of the former King's residence.

Despite efforts to create an image of spatial convergence and temporal synchronisation, the film renders dissimilarities aesthetically in the characters' middle-class environments, suggesting an economic disparity between Tokyo and Seoul. Although U-in owns a roomy apartment in Seoul (which his parents have left him) and 'goes to the office as a hobby' rather than from financial necessity, his surroundings are festooned with provincial icons. In these Korean sequences, there is a curious focus on bodily functions. Indeed, the film's original production title, *Uri-Nation*, conveys half of the narrative's 'bathroom sink realism', which does not flinch in depicting all manner of corporeal abjection, from urinating and masturbating to finger-bleeding and vomiting. Additionally, there are several signifiers of underdevelopment (out-of-order toilets; illegally disposed garbage; U-in's flooded apartment) which cast in comparative relief an obsession with cleanliness, symmetry and order in the *shoji*-panelled Japanese sequences. While U-in spends most of his leisure time surfing porn sites in run-down offices, Aya shops for shoes in a fashionable boutique, and hangs out in chic bars and dance-clubs with her friend Rie. While U-in gobbles down plain Korean noodles at a seedy restaurant, Aya is served an elegant continental breakfast by her health-conscious mother. The economic disparity of their nations generates a schism – one that is insinuated in the still photograph Aya took during her class outing to Seoul. Many Japanese high-school students visit South Korea, just as their parents frequent the country for bargain shopping or sex tours. The reverse is almost unimaginable for most Korean students, who are content with more afford-able trips to local destinations such as Kyŏngju or Pusan. The film irons out this difference by situating their union in Alaska – an exilic space where the two can start from scratch.

The title of P'i Ch'ŏn-dŭk's essay reverberates with the film's principal themes. The almost non-translatable term *inyŏn*, in fact, can only be approxi-mated in English as 'accidental predestination' – an oxymoronic notion akin to secular karma that manages to evoke the temporal disjunction and eventual synchronisation of time and space in *Asako in Ruby Shoes*.[6] A common yet slip-pery term that suggests a kind of quasi-mystical affinity, *inyŏn* refers to any coincidence that cannot be readily explained yet is not altogether unexpected. Strangers might brush past one another on the underground, and their moment-ary connection is said to be a tiny eruption in time and space when all the cosmic coordinates conspire to bring two 'unrelated relations' together. One of the most confounding sequences in *Asako in Ruby Shoes* involves just such an occurrence: though hundreds of miles apart, U-in and Aya appear to bump into each other in the underground. By accentuating the concept of *inyŏn* through the parodic visual citation of P'i's essay, the film draws attention to this notion of 'fateful happenchance', which has become perhaps *the* defining characteris-tic of recent South Korean cinema, observable in everything from *Ditto* (*Tonggam*, 2000) to *Il Mare* (*Siwŏlae*, 2000) – films which depict couples miraculously communicating across temporal vectors by means of, respectively, a ham radio and a 'magic' post-box. Fate, a theme that animates *Asako in Ruby Shoes*, is conjured when Aya reads her horoscope, which accurately predicts a romantic encounter with 'a man from the west'. 'Osaka? Kyoto?' she wonders. In a twist of fate worthy of Krzystof Kieslowski, the film's dénouement brings the two narrative strands together – uniting Aya and this 'man from the west' and lending a blissfully optimistic, albeit chimerical, aura to their predestined co-existence. As unlikely and providential as it may seem, their union gestures ahead to a foreseeable future when U-in and Aya become husband and wife, and thus recalls the title of Japanese essayist Doda Ikuko's best-selling novel about her intercultural marriage to a Korean photographer: *Two Countries Under a Blanket*.

Like that of P'i Ch'ŏn-dŭk's essay, the Korean title of the film – *Sunaebo* ('Pure Love Story') – seems unnecessarily vague. In marked contrast, the (crea-tively translated English-language title departs considerably from the original Korean, explicitly aligning the film with Hollywood through a specific allusion to *The Wizard of Oz*. Like many recent Korean films, such as Cho Kŭm-hwan's *Singing in the Rain* (*Pinŭn sarangŭl t'ago*, 1994) and An Chin-u's *Over the Rainbow* (*Obŏ dŏ reinbou*, 2002), *Asako in Ruby Shoes* bears a familiar title designed to entice a retro-nostalgic audience weaned on American cinema. The title is therefore conciliatory in its attempt to bridge not only different media (literature and film) but also different cultures. 'Sunaebo', however, is a commonplace appellation attached to many *sinp'a*-style melodramas from South Korea's cinematic Golden Age of the 1950s and 1960s.[7] Verging toward generic blandness, the film's Korean-language title – besides gesturing back to such misty-eyed classics as Han Hyŏng-mo's same-titled melodrama, *Pure Love Story* (*Sunaebo*, 1957) – nevertheless articulates the inherent contradictions in any narrative that purports to evoke 'purity' through a show of cultural intermingling and generic hybridity. Geographical migration, spatial movement across borders, produces an identity that is *mixed*, not *pure*. One can see, then, how this 'pure love story', this tale of inter-ethnic romance that knows no borders, depends more on its 'divided loyalties' (the sometimes disorienting oscillation between Japanese and Korean sequences) than on its appeal to any one national sentiment. Brimming with transnational signifiers (*The Wizard of Oz*; *The Umbrellas of Cherbourg*; the Iranian boyfriend; Chinatown; a televised Bollywood musical), *Asako in Ruby Shoes* absorbs a variety of precursor texts and multicultural elements into a synthetic and syncretic cluster that resonates with the demographic mixing of social, racial and ethnic identities. Given this implicit link between intertextuality, hybridity and dissemination, one could conceivably frame the concept of diaspora within the optics of a new 'narrative multiculturalism' – a textual phenomenon that, while certainly not unique to South Korean cinema, is especially salient in *Asako in Ruby Shoes* and other racially and ethnically diverse films which stake a claim in political reconciliation.

Asako in Ruby Shoes's unapologetically upbeat ending suggests that two (geographically) close but (historically and culturally) distant neighbours might put aside their differences and co-exist harmoniously (something apparently achieved two years after the release of the film, when Japan and South Korea co-hosted the 2002 World Cup football championship). The formation of a Japanese–Korean couple allegorising the millennial 'new partnership' between their nations indeed provides a positive alternative to such ethnocentric big-budget extravaganzas as *Anarchists* (*Anak'isŭtŭ*, 2000) and *2009: Lost Memories* (*2009 Losŭtŭ memorijŭ*, 2001) which depict the Japanese negatively and attempt to rationalise anti-colonial violence. At the same time, the fact that such a coupling takes place in neither Japan nor South Korea, but in a third, Edenic space – a cinematic *tabula rasa* on which a new history can be written – attests to the film's impetus to situate the political allegory of inter-ethnic romance within a broader transnational imaginary, one that exists 'neither yesterday nor today'.

REFERENCES

Kim, Soyoung (2001), 'Disappearing South Korean Women', in Kim Soyoung (ed.), *Korean-Style Blockbusters: Atlantis or America*, Seoul: 16–39.
P'i, Ch'ŏn-dŭk (1976), *Essays*, Seoul.

Rector, Gary (2001), 'The Elusive Concept of "Inyŏn": Hungbo's Gourd', *Korea Herald*, April 12.

Rushdie, Salman (1994), 'At the Auction of the Ruby Slippers', in *East, West*, New York.

Rushdie, Salman (2002), 'Out of Kansas', in *Step Across this Line: Collected Nonfiction 1992–2002*, New York.

NOTES

1. See Rushdie (1994: 93).
2. See Rushdie (2002: 13).
3. See Kim (2001: 16–39).
4. The film's anomalous incorporation of 'Inyŏn' was in fact given advance warning through an earlier exchange of dialogue between U-in and former classmate Kuk-jŏng. After accidentally encountering U-in at a bank, she says, 'Meeting and parting are all part of *inyŏn* [fate]'. In response to Kuk-jŏng's question about his love-life, U-in asks her if the name 'Asako' sounds familiar. Kuk-jŏng reminds her slow-witted friend that 'Asako' is the name of the main character in P'i's essay, a staple of Korean middle-school text-books. By planting this nostalgic memory in his mind, the Chinese-Korean woman undoubtedly sparks U-in's imaginative recreation in the scene that immediately follows.
5. Beginning on 28 October 1998, the three-phase process of gradually opening South Korea to Japanese films, cartoons, videos, popular music concerts, compact disks, computer games and broadcasting programmes was implemented. Following the release on 5 December 1998 of Kitano Takeshi's Golden Lion-winning *Fireworks* (*Hana-Bi*, 1997), sixteen Japanese films – including autumnal works by Kurosawa Akira and Imamura Shohei – were theatrically released in South Korea during the first two phases of the opening. After the September 1999 launch of the second stage, the beneficiaries of import allowances expanded from the recipients of the Best Picture and Director Awards at the Cannes, Venice and Berlin International Film Festivals (as well as the Best Foreign Language Film Oscar winners) to all films approved for general audiences by the Media Ratings Board and prize-winners from seventy film festivals around the world. Another step towards unrestricted opening began in June 2000, when any live-action films rated Age 12+ and 15+, as well as award-winning animated features, became eligible for theatrical and video release in Korea. Although the anticipated final phase – complete opening (extending to all Age 18+ rated films) – was postponed in July 2001 owing to a wave of protests against the rightist revision of Japanese history textbooks (which whitewashed the nation's wartime atrocities), the phenomenal success of a few titles, such as Iwai Shunji's *Love Letter* (1995; Korean release: 11 November 1999), and Suo Masayuki's *Shall We Dance* (1995; Korean release: 13 May 2000), had contributed to the mainstream appeal of Japanese cinema, which garnered nearly 8 per cent of South Korea's market-share in 2000. Another small victory came on 28 June 2002, when Miyazaki Hayao's *Spirited Away* hit movie screens. Released in the midst of World-Cup fever, Miyazaki's animated fantasy – unlike the box-office bomb *Ninja Scroll* (the first Japanese animated feature shown theatrically in Korea) – appealed to adolescents and adults alike.
6. For a more supple discussion of this semantic quagmire, see Rector 2001.
7. By selecting an archetypal title ('*Sunaebo*') typically attached to overly sentimental melodramas of the Golden Age, E. J-yong not only alludes to same-titled films of that era but also references the story of Yi Su-il and Shim Sun-ae – a *sinp'a* tale that was adapted from Japanese sources and became the basis for several films such as *Long Cherished Dream* (*Changhanmong*, 1920, 1926, 1969) and *Su-il and Sun-ae* (1931). In a sub-plot of *Asako in Ruby Shoes*, a soldier named Su-il is fleetingly

shown searching for his lover Sun-ae. Unlike her Golden Age forebears, however, Sun-ae is not a melodramatic heroine of devotion and pure love, but an unsympathetic local resident whose illegally disposed rubbish-bags are making U-in's job difficult. Inside the bags are letters from her ex-boyfriend, Su-il, whose tenure in the military has given the unfaithful woman freedom to date other men.

GLOSSARY OF KEY TERMS

Chi-Yun Shin

1997 IMF Crisis An Asia-wide economic depression triggered by the 1997 stock-market crash and subsequent monetary collapse; the debasement of the *baht* in Thailand sparked a series of competitive devaluations (of the *rupiah* in Indonesia, the *ringgit* in Malaysia and the *won* in South Korea) and culminated in a currency crisis of almost global proportions (total loss of wealth estimated at more than two trillion dollars). South Korea was one of the hardest hit by this economic crisis, and its government had to seek assistance from the International Monetary Fund (IMF), which provided $57 billion to help stabilise South Korea's crippled economy. As with most forms of foreign aid, the IMF package was conditional, an intervention that mandated corporate-sector reforms and a reduction of government spending. Ultimately, this restructuring of South Korea's financial institutions drove a wedge between small-business owners and the political élite, between fledgeling entrepreneurs and the *chaebŏls*. The IMF crisis also led to an increase in unemployment (about 1.5 million people) and lent itself to another acronym: 'I'M Fired'. The consequences of the 1997 IMF crisis were compounded by the country's lack of a social-welfare safety net.

3-8-6 (*Sam-p'al-yuk*) **Generation** So-called because they are in their thirties, attended university in the 1980s, and were born in the 1960s, the 3-8-6 Generation refers to the Korean generation who bore the brunt of the combined political and cultural weight of the imperatives of Cold War ideology (in the 1970s), resistance to authoritarian politics (in the 1980s), national-identity struggles and the concern for the corrosive effects of Western capitalist culture on traditional values.

Fourth Republic (1972–79) In 1971, South Korean President Park Chung Hee won office for a third term (he amended the Constitution to abolish the two-term limitation on the Presidency in 1969) but following events both domestic and foreign – e.g. impending American withdrawal from South Vietnam, the new mood of American *rapprochement* with China, coupled with the growing anti-government activities of the opposition parties and university students – combined to toughen his rule. To strengthen his power, during October 1972, the President suspended parts of the Constitution, declared martial law, dissolved the National Assembly and announced a new **Yushin Constitution** which greatly expanded and enhanced the presidential powers. In December 1972, the new Constitution was approved by a national referendum, and Park was elected to a six-year term of office (with no limit on re-election). With his inauguration on 28 December 1972, the Fourth Republic emerged. Following the end of President Park's six-year term of office came his re-election in 1978, but he undoubtedly faced a serious political crisis by the summer of 1979. The opposition stepped up its attacks and now called for Park's resignation and the dismantling of the **Yushin** Constitution. In the midst of this tense situation, President Park was shot and killed by Kim Chae-gyu, director of the **Korean Central Intelligence Agency**, on 26 October, which violently ended the Fourth Republic.

Fifth Republic (1981–87) During the interim period between 1979 and 1981 under Acting President Ch'oe Kyu-ha, following the death of Park Chung Hee, General Chun Doo Hwan, the then Head of the Defence Security Command, consolidated his military and political power, while political unrest in South Korea was gathering momentum. Responding to large-scale riots and protests, including the **Kwangju Uprising** in May 1980, Chun declared martial law, closed the universities, dissolved the legislature, banned all political activity and arrested thousands of political dissidents. Immediately after the sudden resignation of Acting President Ch'oe in August 1980, there was a movement to elect General Chun and, on 2 September, Chun was inaugurated as the new President. The new constitution reflected criticism of the years during which there had been no provision for re-election; there was a limit on the proposed emergency powers of the presidency, but provision was also made for indirect presidential elections by a popularly chosen electoral college. This constitution was approved by a national referendum on 22 October 1980 and, in March 1981, Chun was formally elected President for seven years under the new constitution of the **ROK**'s Fifth Republic, making him the fifth President of South Korea since its founding in 1948. Chun was also the most unpopular leader in post-war Korean history, and his draconian measures were widely deplored.

Sixth Republic (1987–92) The Sixth Republic was established by a general election held in response to people's democratic movements in the spring of 1987. The Sixth Republic, however, under Chun Doo Hwan's successor, Roh Tae Woo, succeeded only in partial democratisation without dismantling repressive state structures, and it continued to suppress freedom of speech.

Banmal Non-honorific language that is normally used by older people when speaking to the younger generation but it can be used among close family members and friends regardless of age – although it is considered to be rude to use *banmal* to younger persons when not acquainted.

Chaebŏl South Korea's family-owned industrial conglomerates (e.g. Hyundai, Samsung and LG group).

Chosŏn Dynasty (1392–1910) Korea's longest-ruling dynasty, the Chosŏn is also called 'Yi Dynasty', after the founder of the kingdom, Yi Sŏng-gye (1335–1408). Former military leader of the Koryŏ Dynasty (918–1392), General Yi led a successful palace coup in 1388 and eventually usurped the throne in 1392. The new kingdom was named Chosŏn, harking back to the Old Chosŏn kingdom fifteen centuries earlier, and its capital was built at Hanyang (now Seoul). The government of the Chosŏn Dynasty was based upon Confucian precepts (transforming the Buddhist-shaped Koryŏ society): the monarch was to be a benevolent ruler; the bureaucracy was to be his (the throne was never occupied by a queen) agent, manned by virtuous and wise officials, and the monarch was to rule the kingdom with the advice and consent of Confucian literati. Confucian doctrines of hierarchy in the Chosŏn Dynasty prevailed within its social structures and institutions. The advent of Japanese colonial rule in 1910 saw the end of the Chosŏn Dynasty. Its failure to defend its sovereignty against the Western and Japanese imperialist onslaught in the late nineteenth century is seen to have cast a pall over Korea's entry into the modern world system.

Chuch'e (Juche) **Ideology** Meaning self-reliance and independence in politics, economics, defence and ideology, *chuch'e* ideology is the organic political thought indoctrinated by the late North Korean leader, Kim Il-sŏng (Kim Il-sung). The term first emerged in 1955 as the North Korean regime drew away from Moscow, and then appeared prominently in the mid-1960s as Kim sought a stance independent of both Moscow and Beijing. The political culture of North Korea has evolved around this solipsistic and highly nationalistic *chuch'e* ideology to the exclusion of all other ideas. By the time of Kim Il-sŏng's death in 1995 and the emergence of his son, Kim Chŏng-il, to leadership, North Korea had developed into a hermetically sealed society with a totally self-referential culture.

Ch'ungmuro A street in Seoul, which formed the Korean film industry's traditional hub, and a byword for the industry.

Comfort Women (*Wianbu*) Sex slaves drafted by the Japanese Imperial Army during the period bracketed by Japan's annexation of Manchuria (1931) and the end of World War II (1945). Between 100,000 and 200,000 women from Korea,

China, the Philippines, Taiwan, Malaysia, Thailand and Indonesia suffered sexual enslavement at military brothels established in occupied zones and front-lines throughout Asia. Between 80 and 90 per cent of the total number of comfort women is estimated to be Korean. Unspoken for nearly fifty years in Korea's authoritarian, patriarchal society, the history of comfort women finally filtered into the domain of public opinion in 1991 when one of the victims, Kim Hak-sun, spoke out about her past to the media. Despite years of inter-Asia protests, law suits and United Nations support, the comfort women issue remains unresolved, as the Japanese government has continuously avoided offering state-level apologies and reparations.

Democratic People's Republic of Korea (DPRK) The official name for the Communist state of North Korea, the DPRK was proclaimed on 9 September 1948, with Kim Il-sŏng as premier. The Soviet Union and its allies soon recognised the DPRK, and the Soviet troops withdrew from North Korea in December 1948.

Dok-do/Takeshima Territory Debate A small island group jutting from the Sea of Japan/East Sea and located 56 miles east of South Korea's Ulnŭng-do, Dok-do has been the focus of an ongoing territorial conflict between two East Asian neighbours who share a long history of hostilities. As the remains of an ancient volcano, these thinly populated, isolated islets would initially seem to be of little importance to either nation. Nevertheless, Dok-do remains important as a potential military defence base, a nautical site with access to a petroleum-rich sea-bed, and – most importantly – a symbol of national pride. Recently designated 'Natural Monument #336' by the **Republic of Korea**, Dok-do first became a tributary of the Silla Kingdom at the beginning of the sixth century. In the late seventeenth century, a jurisdiction dispute broke out which was resolved through Japanese concession of Korean sovereignty. In 1900, Dok-do was officially incorporated into Kangwŏn Province as a satellite island of Ulnŭng-kun under the decree of King Kojong. Beginning in 1905, however, five years before Japan's annexation of Korea, Dok-do (or Takeshima in Japanese) became increasingly dotted with Japanese watchtowers, effectively serving as the Shimane Prefecture naval base during the imperialists' expansion. Despite its reversion to Korea by the Allies following World War II, the Japanese government continued to claim administrative authority until 1998 when the two governments signed an agreement calling for joint ownership of the waters surrounding Dok-do. Despite this diplomatic pact, rival claims to Dok-do continue to proliferate, further widening the geopolitical gulf between South Korea and Japan.

Film Promotion Law A law drawn up in December 1995 to modify and replace the **Motion Picture Law** that had long regulated the local film industry. Going into effect in July 1996, one of the notable measures introduced in the new law was the establishment of a Film Promotion Fund to support the local film industry. The Film Promotion Law also repealed regulations requiring official approval, in advance, from the Ministry of Culture and Sports for exporting Korean films and for co-producing films with foreign companies. The first revision of the Film Promotion Law in the following year replaced the Public Performance Ethics Committee with a civilian board which would assign ratings rather than directly censor films, and the second revision in 1999 reorganised the ratings committee into the **Korea Media Ratings Board**. In general, the reform of film policy throughout the 1980s and 1990s has resulted in much less direct bureaucratic and governmental interference in the film industry.

Han The Korean word *Han* carries a broad sense of a deeply seated Korean experience of oppression and unrequited resentment borne of generations of struggle.

Hanmun Chinese characters; can also refer to difficult and big words.

Hanryu Literally meaning 'Korean wave', the term *Hanryu* was first coined by Chinese journalists to describe the sudden influx of South Korean pop culture, starting with music and then television dramas and films, and its fast-growing popularity among Chinese youths in the late 1990s. The term soon entered the popular vocabulary to include the same phenomenon geographically extended to other parts of Asia, including Hong Kong, Taiwan, Singapore and Vietnam. *Hanryu* is palpable in the region's film festivals dedicated to Korean films, Korean TV dramas aired on the main television networks, Korean songs played on popular local radio, Korean stars featured in local media productions, fan magazines, on television commercials, on street billboards and Internet fan sites devoted to a shared penchant for Korean popular media and stars.

Hwarang The *Hwarang* was a sixth-century élite military troop, consisting of handsome, aristocratic youths, who were trained to be leaders during the Silla Kingdom (57 BC–AD 935). *Hwarang* literally means 'flowering manhood', and is commonly translated as 'flower knights'. Translators who refer to the *Hwarang*'s homosexual tendencies, however, often use the effeminised rendering 'flower boys'.

Inyŏn Fate; 'accidental predestination'; 'fateful happenchance'.

Ipdosŏnmae Literally meaning the 'pre-harvest sale of rice', this term refers to the old practice exercised by mostly poor farmers, who could not wait until the harvest in autumn, of selling their 'unripe' crops at a lower price. *Ipdosŏnmae* is also a derogatory term used in the Korean film industry to refer to the widespread practice (especially in the 1970s) of major film companies selling their films to regional distributors based on a script draft (rather than finished films).

Jop'ok An abbreviation of *jo-jik-p'ok-ryŏg-bae*, which is a legal and rather official term (used in the media, for instance) that means organised, criminal gang members. The term *jop'ok* is not a newly coined expression but it is new in the sense that it came to be used as a more colloquial term for gang members. Also, compared with the already existing Korean colloquial terms for individual hoodlums or hooligans, such as *kkangp'ae* or *gŏndal*, *jop'ok* has an added sense of someone belonging to an organised criminal group. In this respect, *jop'ok* can be seen as the Korean equivalent of Japanese *yakuza*, Hong Kong *triad* or Italian (American) *mafia*. Everyday usage of *jop'ok* coincided with the rising popularity of a new cycle of gangster action films, especially those released since the mid-1990s.

Kihoek yŏnghwa Literally meaning 'planned films', *kihoek yŏnghwa* was introduced by the group of young producers who pushed for a rationalisation of the film-making process in the early and mid-1990s. The planned film essentially involved preselecting a target audience and marketing strategy, and using a long period of script development to improve chances of success at the box-office. Apart from the producer, a separate person would be placed in charge of 'planning' (*kihoek*) to ensure a more thoroughly developed film. Planned films also introduced market surveys into Korean film-making. Proponents of planned films were also heavily involved in film promotion. Following the example of the Hollywood branch offices, they introduced pre-release marketing, whereby advertising for a film would appear weeks or months in advance of its release. Kim Ŭi-sŏk's *Marriage Story* (*Kyŏrhon iyagi*, 1992), for which Shin Ch'ŏl and Yu In-t'aek are credited with planning, remains the most widely cited example of a planned film.

Korean Central Intelligence Agency (KCIA) Security paranoia and the perceived threat of Communist subversion led to the creation under Park Chung Hee (1961–79) of a large, draconian secret police force, the notorious Korean Central Intelligence Agency (KCIA). The KCIA was a spectre in political life throughout the 1960s, 1970s and 1980s, and its nefarious activities extended into the realm of cultural production as well.

Korean Film Commission (KOFIC) KOFIC was set up in 1999 to promote Korean films abroad, replacing the Korea Motion Picture Promotion Corporation (KMPPC). KOFIC consists of a government-appointed civilian board and is funded by the Ministry of Culture and Tourism but, following the Kim Dae Jung government's (1998–2003) 'support without control' guidelines, KOFIC has been allowed greater independence and authority in formulating film policies. While continuing the duties of the KMPPC, KOFIC strengthened the efforts to elevate Korean cinema's international profile and the growth of international sales. For instance, KOFIC sets up pavilions at major international film festivals and markets. It also provides translations and prints, and it pays for the production of subtitles for selected films targeting overseas film markets or international film festivals. In addition, KOFIC subsidises travel costs for film-makers whose films are invited to major film festivals, and it offers cash awards to film professionals who are officially invited to major festival competitions.

Korea Media Ratings Board A second revision of the **Film Promotion Law** reorganised the civilian ratings committee – which replaced a government board responsible for the pre-screening and censoring of films, the Public Performance Ethics Committee in 1997 – into the Korea Media Ratings Board in 1999. The reform of film policy throughout the 1980s and 1990s resulted in much less direct bureaucratic and governmental interference in the film industry, but censorship remains an issue as the Media Ratings Board continues to try to block the release of films with explicit sexual or violent content by assigning them 'Deferred' or 'Restrictive' ratings.

Korean War (1950–53) Korea was liberated from Japanese colonial rule at the end of World War II (1945), but it did not become free and independent. Instead, it was partitioned along the 38th Parallel, with American troops occupying the area south of the line and Soviet troops occupying the area to the north, according to the agreement signed by the Allies. As a consequence, two states emerged in one country during the US–Soviet occupation period (1945–48). The ideological confrontation between the Communist North and capitalist South finally led, in June 1950, to war which lasted for three years. The Korean War was initiated by the North Korean leader, Kim Il-sŏng, with an ambition to unify Korea and put it under Communist rule, yet the counter-attack by the United Nations' forces led by the US, and the intervention of China, altered its nature from a civil to an international war. The tragic war desolated both Koreas and left a legacy of separated families, millions of deaths and atrocities on both sides, and psychologically traumatised several generations of Koreans. Thereafter, both Koreas rebuilt their societies in an atmosphere of security paranoia (the North focused on the threat of the United States and the South on another invasion from the North).

Korea–US Film Agreement In 1985, the Motion Picture Export Association of America (MPEAA) issued a strong complaint to the South Korean government with regard to the country's various restrictions on film imports, and, after subsequent negotiations between the two governments, a Korea–US Film Agreement was signed later that year. The content of the agreement was incorporated into the sixth revision of the **Motion Picture Law,** and consisted of the following: 1. foreign-owned film companies were now allowed to operate on Korean soil; 2. import quotas for foreign films would be abolished, as well as a mandatory ceiling on prices paid for imports; 3. the 100 million *won* tax

($85,000 at 1986 exchange rates) levied on each imported film – which formerly went into a film-promotion fund – would be abolished. Following the agreement, the number of foreign films imported into Korea each year jumped almost tenfold, from twenty in 1985 to 264 in 1989. Most significantly, the revision also paved the way for Hollywood studios to set up their own branch offices within Korea. UIP was the first to register in March 1988, with four others to follow: Twentieth Century Fox in August 1988, Warner Bros. in December 1989, Columbia Tristar in October 1990, and Disney (Buena Vista International) in January 1993.

Kŭnyang 'Just because'; for no particular reason.

Kwangju Uprising In May 1980, after the assassination of President Park Chung Hee by his own chief of the **Korean Central Intelligence Agency** and the rise of Chun Doo Hwan in a *coup d'état*, political demonstrations, protesting against continuing martial law and the illegitimate government, broke out in earnest in Kwangju – the regional capital of Southern Chŏlla province and the traditional stronghold of political opposition. Chun ordered élite paratroopers and other military units forcibly to quell the protest, and this continued for ten days from 18 to 27 May 1980. The resulting bloodshed of at least 500 individuals was suppressed within the Korean media but reported outside of Korea. The official death toll, however, is regarded as far lower than the actual figure which is believed to be close to 2,600.

Minjung **Movement** *Minjung* literally meaning masses or 'common people'. The *Minjung* Movement refers to a national popular campaign for democracy that broke the military dictatorship and culminated in the 1992 presidential elections.

Motion Picture Law A piece of legislation enacted in January 1962 by the military regime under Park Chung Hee. Designed to strengthen censorship and the institutionalisation of the film industry, the law employed various tools to establish a strong control system. Under this legislation, all film companies were required to hold a licence from the government in order to make films, prerequisites of which were to own their studio (space of more than 791 square yards), film equipment (more than three 35 mm cameras, sound recording capabilities, film laboratory facilities and a lighting system of more than 60 kW of power), to have a certain number of crew members or actors and actresses under contract, to own a large amount of capital and to produce a minimum of fifteen films per year. Such stringent requirements forced smaller companies out of business and consolidated the industry into a handful of large companies (which could then be more easily controlled by the government). Meanwhile, the law limited imports by means of a quota which stipulated that companies could import foreign titles only after producing a given number of local films.

The government also exercised strong censorship through a Public Ethics Committee which had the power to censor or modify films as they wished. Any hint of questioning or criticising the government's ideology would result in cuts, an outright ban or the arrest of the personnel involved. The law was revised four times (in 1963, 1966, 1970 and 1973) but it continued to function primarily as a means of controlling and regulating Korean cinema, rather than promoting it.

Mudaep'o A nickname for someone who is headstrong and acts first with no rational thinking.

Mujigae **Parade** Seoul's gay parade, inaugurated in 2000. *Mujigae* is Korean for 'rainbow'.

National Security Law (NSL) A special law, promulgated in December 1948, under South Korea's first President, Syngman Rhee, which made it a crime to seek to consolidate or form a group with the object of disturbing the peace of the nation in collusion with enemies of the state. While South Korea was in name a constitutional republic, Rhee's presidency (1948–60) continued the repressive emergency powers that had evolved during the **Korean War** years, and the NSL allowed the police wide latitude to arrest people for their political views even though it blatantly contradicted the constitutional rights of free speech and assembly. To charge someone as a Communist or Communist sympathiser was an often-used technique of the Rhee government to silence and eliminate its enemies. Later leaders, such as Park Chung Hee (1961–79) and Chun Doo Hwan (1981–87) perfected its use against their political opponents.

Open Door Policy/Good Neighbour Policy The 1998 summit meetings between South Korean President, Kim Dae Jung, and Japanese Prime Minister, Keizo Obuchi, resulted in a joint declaration of their 'new partnership' and paved the way for the Open Door Policy that confirmed South Korea's commitment to opening its ports to Japanese popular culture. The Open Door Policy proved to be a pivotal step towards market liberalisation and government deregulation, setting the stage for a greater diversification of industrial, generic and narrative modes in South Korean cinema. The 1998 lifting of the ban also made the theatrical screenings and video releases of Japanese films in South Korea possible as well as the casting of Japanese actors in Korean films. In addition, it increased the viability of the pan-Asian co-production.

P'ansori Korean traditional operatic drama. The prefix *p'an* refers to an open space and *sori* means sound or song/vocal narrative.

P'okjujok Reckless drivers; a group of drivers who enjoy speeding.

Ppaeint'ŭ Literally 'paint', but used as a derogatory nickname for an aspiring painter or artist.

Pusan International Film Festival South Korea's first international film festival launched in 1996. Held annually in Korea's south-eastern port city of Pusan, the Pusan city government originally supported the Pusan International Film Festival, but the central government also began supporting it in 1998. With strong support from the Korean government, and with the enthusiastic participation of the Asian film communities, the festival has become a leading film event in Asia.

Pusan Promotion Plan (PPP) Set within the **Pusan International Film Festival,** the Pusan Promotion Plan aims to encourage international co-productions by bringing together international film-finance companies and selected film-makers. The PPP, however, is open only to those directors who have achieved recognition abroad through international film festivals.

Republic of Korea (*Taehan min-guk*) Commonly called South Korea, the ROK was formally inaugurated on 15 August 1948, after United Nations-sponsored general elections were held on 10 May 1948. The elected representatives in South Korea formed a National Assembly, adopted a democratic, presidential constitution and then voted for Syngman Rhee (1948–60) as the first president on 31 May 1948. On 12 December 1948, the United Nations General Assembly adopted a resolution that legitimised the ROK as the only lawful government.

Screen Quota System A piece of legislation which stipulates that theatres must screen Korean films for a minimum number of days per year (106 to 146, depending on various factors). The Screen Quota System was retained in the sixth revision of the **Motion Picture Law,** and the government pledged to enforce it more fully as a way of compensating for the changes brought about in the aftermath of the 1985 **Korea–US Film Agreement.**

Segyehwa Literally meaning globalisation (*segye* meaning 'world', and *hwa* meaning 'becoming/turning into'), the *Segyehwa* policy is the ambitious top-down drive for globalisation launched by the Kim Young-sam administration (1993–98) as a survival strategy in the new world order, especially after the agreement of the **Uruguay Round** that pushed for market liberalisation. Formally announced in the Sydney speech of 17 November 1994, President Kim's *segyehwa* campaign involved a wide range of reforms, encompassing political, economic, social and cultural restructuring, while much of its energy was directed towards the rapid internationalisation and globalisation of the Korean economy. The zeal of Korea's economic globalisation also included media and cultural sectors which had been recognised as industries that could produce a huge profit. When the Presidential Advisory Council on Science and

Technology reported to President Kim Young-sam an eye-opening statistic showing that profits from the Hollywood blockbuster *Jurassic Park* (US, 1993) equalled the export revenue of 1.5 million Hyundai cars, and urged him to promote the high-technology media industry as a national strategic industry in May 1994, the government set out plans to support and promote the media industry as the strategic industry for the twenty-first century.

Sinp'a Translated as 'New School', *sinp'a* arose as a popular alternative to the *kup'a* (Old School) drama, *kabuki*, in late nineteenth-century Japanese theatre. Characterised by modern settings and melodramatic plots centring on family tragedy and heterosexual romance, *sinp'a* became a staple form of story-telling in Korean literature, theatre and cinema during the Japanese colonial period (1910–45), a tradition that resurfaced in South Korean melodramas of the Golden Age (1950s to 1960s). Contemporary critics and audiences still use the term to describe – often pejoratively – old-style melodramas filled with unlikely coincidences and fortuitous reversals as well as excessive sentimentality.

'Smile' Movement The Bright Smile Movement is a campaign to show the friendly and kind-hearted nature of the Korean people, particularly during the 2002 Korea–Japan World Cup and Asian Games in Pusan. It also promoted friendship between Koreans and foreigners by organising a series of 'Bright Smile Festivals', in association with the National Council of Better Korea Movement, throughout South Korea prior to the football World Cup. In general, though, the Bright Smile Movement was formed to encourage all people to exchange smiles, with the motto: 'Let's make a brighter world by smiling bright with a joyful heart'.

Sunshine Policy In 2000, President Kim Dae Jung reversed the traditional Cold War logic that kept relations across the 38th Parallel icy and antagonistic since 1953. Known as the Sunshine Policy, this political *rapprochement* with North Korea earned Kim the 2000 Nobel Peace Prize.

Ttanttara A derogatory reference to a musician who performs vernacular music; also refers to an actor, theatrical people.

Uruguay Round Refers to a series of multilateral trade negotiations held between 1986 and 1994. The agreement was reached on 15th December 1993, and it was signed by most of its 123 participating governments on 15th April 1994. The settlement of the Uruguay Round of the General Agreement on Trade and Tariffs (GATT) imposed immense threats to Korea's domestic economy which was soon to face direct competition from foreign companies. The Uruguay Round settlement created the World Trade Organisation.

Yushin **Constitution** The *Yushin* (Revitalising Reform) Constitution created the **Fourth Republic** and provided for an indirect election of the president, virtually guaranteeing Park Chung Hee presidency for life. The Constitution was supported by a series of emergency measures that made illegal even vague criticism of the president or Constitution itself, thus providing the police with wide censorial powers. All publications, newspapers and other public forms of expression, including film, were covered by these laws.

BIBLIOGRAPHY OF WORKS ON KOREAN CINEMA

SooJeong Ahn

Ahn, Byung-Sup (1987) 'Humor in Korean Cinema', *East–West Film Journal*, 2, 1: 90–8.

——(1998) 'Humanism Above All', *Cinemaya*, 42: 40–4.

Armes, Roy (1987) 'The Newly Industrializing Countries', in *Third World Film Making and the West*, Berkeley: University of California Press: 154–6.

Bae, Chang-Ho (1988) 'Seoul in Korean Cinema: A Brief Survey', *East–West Film Journal*, 3, 1: 97–104.

Berry, Chris (1999) 'My Queer Korea: Identity, Space and the 1988 Seoul Queer Film and Video Festival', *Intersections*, 2. May. Online. www.she.murdoch. edu.au/hum/as/intersections/

——(2003a) ' "What's Big about the Big Film?": "De-Westernizing" the Blockbuster in Korea and China', in Julian Stringer (ed.), *Movie Blockbusters*, London: Routledge: 217–29.

——(2003b) 'Full Service Cinema: The South Korean Cinema Success Story (So Far)'. Online. www.gwu.edu/~eall/special/berry-hms02.htm

——(2003c) 'The Documentary Production Process as a Counter-Public: Notes on an Inter-Asian Mode and the Example of Kim Dong-Won', *Inter-Asia Cultural Studies*, 4, 1: 139–44.

Black, Art (2003) 'Coming of Age: The South Korean Horror Film', in Steven Jay Schneider (ed.) *Fear Without Frontiers*, Grange Suite, England: FAB Press: 185–203.

Bowyer, Justin (ed.) (2004) *The Cinema of Japan and Korea*, London: Wallflower Press.

Buck, Elizabeth B. (1992) 'Asia and the Global Film Industry', *East–West Film Journal*, 6: 2: 116–33.

Cho, Francisca (2003) 'The Art of Presence: Buddhism and Korean Films', in

S. Brent Plate (ed.), *Representing Religion in World Cinema: Filmmaking, Mythmaking, Culture Making*, New York: Palgrave: 107–19.

Cho, Hee-Moon (1998) 'Recovering the Past: Rare Films Screened in Korea', *Screening the Past*, 5. Online. www.latrobe.edu.au/screeningthepast

Cho, Young Jeong (ed.) (2003) *Chung Chang Hwa; The Man of Action!*, Pusan: Eighth Pusan International Film Festival.

Choi, Chungmoo (ed.) (1998) *Post-Colonial Classics of Korean Cinema*, Irvine: Korean Film Festival Committee at the University of California.

Chung, Hye Seung (2001) 'From Saviors to Rapists: G.I.s, Women, and Children in Korean War Films', *Asian Cinema*, 12, 1: 103–16.

Ciecko, Anne (2002) 'Ways to Sink the *Titanic*: Contemporary Box-Office Successes in the Philippines, Thailand, and South Korea', *Tamkang Review*, 33, 2: 1–29.

Curnette, Rick (2002) 'Passages of Time: Motifs of Past, Present, Future in Contemporary Korean Films', *The Film Journal*, 1, 2. Online. www.thefilmjournal.com

Desser, David (2003) 'New Kids on the Street: The Pan-Asian Youth Film', *Scope: An Online Journal of Film Studies*. May. Online. www.nottingham.ac.uk/film/journal

Diffrient, David Scott (2000) 'Seoul as Cinematic Cityscape: *Shiri* and the Politico-Aesthetics of Invisibility', *Asian Cinema*, 11, 3: 76–91.

——(2003) 'South Korean Film Genres and Art-House Anti-Poetics: Erasure and Negation in *The Power of Kangwon Province*', *Cineaction*, 60: 60–71.

Ehrlich, Linda C. (1994) '*Why Has Bodhidharma Left for the East?*', *Film Quarterly*, 48, 1: 27–31.

FIPRESCI (Fédération Internationale de la Presse Cinématographique/The International Federation of Film Critics) (2004) *Film Critiques: FIPRESCI Korea* Vol. 3, Seoul: Happy House.

Gateward, Frances (2003) 'Youth in Crisis: National and Cultural Identity in New South Korean Cinema', in Jenny Kwok Wah Lau (ed.), *Multiple Modernities: Cinemas and Popular Media in Transcultural East Asia*, Philadelphia: Temple University Press: 114–27.

Gleason, Timothy R. (2003) 'South Korean Action Films as Indicators of Fear and Hope for Reunification', *Education About Asia*, Spring: 28–32.

Han Sang-Jun (ed.) (2001) *Shin Sang-Ok, Prince of Korean Cinema: Leading the Desire of the Masses*, Pusan: Sixth Pusan International Film Festival.

Hartzell, Adam (2002) 'Hong Sang soo's Unsexy Sex', *The Film Journal*, 1, 4. Online. www.thefilmjournal.com

——(2003) 'Queer Pal for the Straight Gal: *Wanee and Junah* and Queer Friendship', *The Film Journal*, 1, 7. Online. www.thefilmjournal.com

Huh, Chang (1989) 'Anatomy of the Korean Film Industry', *Koreana* 3, 4. Online. www.koreana.or.kr

Huh, Moon-young et al. (eds) (2000) *Kim Soo-yong: An Aesthete Bridging*

Tradition and Modernism, Pusan: Seventh Pusan International Film Festival.

Hyun, Daiwon (2001) 'Renaissance of Korean Film Industry', *Asian Cinema*, 12, 2: 8–19.

James, David E. (2002) 'Opening the Channels of Communication: An Interview with Film Director Park Kwang Su', *Korean Culture*, 23, 2: 10–19.

James, David E. and Kim, Kyung Hyun (eds) (2002) *Im Kwon-Taek: The Making of a Korean National Cinema*, Detroit: Wayne State University Press.

Joo, Jin-Sook and Kim, Mee-Hyun (eds) (2000) *Everlasting Scent of the Classic: Choon-Hyang Jeon*. Pusan: Fifth Pusan International Film Festival.

Kee, Joan (2001) 'Claiming Sites of Independence: Articulating Hysteria in Pak Ch'ŏl-su's *301/302* (1995)', *positions: east asia cultures critique*, 9, 2: 449–66.

Kim, Carolyn Hyun-Kung (2000) 'Building the Korean Film Industry's Competitiveness', *Pacific Rim Law and Policy Journal*, 9: 353–77.

Kim, Dong-ho (2000) 'Pusan International Film Festival: Catalyst for Asian Cinema', *Koreana*, 14, 2: 24–9.

Kim, Elaine H. and Choi Chungmoo (eds) (1998) *Dangerous Women: Gender and Korean Nationalism*, London: Routledge.

Kim, Jinhee (2002) 'Korean Cinema in Transition', *Korean Culture*, 23, 2: 4–9.

Kim, Kyung Hyun (1996a) 'The Fractured Cinema of North Korea: The Discourse of the Nation in *Sea of Blood*', in Xiaobing Tang and Stephen Snyder (eds), *In Pursuit of Contemporary East Asian Culture*, Boulder: Westview Press: 85–106.

——(1996b) 'The Emergence of Auteurism in Recent Korean Cinema', *Korean Culture*, 17, 3: 4–11.

——(2004) *The Remasculinization of Korean Cinema*, Durham, NC: Duke University Press.

Kim, Soyoung (2002) 'Net Documentaries and Blockbusters in South Korea', *Documentary Box*, 20. Yamagata City: Yamagata Documentary International Film Festival. Online. http://www.city.yamagata.yamagata.jp/yidff/docbox/20/box20-2-2-e.html

——(2003) 'The Birth of the Local Feminist Sphere in the Global Era: "Trans-Cinema" and *Yosongjang*', *Inter-Asia Cultural Studies*, 4, 1: 10–24.

Kim, Soyoung and Berry, Chris (2000) 'Suri Suri Masuri: The Magic of the Korean Horror Film: A Conversation', *Postcolonial Studies*, 3, 1: 53–60.

Koh, Helen (2002/2003) 'The Return of South Korean Cinema', *Correspondence: An International Review of Politics and Society*, 10: 48–50.

Korean Film Archive (2003) *Traces of Korean Cinema From 1945–1959*, Seoul: Munhak Sasangsa.

Kwak, Han Ju (2002) 'A Smiling Skepticism: An Interview with Film Director Hong Sang-su', *Korean Culture*, 23, 2: 20–5.

——(2003) 'Discourse on Modernization in 1990s Korean Cinema', in Jenny

Kwok Wah Lau (ed.), *Multiple Modernities: Cinemas and Popular Media in Transcultural East Asia*, Philadelphia: Temple University Press: 90–113.

Lee, Hyangjin (2000a) 'Conflicting Working-Class Identities in North Korean Cinema', *Korea Journal*, 40, 3: 237–54.

——(2000b) *Contemporary Korean Cinema: Identity, Culture, Politics*, Manchester: Manchester University Press.

Lee, Jooran (2000) 'Remembered Branches: Towards a Future of Korean Homosexual Film', in Andrew Grossman (ed.), *Queer Asian Cinema: Shadows in the Shade*, New York: Harrington Park Press: 273–81.

Lee, Yong-kwan and Lee, Sang-young (eds) (1997) *Kim Ki-young: Cinema of Diabolical Desire and Reason*, Pusan: Second International Film Festival.

——(eds) (1999) *Yu Hyun-Mok: The Pathfinder of Korean Realism*, Pusan: Fourth Pusan International Film Festival.

Lee, Yong-kwan (2000) 'Three Readings: One Text: Im Kwon-taek's *Chunhyang*', *Cinemaya*, 49: 17–19.

Lee, Young-Il (1988) *The History of Korean Cinema: Main Current of Korean Cinema*, Seoul: Motion Picture Promotion Corporation. Translated by Richard Lynn Greever.

Lent, John A. (1990) *The Asian Film Industry*, Austin: University of Texas Press.

——(1995) 'Lousy Films Had to Come First: Im Kwon-taek, Korean Director', *Asian Cinema*, 7, 2: 86–92.

Leong, Anthony C. Y. (2003) *Korean Cinema: The New Hong Kong: A Guidebook for the Latest Korean New Wave*, Victoria: Trafford Publishing.

Leong, Toh Hai (1996) 'Postwar Korean Cinema: Fractured Memories and Identity', *Kinema*, Fall. Online. www.arts.uwaterloo.ca/FINE/juhde/kfall96.htm

McHugh, Kathleen A. (2001) 'South Korean Film Melodrama and the Question of National Cinema', *Quarterly Review of Film and Video*, 18, 1: 1–15.

Min, Eungjun (1998) 'A Theoretical and Historical Analysis of the National Cinema Movement in Korea', *Journal of Asian Pacific Communication*, 8, 2: 165–180.

Min, Eungjun, Joo, Jinsook and Kwak, Han-Ju (2003) *Korean Film: History, Resistance, and Democratic Imagination*, Westport: Praeger Publishers.

Noh, Kwang Woo (2001) 'Formation of Korean Film Industry under Japanese Occupation', *Asian Cinema*, 12, 2: 20–33.

——(2003) 'Transformation of Korean Film Industry During the U.S. Military Occupation Era (1945–1948)', *Asian Cinema*, 14, 2: 91–101.

Paquet, Darcy (2002) '*My Beautiful Girl, Mari*, and the Rebirth of Korean Animation', *The Film Journal*, 1, 2. Online. www.thefilmjournal.com

Park, Ed (2002) 'Cries and Whispers: Note on Recent Korean Cinema', *Cinema Scope*, 12: 40–42.

Park, Seung Hyun (2000a) 'Structural Transformation of the Korean Film Industry, 1988–1993', *Asian Cinema*, 11, 1: 51–67.

——(2000b) 'The Memory of Labor Oppression in Korean Cinema: The Death of a Young Worker in *Single Spark* (1995)', *Asian Cinema*, 11, 2: 20–3.

——(2002) 'Film Censorship and Political Legitimation in South Korea, 1987–1992', *Cinema Journal*, 42, 1: 120–38.

Pok, Hwang-mo (1999) 'On Korean Documentary Film', *Documentary Box*, 10. Yamagata City: Yamagata Documentary International Film Festival. Online. www.city.yamagata.yamagata.jp/yidff/docbox/10/ box10-3-e.html

Rayns, Tony (1994) 'Korea's New Wavers', *Sight and Sound*, 4, 11: 22–5.

——(1994b) *Seoul Stirring: 5 Korean Directors*, London: Institute of Contemporary Arts.

——(1998) 'Cinephile Nation', *Sight and Sound*, 8, 1: 24–7.

——(2000) 'Sexual Outlaws', *Sight and Sound*, 10, 2: 26–8.

Rist, Peter (1998) 'An Introduction to Korean Cinema', *Offscreen*. Online. www.horschamp.qc.ca/offscreen

——(2001) 'Neglected "Classical" Periods: Hong Kong and Korean Cinemas of the 1960s', *Asian Cinema*,12, 1: 49–66.

Rutherford, Anne (2000) 'Arrested Motion: Leaps and Bounds in the Korean Detective Film', *Senses of Cinema*, 7. Online. www.sensesofcinema.com

Seo, Hyun-Suk (2002) 'To Catch a Whale: A Brief History of Lost Fathers, Idiots, and Gangsters in Korean Cinema', *The Film Journal*, 1, 2. Online. www.thefilmjournal.com/whale.html

Server, Lee (1999) *Asian Pop Cinema: Bombay to Tokyo*, San Francisco: Chronicle Books.

Shim, Doobo (2002) 'South Korean Media Industry in the 1990s and the Economic Crisis', *Prometheus*, 20, 4: 337–50.

Song, June (1993) 'Korea's New Cinema', *Korea Focus*, 1, 3: 46–50.

Standish, Isolde (1992) 'United in Han: Korean Cinema and the "New Wave"', *Korea Journal*, 32, 4: 109–18.

——(1994) 'Korean Cinema and the New Realism: Text and Context', in Wimal Dissanayake (ed.), *Colonialism and Nationalism in Asian Cinema*, Bloomington: Indiana University Press: 65–89.

Willemen, Paul (2002) 'Detouring Through Korean Cinema', *Inter-Asia Cultural Studies*, 3, 2: 167–86.

Wilson, Rob (1991) 'Filming "New Seoul": Melodramatic Constructions of the Subject in *Spinning Wheel* and *First Son*', *East-West Film Journal*, 5, 1: 107–17.

——(1994) 'Melodramas of Korean National Identity: From *Mandala* to *Black Republic*', in Wimal Dissanayake (ed.), *Colonialism and Nationalism in Asian Cinema*, Bloomington: Indiana University Press: 90–104.

——(2001) 'Korean Cinema on the Road to Globalization: Tracking Global/Local Dynamics, or Why Im Kwon-Taek is not Ang Lee', *Inter-Asia Cultural Studies*, 2, 2: 307–18.

Yecies, Brian and Shim, Ae-Gyung (2003) 'Lost Memories of Korean Cinema:

Film Policies During Japanese Colonial Rule, 1919–1937', *Asian Cinema*, 14, 2: 75–90.

Yi, Hyangsoon (2003) 'Old Masters and New Cinema: Korean Film in Transition'. Online. www.gwu.edu/~eall/special/HMS02-Yi.htm

Yi, Hyo-in and Yi Chong-ha (eds) (1996) *Korean New Wave: Retrospectives from 1980 to 1995*, Pusan: First International Film Festival.

Yu, Gina (2000) 'Renaissance of Korean Movies', *Koreana*, 14, 2: 4–15.

WEBSITES

Asian Cinema Weekly. www.kinoasia.com
Asia-Pacific Media Center. www.asianfilms.org
CineKorea. www.cinekorea.com
The House of Kim Ki-young. www.knua.ac.kr/cinema
Jeonju International Film Festival. www.jiff.or.kr
Korean Film Archive. www.koreanfilm.or.kr
Korean Film Commission. www.kofic.or.kr
Korean Film Page. www.koreanfilm.org
Korea Foundation. www.kofo.or.kr/koreana
Korean Independent Film and Video Maker's Forum (Indieforum).
   www.indieforum.org
Kwangju International Film Festival. www.giff.or.kr
Puchon Fantastic Film Festival. www.pifan.or.kr
Pusan International Film Festival. www.piff.org
Seoul International Cartoon and Animation Festival. www.sicaf.or.kr
Seoul Net and Film Festival. www.senef.net
Women's Film Festival in Seoul. www.wffis.or.kr

INDEX

Note: **bold** denotes an illustration